DISCIPLINED GROWTH STRATEGIES

INSIGHTS FROM THE GROWTH TRAJECTORIES OF SUCCESSFUL AND UNSUCCESSFUL COMPANIES

Peter S. Cohan

Apress®

Disciplined Growth Strategies: Insights from the Growth Trajectories of Successful and Unsuccessful Companies

Peter S. Cohan
Marlborough, Massachusetts, USA

ISBN-13 (pbk): 978-1-4842-2447-2   ISBN-13 (electronic): 978-1-4842-2448-9
DOI 10.1007/978-1-4842-2448-9

Library of Congress Control Number: 2017932383

Managing Director: Welmoed Spahr
Editorial Director: Todd Green
Acquisitions Editor: Robert Hutchinson
Development Editor: Laura Berendson
Coordinating Editor: Rita Fernando
Copy Editor: Karen Jameson
Compositor: SPi Global
Indexer: SPi Global
Cover image designed by eStudio Calamar

Distributed to the book trade worldwide by Springer Science+Business Media New York, 233 Spring Street, 6th Floor, New York, NY 10013. Phone 1-800-SPRINGER, fax (201) 348-4505, e-mail orders-ny@springer-sbm.com, or visit www.springeronline.com. Apress Media, LLC is a California LLC and the sole member (owner) is Springer Science + Business Media Finance Inc (SSBM Finance Inc). SSBM Finance Inc is a **Delaware** corporation.

For information on translations, please e-mail rights@apress.com, or visit http://www.apress.com/rights-permissions.

Apress titles may be purchased in bulk for academic, corporate, or promotional use. eBook versions and licenses are also available for most titles. For more information, reference our Print and eBook Bulk Sales web page at http://www.apress.com/bulk-sales.

Any source code or other supplementary material referenced by the author in this book is available to readers on GitHub via the book's product page, located at www.apress.com/9781484224472. For more detailed information, please visit http://www.apress.com/source-code.

Printed on acid-free paper

Apress Business: The Unbiased Source of Business Information

Apress business books provide essential information and practical advice, each written for practitioners by recognized experts. Busy managers and professionals in all areas of the business world—and at all levels of technical sophistication—look to our books for the actionable ideas and tools they need to solve problems, update and enhance their professional skills, make their work lives easier, and capitalize on opportunity.

Whatever the topic on the business spectrum—entrepreneurship, finance, sales, marketing, management, regulation, information technology, among others—Apress has been praised for providing the objective information and unbiased advice you need to excel in your daily work life. Our authors have no axes to grind; they understand they have one job only—to deliver up-to-date, accurate information simply, concisely, and with deep insight that addresses the real needs of our readers.

It is increasingly hard to find information—whether in the news media, on the Internet, and now all too often in books—that is even-handed and has your best interests at heart. We therefore hope that you enjoy this book, which has been carefully crafted to meet our standards of quality and unbiased coverage.

We are always interested in your feedback or ideas for new titles. Perhaps you'd even like to write a book yourself. Whatever the case, reach out to us at editorial@apress.com and an editor will respond swiftly. Incidentally, at the back of this book, you will find a list of useful related titles. Please visit us at www.apress.com to sign up for newsletters and discounts on future purchases.

—*The Apress Business Team*

To Robin, Sarah, and Adam

Contents

About the Author. ix

Acknowledgments xi

Introduction xiii

Chapter 1:   Introduction 1

Part I: Exploring the Five Dimensions of Growth 21

Chapter 2:   Growth via New or Current Customers 23

Chapter 3:   Growth via New or Current Geographies. 57

Chapter 4:   Growth via Building or Acquiring New Products 89

Chapter 5:   Growth from Current or New Capabilities. 123

Chapter 6:   Growth via Culture 165

Part II: Constructing Growth Trajectories 187

Chapter 7:   Growth Trajectories. 189

Chapter 8:   Growth Road Maps 211

Chapter 9:   Notes. 241

Index 269

About the Author

Peter S. Cohan is a Lecturer of Strategy at Babson College where he teaches strategy and entrepreneurship to undergraduate and MBA students. He is the founder and president of Peter S. Cohan & Associates, a management consulting and venture capital firm. He has completed over 150 growth strategy consulting projects for global technology companies and invested in 7 start-ups—3 of which were sold for over $2 billion. He has written 11 books and writes columns on economic policy, stocks, and entrepreneurship for *Forbes, Inc.,* and the *Worcester Telegram & Gazette*. Prior to starting his firm, he worked as a case team leader for Harvard Business School professor Michael Porter's consulting firm and taught at MIT, Stanford, and the University of Hong Kong. Since 2001, he has taught undergraduates and MBA students at Babson College. He earned an MBA from Wharton, did graduate work in computer science at MIT, and holds a BS in Electrical Engineering from Swarthmore College.

Acknowledgments

This book has benefited greatly from the help of many people.

I could not have embarked on this project without the enthusiastic support of Keith Rollag who chairs the Management Division at Babson. Len Schlesinger, former Babson College president and currently Baker Foundation Professor at Harvard Business School was particularly helpful in providing insightful suggestions about how to structure the chapters. My Management Division colleagues Dwight Gertz, Wendy Murphy, and Jonathan Sims all provided helpful suggestions. Thanks also go to my college classmate, Chris Lamb, for his insightful feedback on many chapter drafts. Finally, thanks go to my Babson students who inspired this book with their struggles to develop effective growth strategies for the many companies we studied.

Without Apress this book would not exist. I am most grateful to Robert Hutchison for his enthusiastic support of the idea for this book and for the outstanding project management and editing help from Rita Fernando Kim and Laura Berendson.

Finally, I could not have completed this book without the help of my wife, Robin, who patiently read and commented on many of the chapters; and my children, Sarah and Adam, who always make me proud.

Introduction

I was the poster child for a confused adolescent. In college, I stumbled through a series of seemingly random career aspirations—concert pianist, poet (my father dissuaded me from this career choice by asking to look up 'poet' in the Yellow Pages), and architect—before realizing in my senior year that I wanted a career that combined my interests in computers and business strategy.

So I set my sites on becoming a strategy consultant—helping companies identify, evaluate and profit from growth opportunities—which I have done in various guises ever since.

Back then, consulting firms hired newly minted MBAs, rather than college graduates as they do these days.

While doing graduate studies in computer science at MIT, I met with the director of career counseling at its Sloan School of Management who introduced me to Index Systems, a consulting firm founded by four former Sloan School professors.

I found out that consulting firms hired very talented people and provided opportunities for traveling and working on a variety of interesting projects. Index focused on helping managers use technology to boost business performance.

I decided that I was most interested in strategy work, so after earning an MBA at The Wharton School, I went to work for Monitor Company—a strategy consulting firm cofounded by Harvard Business School strategy guru, Michael Porter.

My years there were a supremely intense learning experience. Thanks to what partners saw as a talent for turning Porter's ideas into processes for leading client teams, I was quickly promoted to managing consultant teams.

Ultimately, the demanding travel burned me out and I spent the next few years working as an internal consultant in the banking and insurance industries.

In 1994, I took a chance and started my own consulting firm that provided strategy consulting for large, high-technology companies. This happened at a lucky time in economic history—the Internet was emerging as a major force for business growth.

My consulting business boomed, I wrote several books—including *Net Profit*—which made me a regular on TV networks such as CNBC and an in-demand speaker at business conferences around the world.

I also began investing in start-ups—since then, I have funded seven private companies. Three of those were sold for over $2 billion.

In 2001, I began teaching at Babson College—which *U.S. News and World Report* has ranked the top U.S. entrepreneurship school for the last two decades.

After teaching part time, I became a full-time lecturer in 2014 and was promoted to a Lecturer of Strategy in 2016. I teach MBA and undergraduate courses such as Strategy and the CEO, Strategic Decision Making, Strategic Problem Solving, and Foundations of Entrepreneurial Management.

I also created and lead offshore Start-Up Strategy electives to Hong Kong and Singapore, Israel, Spain and Portugal, and Paris. In these courses, students visit with start-ups, venture capitalists, and accelerators and conduct six-week consulting projects for start-ups.

This brings me to why I wrote this book. In almost every course, I assign students the challenge of analyzing a company's problems and figuring out how to solve them.

By far the most frequent problem they encounter is that the company is not growing profitably. Sadly, their solutions to that problem are at best uneven in their originality and likely effectiveness.

This problem is not limited to students—the vast majority of CEOs struggle unsuccessfully with the challenge of how to revive a moribund company or how to sustain the growth of a company that has done well in the past.

I realized that it's unfair to expect students to come up with great growth strategies unless they have a practical road map for doing so.

In February 2016, I wrote a "Note on Growing Faster" to help remedy the problem. A more concise version of the "Note" was published as "Five Commandments for Faster Growth."[1]

But I concluded that in order to provide sufficient depth into how to craft successful growth strategies, I should write a book.

Disciplined Growth Strategies Road Map

If your organization needs disciplined growth, this book will explain how to achieve it in two parts.

Part I. Exploring the Five Dimensions of Growth

Chapters 2 through 6 examine how companies pursue growth along each of the five dimensions of growth—customers, geographies, products, capabilities, and culture.

For each of these chapters, Part I covers the following topics:

- Definitions of key terms and concepts, where appropriate.

- Summary of key principles for achieving growth through the dimension addressed in the chapter.

- Case studies of successful and unsuccessful large and small companies pursuing growth from the current or a new growth vector.

- Lessons learned from the cases about what to do and what to avoid.

Part II. Constructing Growth Trajectories

This second part of the book consists of its concluding chapter in which we will explore how companies chain together some or all of these dimensions into growth trajectories. Drawing on an analysis of Forbes 2000 companies, Chapter 7 does the following:

- Identifies the fastest and slowest growing companies.

- Describes the growth trajectories of the fastest and slowest growing companies.

- Analyzes the logic underlying the decisions to follow those growth trajectories.

- Highlights the most useful takeaways for leaders in what principles to pursue and which to avoid in constructing growth trajectories.

Chapter 8. Road Maps

Road maps for leaders to capture growth from each dimension using examples from the cases in the chapter.

---

[1]Peter S. Cohan, "Five Commandments for Faster Growth," *Knowledge@Wharton*, May 9, 2016, http://knowledge.wharton.upenn.edu/article/five-commandments-for-faster-growth/

Introduction

One of the most important challenges that leaders face is to devise and execute strategies that speed up revenue growth. Not growing fast enough can be
costly for executives and investors. Take the example of LinkedIn, the business
social network service. After markets opened on February 5, 2016, investors
hacked 44% from the company's shares. The reason was easy to understand,
yet difficult to remedy. LinkedIn lowered its expectations for the year's growth
in revenue (from 35% to 20%) and adjusted earnings (from 41% to 7%)—well
below what analysts expected. This slashed a cool $1 billion from the net
worth of LinkedIn's founder, Reid Hoffman, and forced its CEO, Jeffrey Weiner,
to ponder important questions that must be answered before investors could
hope to recoup what they had lost.

Where would faster growth come from? Could it be spurred by improving
LinkedIn's offerings? By selling its current products to new customers, or in new
geographies? By inventing new products for its existing customers? By adding
entirely new classes of products, or creating a new growth culture? Ultimately,
LinkedIn failed to answer these questions. On June 13, 2016, Microsoft paid a
50% premium over the previous day's price—$26.2 billion—to acquire LinkedIn.
The deal restored LinkedIn shareholders to where they were before that fateful
February day. And it let Weiner off the hook. He was no longer under pressure to conceive and implement an effective growth strategy for LinkedIn—that
would become the responsibility of Microsoft CEO, Satya Nadella.

LinkedIn's growth challenge was just one side of the growth coin. The other
is growing too fast—in a manner that boosts short-term revenues and stock
price but is ultimately unstainable and leads to collapse. A case in point is Laval,

© Peter S. Cohan 2017
P. S. Cohan, *Disciplined Growth Strategies*, DOI 10.1007/978-1-4842-2448-9_1

Quebec-based pharmaceutical manufacturer Valeant Pharmaceuticals. Former McKinsey consultant Michael Pearson advised Valeant as an outside consultant in 2007—and took over as its CEO in 2008. In the seven years that followed, Pearson cut risky R&D (research and development) and made acquisitions—drastically raising the prices of its existing approved drugs. The result was a more than 1,000% spike in Valeant's stock price through early 2015—winning Pearson a $1 billion fortune. Valeant fell apart in September 2015 when its drug pricing policies came under attack—slashing 90% from the stock's 2015 peak value. Pearson was dismissed from Valeant's CEO slot. While LinkedIn's disappointing growth demonstrates the challenges that face executives who can't achieve enough growth, Valeant's implosion shows the high price that leaders pay for growing too fast with a strategy that can't be sustained.

The unfortunate truth is that very few executives can think of creative, practical solutions to such questions. To me this suggests a crying need for growth discipline. By this I mean a systematic process for brainstorming, evaluating, choosing, and implementing growth strategies that produce the kind of better-than-expected revenue and profit growth that boosts shareholder value—and makes it easier for leaders to attract and motivate top talent.

Why Growing Faster Matters

Growth creates opportunities for your people to develop their skills. It attracts the best talent to your company (and away from rivals), and it creates wealth for you and your investors. Moreover with the world economy struggling to grow at all, start-ups and public companies are increasingly falling into two categories—the vast majority that are stagnating and declining, and a tiny minority that are enjoying accelerating growth. Languishing public companies become fodder for so-called activist investors who buy a small stake, lobby hard for splitting the company into pieces, and clamor for board seats.

Consider the case of DuPont. In 2014, veteran activist investor, Nelson Peltz, bought a 2.7% stake in the chemical conglomerate and demanded that it break itself into pieces. While Peltz lost a proxy battle in May 2015, he won the war in October 2015 when DuPont's CEO, Ellen Kullman, resigned under pressure after a 46% drop in quarterly profits from the year before. Ultimately, Peltz got a split up—but not in the form he wanted. In December 2015, DuPont and Dow Chemical merged at a value of $120 billion with the idea that they would cut $3 billion in costs and two years later split into three public companies focusing on agricultural, materials, and so-called specialty products.

For top executives, such interventions are hugely distracting and often career ending. The desire to avoid such distractions should spur CEOs to lead their companies to much faster growth that boosts their stock price to a level that makes it harder for activist investors to flip for a quick profit. Shrinking private companies are even more vulnerable. Chances are good that they will not attract investment, will burn through their remaining cash, and shut down. Simply put, boards must ensure that their CEO is achieving rapid growth or has a compelling plan to deliver it. Otherwise, they should find a CEO who can.

Growth Challenge Varies by Company Size and Growth Trajectory

Growing faster is always a difficult challenge.

However, as illustrated in Figure 1-1, the nature of that challenge varies depending on the size of the company and its growth trajectory.

Company Size	Small	When will initial market be saturated? Should new growth opportunities be considered?	Can strengths be applied to another product or is it time to find an acquirer?
	Big	What new source of growth is in the works? Is there room to grow in current markets?	Will an acquisition boost growth? Can we gain share in a new market? Is it time to sell?
		Growing	Declining

Growth Trajectory

Figure 1-1. Growth Challenges by Company Size and Growth Trajectory

Here are examples of each:

- SimpliVity (small, growing). This Westborough, Massachusetts-based data storage supplier had grown to nearly 800 employees by December 2015 with revenues increasing 50% in the third quarter of 2015. By November 2016, SimpliVity's CEO, Doron Kempel, faced three challenges. Its biggest partner, Cisco Systems, was building a product to compete with SimpliVity's. Its larger rival, Nutanix, had gone public—raising significant capital that it could invest in sustaining its market lead. And SimpliVity was so eager to raise new—but its stock had since dropped considerably. Capital that rumors surfaced that it might be acquired for as much as $3.9 billion by Hewlett Packard Enterprise (HPE). In January 2017, HPE acquired SimpliVity for a disappointing $650 million in cash.[1]

---

[1]Peter Cohan, "Hewlett Packard Enterprise Pays $650 Million In Cash For SimpliVity," Forbes, January 17, 2017, http://www.forbes.com/sites/petercohan/2017/01/17/hewlett-packard-enterprise-pays-650-million-in-cash-for-simplivity/

- Fiksu (small, declining). This Boston, Massachusetts-based mobile app marketing algorithm developer had grown from less than $1 million in 2010 to $100 million in a mere 3 and one-half years with only $17.6 million in venture capital. But in 2015, Fiksu hit the wall. As that year dawned, Fiksu was planning to double staff to 500 and go public. Yet by April 2015 it had called off its IPO and announced plans to fire 10% of its staff. By September 2015, it had dismissed 25 more people. Intense price competition from better-funded rivals slammed the brakes on Fiksu's growth. Micah Adler, Fiksu's MIT-educated CEO, hoped to revive the company's growth by applying its algorithm-development skills to a new market – analyzing consumer data to help advertisers target more effectively. However, by March 2016, Fiksu was quietly folded into another company—a disappointing result for its investors. Adler said, "Eighty-five cents of every new online advertising dollar goes to Google and Facebook. It's harder and harder for small companies to compete."

- Amazon (big, growing). Seattle-based Amazon is a $100 billion e-commerce and cloud service provider that continues to grow at over 20% annually—despite earning barely perceptible profits. Since it needs to add over $20 billion in revenues to sustain that pace, Amazon's CEO Jeff Bezos faces a huge challenge in sustaining that growth. Can he invest in the right blend of new services, new capabilities, and new geographies to sustain that 20% growth?

- Apple (big, declining). Apple used to be the world's largest company as measured by stock market capitalization—but Alphabet (Google's parent) took over that spot for a few weeks in February 2016. And that's because Apple has not been able to come up with a new product—on the order of the iPod, iPhone, or iPad—that took significant market share from large, established markets like MP3 players, cell phones, and tablets, respectively. With Apple becoming dangerously dependent on a slowing market—selling iPhones in China—can it invent a new product that will accelerate its revenue growth?

What Is a Growth Opportunity?

There are plenty of huge markets in the world—for example, there are over $1 trillion worth of student loans—but market size alone does not mean it's a growth opportunity for your company. If the market is big and getting smaller, you may want to avoid it. If there is intense price competition in a market, there may be very little profit available for your company. And even if there is high profit potential in the market, it will mean little to your company if you lack or cannot create the skills needed to gain a significant share of that market. Moreover, even if the market is attractive and you have or can obtain the skills needed to take share, does the risk-adjusted return required to compete in that market justify the investment?

When considering growth opportunities, you should brainstorm without constraint. But before committing resources, rank the ideas based on the following definition: a growth opportunity exists for your company if it passes four tests:

- It relieves human pain—there is a chance to put a smile on the faces of unhappy people.

- There's a big market—many such people in pain will pay for a product to make them happy. For a start-up, a big market would be $1 billion—but to be attractive to a large company, a market would have to be correspondingly larger.

- You have the right capabilities—your company can design, build, distribute, and service the product. Or, as we will explore in the case of Netflix, it can create the right capabilities.

- You have an advantage—you are ahead of current and potential rivals in the race to make those people happy.

Anticipate Expiration of Current Growth Opportunities and Invest in New Ones

Moreover, in considering growth opportunities, decision makers must remember that they expand and contract over time. Every industry goes through life cycles—starting with slow initial acceptance, followed by very rapid growth, maturity, and decline. Some industries—for example, semiconductors—go through these cycles much faster than others—such as railroad cars. However, thanks to the way technological innovation has spread to more industries over the last several decades, no company is immune from the threat that its success surfing one technological wave will make it very difficult for the company to sustain that success in subsequent waves. As illustrated in Figure 1-2, leaders should think of their industry as a series of S-curves that will emerge as technology makes possible huge increases in customer value—what I call a Quantum Value Leap (QVL).

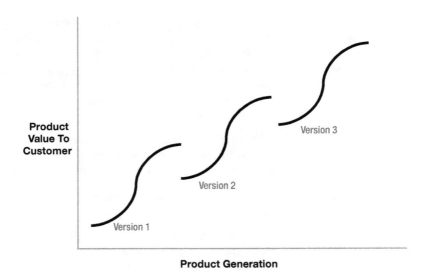

Figure 1-2. S-Curve Generations Boost Value to Customers

A QVL gives customers a reason to take the risk of switching to a new product from the one they are using now. Those risks can be considerable—especially if a business has changed its operations to use a supplier's current product. For example, in order to use so-called Enterprise Resource Planning (ERP) software, companies needed to pay millions of dollars to suppliers like SAP to license the software, millions more to a consulting firm to install it, and devote countless hours to training employees on how to change the way they operate in order to take advantage of the ERP system. Such a company would be unwilling to switch to a new ERP supplier unless it was obvious that the new technology would provide so much of a boost to its profits that it would be worthwhile to incur the costs of buying and installing the new product and taking the risk that it might not work properly.

Such a new technology would have to occupy the starting point of a new S-Curve. And the question for incumbent suppliers is whether they can envision that new S-Curve and supply it, or whether they would prefer to focus on milking the cash from the maturing one from which it derives the bulk of its revenue. For its part, SAP saw that companies like Salesforce were gaining market share from rivals such as Seibel by building a new S-Curve that would enable companies to rent continuously updated software that operated on outsourced hardware for a lower monthly fee.

Moreover, Salesforce changed the risk profile of corporate software purchasing. An IT executive who bought Seibel's product would pay millions of dollars and wait three years before the product's success or failure was clear. By that time, a sales manager could be out of a job. By contrast, Salesforce sold its service directly to sales managers who would need to wait only a few months before it was clear that it worked—a much less risky decision for sales managers.

By January 2016, SAP had implemented its own product on the Software as a Service (SaaS) S-Curve. And that product—S/4 HANA—promised to reduce by 40% the amount of computing power companies needed to employ, according to SAP co-founder Hasso Plattner. The success of S/4 HANA was so great that it accounted for 75% of SAP's cloud revenue during the fourth quarter of 2015—three quarters after it was introduced. One such customer, Airbus said at a June 2015 SAP customer meeting in France that it had sped up "reporting performance five-fold and data load time four-fold" after replacing its Oracle product with SAP HANA. While SAP did not lead the charge to the SaaS S-Curve, it did follow fast enough to gain a meaningful share of its growth phase.

Executives must know where they are on the current S-Curve and which technology will propel the next one. And they must develop the strategic discipline needed to use the profit generated by the current S-Curve to invest in the capabilities needed to tap the growth opportunities from the next one. The key to successfully making the transition from one S-Curve to the next is to do the opposite of what Clayton Christensen recommended in his book, *The Innovator's Dilemma*. Rather than housing the new technology in a separate subsidiary charged with killing the parent as he recommends, the CEO should manage the transition to the new S-Curve within the company. As described below, a case in point is Netflix's transition from a DVD-by-Mail service to an online streaming supplier.

Three Myths of Corporate Growth

While boosting growth is an imperative for all CEOs, achieving that end is made more difficult because decision makers are blinded by three powerful myths—drawn from *Grow to be Great* coauthored by Babson College senior lecturer Dwight Gertz. Ultimately, these myths are manifestations of confirmation bias—the notion that people seek out information that confirms what they believe and disregard information that challenges those beliefs.

Big Companies Can't Grow

Conventional wisdom is that start-ups sprint and big companies plod. To be sure, there is no comprehensive data on the growth rates of start-ups since they are privately held. Moreover, the ones that say that they are growing are much more eager to highlight their skyrocketing percentage growth rates, which often mask how small their revenues were and still are. While there are plenty of big companies that grow very slowly, there is much to learn by comparing big companies that are growing faster than 20% a year with peers whose growth is stagnant.

Table 1-1 provides a few illustrations of fast-growing big companies and their slower growing peers.

Table 1-1. Revenues and Growth Rates of Slow- and Fast-Growing Big Companies

	2015 Revenues ($B)	2015 Revenue Growth Rate	One-Year Stock Price Change
WalMart	$482	-1%	-21%
Amazon	107	22	44
Yahoo	5	2	-29
Google	75	18	26
CBS	13.9	6	-22
Netflix	6.8	23	38

Source: *Yahoo! Finance, accessed February 28, 2016*

My Industry Is Not Growing, So Neither Can Our Company

In almost every industry, some participants are growing much faster than the average company. Yet some CEOs believe that it is unreasonable for investors to expect their companies to grow faster than their industries—especially if they are large participants. Nevertheless, in many large industries that are growing relatively slowly, there are frequently significant companies that are growing faster—in some cases many times more rapidly than their peers.

Table 1-2 provides eight illustrations of large, slowly growing industries that host major companies growing many times faster than the average participant.

Table 1-2. Fast-Growing Participants in Large, SlowlyGrowing Industries

Industry	2015 Industry Revenues ($B)	2010 to 2015 Growth Rate	Fast Grower	2010 to 2015 Growth Rate
Fast Food	225.1	2.5%	Chipotle	15.4%*
Home Building	104.8	5.8	DR Horton	25.7
Credit Card Issuing	117.8	2.4	American Express	4.2
Security Software	10.4	3.4	Imperva	25.3
Soda Production	43.1	-1.2%	Monster Beverage	13.2
Computer Manufacturing	10.3	-13.3	Oracle	7.8
Medical Device Making	44.8	5.8	Medtronic	9.8
Dating Services	2.4	5.0	Zoosk	26.6

*Source: IBISWorld US, accessed February 28, 2016. *Chipotle Growth from 2011 to 2015*

The Only Way We Can Grow Is through Acquisition

Big company growth can come from many sources—products developed internally, partnerships, and acquisitions. Gertz and Baptista analyzed a sample of profitably growing companies and found that 61% of revenue growth was generated internally while only 39% of the growth was attributed to acquisitions. And while acquisitions usually fail, the ones that succeed do so because the acquiring company and the target need each other's capabilities to succeed. For example, during the 1990s, Cisco Systems regularly made over 60 acquisitions a year, and its most successful acquisitions were able to tap its powerful corporate sales force to turn an acquired company's technology into a $2 billion a year product.

Growth Comes from Five Dimensions

If you'd like your company to grow faster, what should you do? Follow a strategic growth discipline. And that discipline starts with a systematic approach to brainstorming, ranking, choosing, and investing in growth opportunities. Companies can find growth along five dimensions, ranging from the most basic to the most challenging. As depicted in Figure 1-3, these dimensions can either be the same as those in a company's existing practices, or reflect new and different parameters.

- Customers
- Geographies
- Products
- Capabilities and/or
- Culture

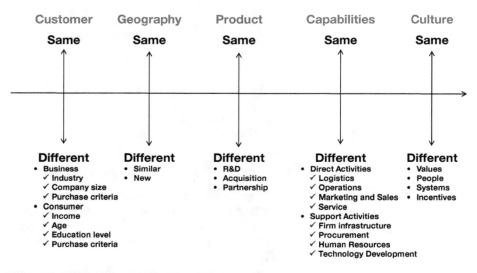

Figure 1-3. Five Dimensions of Growth

Let's look at examples of how companies have tapped these dimensions for growth, summarize the key insights from these cases, and recommend how leaders can apply them.

Customers: Same or Different

If you're already selling a product now, you may be able to grow faster by selling new products to your existing customers. Or faster growth may come from selling your current products to a new group of customers. To evaluate this decision, it helps to have a map of your customers. And the nature of that map varies depending on whether you sell your product to individuals or organizations. For example, if individuals buy your product now, you should try to identify whether most of those customers share common attributes such as the following:

- Age range
- Gender

- Income level
- Education level
- Attitude toward technology
- Political leanings

Consumers who share common attributes are market segments. If organizations buy your product, you ought to be able to segment your customer base by seeing how they cluster among a different set of attributes such as the following:

- Number of employees
- Industry
- Geography
- Attitude toward technology
- Financial condition

Can you take a bigger share of your current market or should growth flow from a new group of customers? One start-up is seeking growth by winning more business from its current customers. I invested in SoFi, a consumer lender based in San Francisco, which uses a unique marketing strategy to grow fast—from $168 million worth of loans in 2013 to $7 billion by January 2016. What makes SoFi different from a bank is that it picks customers who are graduates of top schools like Stanford and Harvard. Such customers tend to have better loan repayment rates and are more likely to have successful careers that make them lucrative financial services customers throughout their lives.

SoFi holds parties for its customers in cities around the United States. Such parties encourage its customers—millennials who graduated from top schools—to build relationships with each other and to bring in potential customers from among their peers. The company seeks to turn this cohort into lifelong customers by making them "feel as if they belong to an exclusive club," according to Bloomberg. As CEO Mike Cagney said, "We can do some things that really get you to start to rethink how your relationship with a financial services firm should work. We're trying to make these guys dinosaurs. And hopefully I'm the meteor by which they all die." While SoFi had made $7 billion worth of loans by January 2016—it had only won a tiny share of the $3.5 trillion (December 2015) market for consumer installment loans.

Thinking about segments should lead executives to ask questions such as:

- In which segments are the 20% of my customers that account for 80% of our revenues?
- Which segments do the other customers that account for the remaining 20% of our revenues occupy?

- Are our most important segments saturated?
- If so, are there less saturated segments that would be eager to purchase our current products?
- If not, how can we boost our share of the less saturated segments?

To decide whether your company has a chance to accelerate its growth from current or new customers, address these questions by taking six steps:

- Segment your current customers.
- Identify how much of your revenue comes from each segment:
  - Analyze the broad trends—such as evolving customer needs, changing economic conditions, or new technology—that might boost (or contract) growth in these segments.
- Estimate your company's share of the most important segments:
  - For saturated segments, identify new segments that would be interested in buying your product and interview potential customers in those segments to gauge their level of interest.
- For unsaturated segments, determine the most effective marketing strategies for achieving further penetration.
- Assess the cost, fit with your company's skills, and time to market of the options.
- Pick the option with the lowest cost, best fit, and quickest time to market.

Geography: Same or Different

If your company's product is selling well in the markets where you currently operate, consider whether future growth could come from the locations where you currently operate—or by expanding your company's geographic scope. If you have a small share of your current geographic market, more share of that market could be no further away than boosting your marketing budget, adding more distribution partners, and/or hiring more salespeople.

Sometimes growth can come from taking your show on the road. When Starbucks decided to open coffee shops in China in 1999, it did so in the face of naysayers who assumed that with its thousands of years of tea-drinking culture, the Chinese would be the last people to drink coffee. But 16 years after entering the Chinese market, Starbucks operated 2,000 stores in 100 Chinese cities. Moreover, Starbucks anticipated adding 1,400 more such coffee shops by 2019—including 500 alone in the current year. Starbucks carefully studied the market and saw an opportunity to "introduce a Western coffee experience, where people could meet with their friends while drinking their favorite beverages," according to *Forbes*.

Starbucks decided not to threaten China's tea-drinking culture through advertising and promotion. Instead it selected "high-visibility and high-traffic locations to project its brand image," noted *Forbes*. Starbucks introduced drinks that included local ingredients such as green tea and made young Chinese feel "cool and trendy" through what *Forbes* noted was its stores' "chic interior, comfortable lounge chairs, and upbeat music." Starbucks also used its best baristas as brand ambassadors to China—they trained its Chinese employees and helped establish the company's culture there.

Here are five steps to get you started on sourcing growth from new countries:

- List four countries that best match with your current markets.

- Identify how your product can boost the profits of your distribution partners in those countries.

- Ask potential end users of your product to rank the criteria—for example, price, quality, service —they use to compare suppliers.

- Analyze how well your company does on these criteria relative to competitors.

- Position your product to outperform competitors on the ranked criteria.

Products: Same or Different

One of the most basic sources of growth is to sell new products to your existing customers. The new product can come from acquisition, partnership, or your own product developers. As Northwestern University Kellogg School of Management Professor Mohanbir Sawhney, explained, not all growth is good. Bad growth—such as that caused by subprime lending or acquisitions that add needlessly to a company's complexity—produces short-term revenue growth but longer-term collapse. Good growth, says Sawhney, is organic—from "increased share of [a customer's] wallet, stealing share from competitors, or increasing the size of the market [and maintaining your share]." A case in point is Reliance Jio Infocomm, an insurance claims management firm on whose board he serves. The company gained a bigger share of wallet by adding new services beyond claims management—such as policy administration, underwriting, paying claims, and terminating policies—which its customers wanted.

If you decide that selling the same product to new customers is the way to go, which new customers should you pick? They might be people who have the same pain as your existing customers—say people in New York—who you have not yet tried to contact—for example, Connecticut residents. If you decide that the best growth path may be from selling new products to your current customers, here are four steps that will help you build the right product:

- Ask your customers to tell you their goals and the biggest barriers to achieving them.

- Brainstorm new product ideas that would help your customers leap over these barriers.

- Build a prototype of the best ideas and get customer feedback.

- Turn the most promising ideas into your next product.

If you find it might be faster or better to acquire a company that makes the new product, follow these seven steps:

- Observe the most pressing external and internal challenges facing your current customers and whether they are buying new products or services to help address those problems.

- Identify a list of companies who provide that product or service.

- Determine whether that new market would be sufficiently large and profitable to warrant further examination.

- Assess the capabilities needed to gain a significant share of that market.

- Evaluate whether a merger with one of those companies could yield a competitor with stronger capabilities.

- Investigate how difficult it would be to integrate the candidates' companies into yours.

- Estimate the investment required to acquire the best candidate and its net present value.

Capabilities: Same or Different

Capabilities are business activities—such as new product development, supply chain management, selling, marketing, and service—that help a company to win and sustain long-term customer relationships. When a company introduces its first successful product, it usually builds up the capabilities it needs to meet customer demand as the S-Curve shifts from initial adoption through to maturity and decline. If the company is fortunate, the skills that it develops for the first product will help the company to introduce future products.

This is what Apple was able to do for three products in a row. Under Steve Jobs, Apple was great at product design, marketing, supply chain (led by current Apple CEO, Tim Cook), and building content ecosystems. It first applied those skills to building a better MP3 player—the iPod. Apple first designed a much more satisfying piece of hardware. It also overcame objections to breaking albums into singles by citing the lost revenue from peer-to-peer sharing networks like Napster. As a result, Apple negotiated a deal with producers to make available to consumers a wide selection of music and other audio products. In January 2001, Apple launched this content ecosystem dubbed iTunes that made people want to buy the iPod when it was introduced that October. Moreover, Apple built a supply chain—mostly centered on Foxconn, which could manufacture and ship the product to Apple's retail stores. And Apple applied its advertising and marketing skills to ignite people's desire to buy the product.

With some modifications, Apple applied the same set of skills to build its version of a cell phone—the iPhone—and a tablet, the iPad. To make the iPhone compelling, Apple created a content ecosystem—the App Store—that offered economic incentives for developers. Moreover, Apple persuaded AT&T to be the first telecommunications carrier to support the iPhone—another manifestation of Apple's partnering capability. Since it introduced the iPad in 2010, the question for Apple is whether that same set of capabilities can enable the company to capture a new growth opportunity to replace the profit that will be lost as the iPhone matures. Perhaps Apple's capabilities are less useful now that Steve Jobs is no longer its CEO. And that could mean Apple needs a new CEO or needs to create new capabilities in order to capture new growth opportunities.

Netflix has not enjoyed the luxury of being able to rely on its capabilities for three products in a row. Instead, Netflix added new capabilities in order to shift from DVD-by-Mail to online streaming. Investors approve—its stock price more than tripled in the five years ending January 2016. DVD-by-Mail depended on such capabilities as the wholesale purchasing of a wide variety of DVDs, as well as building and operating a system to track customer orders and route delivery and pickup of DVDs between Netflix and customers' mailboxes.

When Apple introduced the iPhone in 2007, Netflix CEO Reed Hastings realized that DVD-by-Mail would go the way of the Dodo—and soon people would demand to watch videos on their smartphones. Hastings also realized that Netflix would encounter an insurmountable challenge—obtaining early access to movies and TV programs produced by others. So rather than depend on suppliers who viewed it as a rival, Netflix produced its own content. While creating that capability was a huge challenge, the popularity of shows like *House of Cards* and *Orange Is the New Black* suggests that Netflix succeeded. Hastings bet over $100 million—ordering 26 episodes of *House of Cards* (based on a BBC original that came up for auction in 2012).

This bet flowed from Netflix's 2012 analysis of the habits and preferences of its 29 million subscribers. Hastings concluded that Netflix would be able to recoup its *House of Cards* investment because so many of its subscribers watched Kevin Spacey and David Fincher movies and political thrillers. But along with the bet on producing its own content would come a phasing out of capabilities on which it depended to operate its DVD-by-Mail business—such as wholesale purchasing of DVDs and operating a network to pick up and deliver those DVDs to customers' mailboxes. While phasing out those activities, Netflix needed to add another new one—the ability to partner with a complex array of broadband service providers. Given that its consumers consume as much as 37% of all bandwidth during peak streaming hours, such partnerships are essential for Netflix's ability to operate its online streaming service.

If you see such a growth opportunity, here are four steps to make this work for your company:

- List the skills needed to succeed in the new market.

- Assess the fit between those skills and the ones at which your firm excels.

- Develop a plan to hire or partner to get the skills you'll need.

- Manage the process of changing your company's skills.

On the other hand, if you are looking for new markets where your skills would enable you to take market share, do the following:

- Make a list of skills at which your company excels.

- Look at big markets where those skills could yield a better product.

- Build a prototype of that product and get feedback from potential customers.

- Estimate the time and cost needed to bring that product to market.

Culture: Same or Different

In some companies—think Apple under Steve Jobs—the CEO was the source of new product ideas. That works well until the CEO stops coming up with good ideas or leaves the company. To supplement the CEO's creativity, other companies encourage all employees to come up with growth ideas. For example, 3M is famous for letting employees spend 15% of their time on projects that interest them—that's how the Post-It Note was born (it solved an employee's problem with bookmarks falling out of his church hymnal). 3M encourages its people to come up with new ideas and pressures its divisions to derive 30% of their revenues from products introduced in the last three years.

Can you change your culture to encourage your employees to create more growth opportunities? Intuit, the maker of accounting software such as TurboTax and Quicken, created an idea collaboration portal that lets employees post ideas, get feedback, coaching and suggestions—and even sign up people to help implement these. And the beauty of this portal is that all this idea generation can happen without a manager getting involved. According to Intuit's founder, Scott Cook, by 2012 this portal had turned 30 ideas into "shipping products and features" that boosted Intuit's revenues. Cook, who joined Bain & Co. after earning his Harvard MBA, described his passion for assuring that Intuit was capable of both strengthening its core business and creating innovative new ones. His key finding was that big companies must create a culture of frugal experimentation.

This was a problem that Cook began studying in 2008. He believed that there was no market category that kept growing for so long that an incumbent company could avoid eventually perishing unless it hitched its wagon to a new market. As an example, Cook cited Microsoft that "has been unable to invent successful new disruptive businesses—causing its growth to slow down." Cook found it strange that large successful companies could not invent new industries. After all, he reasoned, they had the best people, a high profit flow, the largest customer base, and the broadest channels of distribution. And yet, Cook noted, if you look at enterprise and consumer technology companies, the game-changing innovations almost never come from the big incumbents such as Oracle, SAP, and Microsoft. With the exception of Apple in the 2000s, all the big innovations came from start-ups.

Cook decided to investigate whether there were any large companies that have been able to buck this trend. Cook studied companies such as Hewlett Packard, 3M, Procter & Gamble—where he worked, and Toyota Motor. He found that the common thread during the periods of their most successful product and process innovations was the systems they put in place to encourage employees to conduct frugal experiments.

Cook did not see himself as being a product champion like Jobs or Amazon founder and CEO Jeff Bezos. Instead, he strived to create a company that would be able to continue to create new growth businesses long after he had left Intuit. Intuit invented new businesses by creating an environment that encouraged people there to come up with new business hypotheses and test them against feedback from customers. One example was a debit card for people without bank accounts. An Intuit finance employee—not a "product person"—noticed that the people who need tax refund checks the most are often ones who don't even have bank accounts. She came up with the idea of giving those people debit cards: Intuit would accept the tax refunds into its accounts and transfer the funds to the debit card. She thought of the idea in February and wanted to test it by April 1, before tax season ran out on April 15.

CEO Cook criticized the kludgy web site she developed, but the employee argued that it was better to get something crude that would test her idea than to wait another 10 months. She expected 100 takers but got 1,000. And the surprise was that half of those who wanted the debit card already had bank accounts. In this way, Intuit discovered that the need for this product was much greater than it had reckoned. One interesting feature of this story is that Cook was not wild about the web site that the employee had developed but she was able to pursue her idea anyway. This echoes one of Cook's findings when he studied Hewlett Packard.

His conversation with the author of a 650-page book on its history revealed that seven of the eight big new businesses that HP invented came "from the bottom" and were opposed by CEO David Packard. The pattern Cook has found is that in all these cases, three things were true:

- The company "liberated the inventive power of new people."
- It created a "culture of experimentation."
- It changed the role of the boss from a decider of whether to pursue or cancel innovation projects to an installer of systems that encourage endless cycles of hypothesis generation, testing with customers, and learning from the gap between quantitative expectations and measured market truth.

Cook believed that there was nothing more rewarding to employees than to see their idea being used by people. To that end, Intuit created an idea collaboration portal that let employees post ideas, get feedback, coaching, and suggestions—and even sign up people to help implement it. And the beauty of this portal was that all this idea encouragement could happen without a manager getting involved. According to Cook, by 2012 this portal had turned 30 ideas into "shipping products and features" that boosted Intuit's revenues. Cook's system sounds eminently doable at big companies around the world—if their executives are willing to adopt it. Here are Cook's eight steps for creating a culture of innovation:

- Leader's vision. A culture of experimentation starts with the CEO's vision. In Cook's case, the vision is to change peoples' financial lives so profoundly that they can't imagine going back to the old way.

- Strategy-by-experiment. Rather than trying to curry favor with their bosses, Cook believes it's essential to enable people to make data-based decisions. This means encouraging them to conduct experiments and collect data on customer behavior.

- Leap of faith assumptions. Cook encourages people to identify the two or three key assumptions that have to be true for the idea to succeed but might not be. Then people must find a way to test those assumptions with customers at a low cost in a very short time frame.

- Numeric hypothesis. Next Cook wants people to come up with an estimate of, say, the number of customers that will order the new product.

- Experimental run. The employee should then run the experiment to test whether that numeric hypothesis is right or not.

- Analysis of variance. Then Cook wants people to analyze the gap between the hypothesis and the actual results and dig deep to find the reason for that gap.

- Surprise celebration. Cook is adamant that people should not try to bury surprises to keep from being embarrassed but to savor them because they expose a market signal that has not yet been detected.

- Decision. Finally, people should make a decision about whether to pursue the idea or pivot.

Thus success of this process depends on a blend of confidence in a new idea coupled with intellectual humility when it comes to testing and refining it. Cook believes that one of his roles is to model this behavior so it will permeate Intuit. If you choose to follow in Intuit's path, you may need to create a new culture to encourage all your people to come up with growth ideas. Here are four steps you can use to create such a culture:

- Make a list of your values—one of which should be customer innovation.

- Use a hiring process that favors people who share those values.

- Give employees time to brainstorm new products that will make customers better off.

- Provide resources to commercialize the best products and reward those who succeed—as well as the noble failures.

Summary

In a slowly growing world, there are two kinds of leaders—the innovators and the loungers. Investors and talented employees flock to the fast-growing companies and leave the rest. Read on to learn how you can use the five dimensions of growth to be the leader who wins those rewards for your company.

Exploring the Five Dimensions of Growth

Growth via New or Current Customers

The most obvious place for many companies to look for growth is to sell more to the customers who have already bought their products. The problem with trying to sell more to people who already buy your product is that they might turn you down for several reasons:

- *They are unhappy with your company's product or its customer service.* If this is the reason, you should find out why and improve fast.

- *Your product is working fine for the time being and they do not need to buy anything now.* In this case, you should explore whether you can grow by selling the customer a product that satisfies a need related to your initial product or by finding more people like your current customers who will buy your current product.

© Peter S. Cohan 2017

P. S. Cohan, *Disciplined Growth Strategies*, DOI 10.1007/978-1-4842-2448-9_2

- A competitor has offered your customer a better value—for example, better performance and/or a lower price for comparable performance—and the customer will swap your product for the competitor's. In this case, you might consider whether you can offer your customer a better value than your rival—or acquire the rival.

But if your current customers are happy, the growth path of least resistance is selling your current product to people who have not yet purchased it.

Defining Customer Groups

To find these customers, executives ought to think about market segments—groups of customers that share common traits. As we saw in Chapter 1, these common traits vary depending on many factors. However, it helps to start by grouping business customers and consumers. Companies I've interviewed and advised as a consultant tend to group business customers along the following dimensions:

- **Industry.** Many information technology (IT) companies tend to focus their initial sales efforts on banks and insurance companies. Such companies often find it easiest to grow by selling to potential customers in the same industry.

- **Size.** Many companies distinguish between selling to the largest, say, 1,000 companies ranked by revenues from selling to so-called small and medium-sized enterprises (SMEs). When IT upstarts challenge big rivals like IBM, they may initially find it easier to focus on selling to SMEs, which tend to buy from channel partners. In so doing, the upstarts may generate revenues more quickly than they would were they to compete against incumbents' most well-compensated sales people—the ones who sell to the biggest companies.

- **Appetite for risk.** Within each industry, some companies like to be the first to try the latest technological innovation while most of them tend to be more conservative—waiting for the so-called early-adopters to be the guinea pigs. Companies often listen to early-adopters to help inspire their development of new products.

- **Price sensitivity.** Some business customers always seek to purchase a product at the lowest possible price while others are willing to pay a price premium for better quality. A company should pick customers who represent the best fit with its pricing strategy. Simply put, a company that sells its product at the lowest price should target the most price-sensitive customers and vice versa.

Consumers can be grouped—mostly along different dimensions than companies. These include:

- **Age range.** Consumers are often grouped based on generational differences. For example, Baby Boomers (those born between 1945 and 1975) and Millennials (born between 1983 and 1995). Such groups of consumers may share common traits that can guide companies seeking to separate them from their money.

- **Income.** The last few decades have featured an increasing flow of wealth to a narrow segment of society with many in the middle losing economic ground. Companies seeking to reach consumers in different income strata should recognize that their purchase decisions will be motivated by their position on attributes such as price sensitivity and status signaling.

- **Product occasions of use.** Consumers may find many uses for a company's product. For example, while many consumers eat cold cereal for breakfast, others eat cereal during lunch or dinner times. If a cereal company were marketing its product based on the assumption that people only consume its product in the morning, it could grow by encouraging those who eat cereal at other times of day to buy its product.

- **Purchase process.** Different consumers may buy a company's product in many different ways. Some go to an online site to compare prices and user ratings and pick the one with the best ratings. Others walk into a retail store and purchase the first product they see. In many cases, companies can benefit by grouping potential customers based on differences in the way they make purchases.

- **Appetite for risk.** Like companies, some individuals like to be the first to try a new product. For example, when Apple first announced its Watch, I asked about 200 of my students whether they would purchase it. Of those, one or two said they would because they wanted their peers to know they had purchased it. Most of the students said they were skeptical that the Watch could offer benefits worth purchasing. Companies should target their new products to these consumer early-adopters.

Principles of Growth from Current or New Customers

To grow faster, companies must find unmet customer needs and satisfy those needs better than do rivals. Achieving that goal requires CEOs to be intellectually humble—which means that they investigate with an open mind, rather than assuming that strategies that worked for them in the past will result in future success. Indeed intellectual humility when applied to identifying unmet customer needs and satisfying those needs more effectively than competitors do is essential whether a company is large or small.

For large companies seeking to achieve growth by selling to current customers, there is no more important principle than a willingness to listen with an open mind to what customers want and finding a way to overcome a company's internal inertia in order to deliver a product that satisfies those unmet needs. Indeed for large companies, a long-tenured CEO or one who has spent her entire career at the company may be unable to recognize that customer needs have changed or may try to respond to those changes without making fundamental changes to the company's product mix or operations. This theme is particularly pronounced in the cases we will explore that pair McDonald's and Subway.

Large companies seeking growth by selling to new customers ought to seek insight into the unique needs of those new customers. While this sounds simple in concept, the insight gained may cause business leaders to recognize a gap between the needs of the new customers and the company's ability to deliver a better solution to those unique needs. As we see in the cases of Criteo and Kodak in this chapter, if that new strategy endangers the way that the company has made money in the past, the company may choose to respond in a way that causes the company to lose market share. However, if the company delivers a new product that outperforms competing ones in the minds of those new customers, it will gain market share and boost its revenue growth rate.

These principles also apply to small companies. But given their more precarious financial condition, small companies are more subject to the specific strengths and weaknesses of their CEOs. If a small company's CEO has superior insight than rivals into how unmet customer needs are likely to evolve and how to satisfy them uniquely, then that small company has a much greater chance of getting large quite rapidly. Conversely, if a small company's founders are weak in skills required to deliver a better product to satisfy customers' unmet needs, they are likely to drive the company out of business without even realizing why. Ultimately growth from current or new customers is a result of winning a contest between the company and competitors to provide those customers with the best value in the industry.

Case Studies

By examining case studies that pair successful and unsuccessful efforts we can gain insight into how executives have tried to grapple with the issues we discuss in this chapter in mapping a growth strategy based on selling to new or existing customers.

In the remainder of this chapter, we examine case studies to illustrate four principles of growth through new products:

- **Large companies seeking growth from current customers** should monitor and adapt to changing customer tastes.

- **Large companies seeking growth from new customers** should identify ranked customer purchase criteria in the new segment and deliver a competitively superior value proposition.

- **Small companies seeking growth from current customers** should pick customer groups with a high willingness to pay, deliver excellent service, and encourage them to recommend the company to members of their network.

- **Small companies seeking growth from new customers** should conduct research to rank their purchase criteria, analyze competitor offerings, and deliver superior value.

Principle One Large companies seeking growth from current customers should monitor and adapt to changing customer tastes.

Compared to start-ups, big companies combine disadvantages and advantages when it comes to adapting to changing customer needs. A big company may have existing assets—such as a large and powerful distribution channel—which it can use to get access to consumers. But it may simultaneously suffer from leadership that is locked into an old way of operating the company that keeps it from listening to customers and adapting to their changing needs.

In theory the easiest path for future growth should be winning more business from current customers. That's because a well-run company would be rewarding its people for understanding its customers and anticipating their changing needs. However, in practice what makes the difference between success and failure in tapping growth from current customers is the CEO's willingness to adapt to change. Companies whose CEOs have come up through the ranks often have difficulty changing the company to seize new growth opportunities. CEOs who come in from the outside may have good ideas but may struggle to get them implemented. And big company CEOs with the right blend of internal and external experience may be best positioned to envision and execute effective strategies for growth from current customers.

Successful: McDonald's All-Day Breakfast

Introduction

Adapting to change quickly and effectively can be especially helpful for big companies seeking growth from current customers. A case in point is McDonalds, which introduced all-day breakfast in response to social media requests from its current customers within six months. By the fourth quarter of 2015, that change propelled its growth above 5%—more than double analysts' expectations.

Case Scenario

In a 2015 bid to boost growth, McDonald's sold a product it was already selling—but only in the morning—to a mixture of new and existing customers by answering their call for all-day breakfast.

In January 2016, McDonald's beat Wall Street earnings expectations for the fourth quarter of 2015—enjoying 5.7% same-store-sales growth in North America—well ahead of the 2.7% growth Wall Street had expected, leading to a 35% profit pop and propelling its stock to an all-time high after a two-year slump. How did it do so? McDonald's USA Chief Marketing Officer Deborah Wahl said, "Customers were saying to us 'Hey, McDonald's, this is the next big thing. This is what we want from you. This idea came from our customers. We said this really is the people's launch, that's what this is all about." As one analyst told CNBC, "I think the key takeaway with the all-day breakfast is the fact they were able to roll it out in a matter of six months. That wasn't something we saw under previous leadership, and I think that bodes well for a lot of the new initiatives."

Moreover, the initial success of all-day breakfast motivated McDonald's to expand it. McDonald's Corp. decided to go bigger with all-day breakfast. In a bid to maintain the hype—and the sales gains—the chain was planning to add McGriddles and more breakfast sandwiches to its all-hours menu. The change would take place across the United States in September 2016, almost a year after all-day breakfast was first introduced, the Oak Brook, Illinois-based company said in a statement. In July 2016, McDonald's announced plans to expand its full-day breakfast menu to all U.S. locations and to offer three varieties of McGriddles—a sandwich that uses maple-flavored pancakes as buns—to its previous all-day breakfast menu consisting of English muffin- and biscuit-based sandwiches.

Yet this turnaround was so dramatic because McDonald's had gotten locked in to a rigid approach to managing itself. And that approach probably seemed justified to experienced executives who had grown up inside its system based on its legendary success. Between 1948 and 2014, its emphasis on quick service and a standardized menu propelled it from a single store to more than 35,000 outlets across the world. But by July 2014, global sales began to decline due to problems around the world. For example, sales in China fell sharply after one of its suppliers was discovered in July 2014 to be using expired and contaminated chicken and beef. After that, several Japanese customers reported finding bits of plastic and even a tooth in their food.

In the United States, Burger King gained market share with a simpler and cheaper version of the McDonald's menu. And "fast-casual" restaurants such as Shake Shack and Chipotle Mexican Grill were taking customers from McDonald's with their slightly better quality food, a high level of customization (such as the option to choose the ingredients in a burrito or burger), and some table service. All these problems began to be solved when McDonald's appointed Steve Easterbrook CEO in January 2015.

Dean DeBiase, Adjunct Lecturer of Innovation & Entrepreneurship at Northwestern University's Kellogg School of Management taught in a part-time MBA program on corporate innovation that included an immersion program in which students developed new products for McDonald's.

In this way, he had a chance to observe how Easterbrook had turned McDonald's around. Easterbrook is a great leader for McDonald's. "Steve has the outlook of a younger generation. He left and came back which gave him a global perspective and insights into how to succeed in smaller markets. He is a rugged individualist who inspires people, holds them accountable, and gets things done," explained DeBiase. Easterbrook also excels at driving changes that benefit all of the company's stakeholders. "Steve is a smart operator who is using insights from social media to understand what consumers want and helping franchisees and employees to see why they will be better off if they get on board with the need to adapt to consumers' changing tastes," he said.

A case in point is the introduction of all-day breakfast, which contributed to McDonald's big growth spurt in the first quarter. There was clear evidence for years that consumers were asking for the change. But Easterbrook was able to help franchisees see that the resulting revenue growth would warrant the investment they'd have to make to change their supply chain, information technology, and employee training. One reason Easterbrook was able to make the case was that McDonald's could try out the all-day breakfast in its test kitchens so it would be able to provide detailed answers to the questions franchisees had about how the change would affect their operations. Easterbrook used the forum of the regular franchisee meetings to help get them on board with the change he wanted to make. "Steve used the meetings to encourage the franchisees to think openly about how their lives would change over the next decade," according to DeBiase.

Case Analysis

Easterbrook's example also offers four lessons for companies seeking to boost growth by selling to current customers.

1. Listen to customers for inspiration on sources of growth.

2. Test out your best growth ideas to iron out the kinks before introducing them.

3. Craft your case for change to appeal to the interests of your company's stakeholders—such as partners, customers, and employees.

4. Inspire people to embrace the growth idea and hold them accountable for making it happen.

Unsuccessful: Subway Shrinks by Losing Touch

Introduction

Success can lead to failure—especially if the company in question is big and chooses to ignore up-start rivals that take its customers. That's what Subway did. With 43,945 sandwich shops in 110 countries in 2015, Subway U.S. sales fell 3% in 2014 from the previous year's $13.3 billion—faster than any other of America's top 25 food chains, according to the *Washington Post*.

Case Scenario

Due to profit pressures, franchisees—who sold an average of $437,000 worth of subs, sodas, and cookies in 2015—were unable to adapt to competitive pressure by boosting ingredient quality and paying workers more to improve service. But more than any other lesson behind Subway's decline is the high cost an organization pays when it trades off listening to changing customer needs and competitive pressures in favor of short-term profit goals. Perhaps one reason that Subway shrank is that decades of success produced a creeping belief that it could do no wrong. After all, Subway grew for decades by offering American consumers healthier alternatives at lower prices compared to the likes of McDonald's and Burger King.

But by early 2015, Subway began to lose market share to rivals such as Chipotle Mexican Grill and Firehouse Subs that offered "fresher, healthier, build-your-own meals" than did Subway, noted the Post. These rivals redefined the meaning of healthy food—leading consumers to switch away from Subway. How so? While these rivals provide diners with fresh-cut meat heated by steamers, Subway continued peeling the meat off wax paper and heating it in a microwave. In pursuit of fresh growth, Subway chose to keep doing what had made it successful in the past—opening new stores—rather than going a step further in redefining freshness beyond Chipotle and Firehouse. As Darren Tristano, executive vice president of industry researcher Technomic, said, "Subway's strategy has only been to open more stores, and ultimately those stores just cannibalize each other."

By 2016, Subway had been around for 51 years. In 1965, 17-year-old Fred DeLuca borrowed $1,000 from Peter Buck, a doctor, to open Pete's Super Submarines in Bridgeport, Connecticutt. Things went slowly until 1974 when they changed the name to Subway. By 2013, Subway was opening 50 new shops a week—in hundreds of U.S. colleges, malls, and military bases. And Subway stepped up its growth ambitions—seeking 30% growth in a year. In 2014, the then 66-year-old CEO DeLuca set a goal of adding 8,000 new American franchises to Subway's existing 27,000. But while franchisees liked the relatively low upfront investment of $116,000—10% of McDonald's, Franchise Grade, a franchisee polling and review service, ranked Subway number 468 in its 2015 report.

Prices of existing franchises were discounted to "the price of a car, as a sign that some owners wanted out. And as sandwich sales shrank, the pressure on franchisees increased," according to the Post. And workers' wages stayed low because franchisees—who paid the Subway parent company a $15,000 start-up franchise fee plus 12% of weekly sales—were under the gun to keep boosting profits as sales declined and the costs of keeping up with changing ingredients and menus rose. Subway's reputation as a place to buy a healthier lunch had weakened. Technomic surveyed Americans who "found Subway's food taste, flavor and visual appeal sagged" between 2014 and 2015, according to the Post thanks to "intense competitive pressure from other sandwich concepts."

Andrew Alvarez, a food analyst with IBISWorld concluded that Subways' efforts to respond to its rivals—by adding items like hummus and a creamy sriracha sauce—were insufficient. "We're in a new environment—the Chipotle environment—with a new type of rhetoric, quality and marketability. Subway's platform, its presentation almost looks primordial," said Alvarez.

Subway's strategy of boosting revenues by adding new stores and new menu items fell flat. In 2015, its sales declined 3.4% from the year before due to continued competitive pressure from Jimmy John's, Jersey Mikes, and Firehouse Subs—some of whom saw sales soar as much as 30%. Moreover, Subway raised prices on its footlong subs from $5 to $6 without boosting perceived freshness or quality, which also caused customers to turn away.

Sadly, DeLuca was taken ill while visiting stores in 2013 and was discovered to be suffering from leukemia from which he died in September 2015. Prior to his death, DeLuca appointed his sister, Suzanne Greco, as president to run Subway's day-to-day operations.

Case Analysis

Subway's declining revenues reveal three fatal flaws that companies should seek to avoid if they want to grow from selling more to customers in their current market segments.

1. CEO suffers from confirmation bias—the tendency to ignore information that does not reinforce the CEO's mental model. In Subway's case, the bias is that growth comes from aggressively selling more franchises.

2. CEO ignores competitors who are redefining the industry value proposition and taking away customers.

3. CEO measures success through short-term profit goals—thus creating a doom loop when sales drop that requires cutting product quality and service, which leads to further sales declines.

The success of McDonald's and the struggles of Subway reveal the importance of a basic insight that is very easy for big companies to forget—the customer is the boss. If a company wants to grow by selling to more customers within its core segments, it must listen to changes in customers' needs and keep a close eye on what competitors are doing to satisfy those changing needs. Moreover, it is never enough merely to notice that customer needs are changing. Instead, an effective CEO must create a sense of urgency about the importance of taking effective action quickly to capture the growth opportunity. The McDonald's case demonstrates what happens when these ideas are put into practice while the Subway story illustrates the perils of ignoring them.

Principle Two   Large companies seeking growth from new customers should identify ranked customer purchase criteria in the new segment and deliver a competitively superior value proposition.

When a large company seeks growth from a new customer group, the most important mistake to avoid is assuming that the strategy that worked for your current customers will also work for the new ones. Avoiding that mistake depends on a company's willingness to think about the new customer group as if it were starting the company from scratch—with the hope that some of the skills and resources that worked so far will help in the new venture. More specifically, targeting new customers will be most effective if the company deeply analyzes the specific needs of the new customers and examines how well customers perceive that the rivals meet those needs.

To do that, as we'll see later in the chapter, companies should listen to potential customers describe and rank the factors—I call them customer purchase criteria—which they use to compare competing suppliers. Moreover, companies ought to heed what those potential customers say about why their winning supplier outperforms rivals and whether there is a realistic opportunity for growth—where the company can satisfy customers' unmet needs more effectively than rivals.

Successful: Criteo Penetrates the Middle Market

Introduction

A French mobile advertising service provider, Criteo, followed this path when it added so-called middle market companies to its initial big-company customer base. For example, in the second quarter of 2015, Criteo—which operates a system to let corporate clients boost sales by targeting consumers through desktop and mobile advertising——boosted its revenue excluding traffic acquisition costs (TAC) by 65% to $120 million as it added 730 mid-market customers to total about 8,500.

Case Scenario

Criteo expected more growth from these new customers. "Mid-market has been particularly strong this quarter both in contribution to our overall growth and net client additions. We expect we will see more and more new clients coming from the mid-market," said CEO J. B. Rudelle. Indeed, Criteo fulfilled Rudelle's commitment— maintaining its rapid growth throughout 2015. Its revenues grew 60% to $1.3 billion and Criteo earned a 5% net margin—serving more than 10,000 clients while retaining over 90% of them. Criteo grew quickly because of a fundamentally different way of grouping consumers, which led to a different set of product features that met the unique needs of these newly defined segments.

More specifically, instead of clustering consumers based on demographic variables like age or income, Criteo grouped them based on what they wanted to buy. "Instead of targeting people based on who they are (their age, gender, home address, marital status, etc.), we concentrate on what they want (a new phone, a sofa, a beach vacation, etc.)," explained Rudelle.

While this may seem obvious, recent developments in technology have made it possible. First, Criteo was able to "capture shopping intent" through search keywords, digital purchase history, online shopping carts, and other signals from consumers' desktop and mobile devices. This enabled Criteo to predict what consumers would want to buy more accurately than in the past. Secondly, Criteo was able to provide its clients with real-time sales information by product that helped them to measure their return on marketing expenses. As Rudelle explained, "Thanks to break-through technologies, it's now increasingly possible to make this link not only with precision for each consumer, but in real-time. This ability to close the loop allows for optimized media buying in a way that was only possible to dream of before." Ultimately, Criteo's growth comes from its ability to persuade clients that it can deliver a higher return on their marketing investment than do rivals.

As Eric Eichmann, president and COO of Criteo said, "From our perspective, we have 8,500 clients-plus who are willing to work with us and we have a consumer database that connects [data] through us. There are not many people who have that installed base who could fuel that cross-device database, and we think this complements

*efforts by Google and Facebook. Measurability is absolutely key to our business,"
Rudelle said. "We're investing in our technology to show more performance. The best
demonstration of this is mobile. We wanted to make sure we could measure ROI in
mobile both in browser and in-app. We believe as advertising becomes more focused
on performance and ROI, we will benefit." Indeed Criteo was able to sustain its growth
through the first quarter of 2016—posting a 36.4% increase in revenue—with 45%
coming from existing clients and 55% from new ones—a total of 760 new clients.*

Case Analysis

The Criteo case study reveals four critical lessons for executives seeking
growth by selling to new customers:

- **Pursue growth with an open mind.** The CEO must
  be willing to assume that the needs of customers and the
  requirements for gaining market share will be different in
  the new market than they were for the company's core
  business.

- **Find customer's pain.** The company must listen to customers in the new segment to identify the unmet needs
  that competitors may not be trying to address.

- **Solve the problem in a way that will delight customers.** The company must have a vision for how technology can be used to address the unmet needs of these
  new customers in a way that will provide the customers
  with measurable benefits.

- **Turn the vision into sales growth.** The company must
  bet capital and product development resources on the
  vision, build the product, present it to customers, and
  close deals.

Unsuccessful: Eastman Kodak Files for Bankruptcy

Introduction

One of the biggest reasons that large companies fail to win customers in new
markets is that their previous success installs organizational blinders on their
top executives. These blinders lead executives to view anything new through
a specific mental model that flowed from what made the firm successful in
the past.

The longer the company has been successful with the same business strategy,
the more effective those organizational blinders. That's especially true if the
company is located in a relatively remote area where the best way to enjoy

an economically comfortable life is to get a job at such a company and slowly rise through the ranks by following all the clearly articulated cues for achieving career success at the company.

The key point is that success can lead to failure because it molds a mental model that turns important market signals—such as changing customer needs, new technologies that create better value for customers, and the growing market power of new competitors—into information that must be ignored at the risk of being thrown off the corporate fast track. If one were to ask an individual employee whether such market signals demanded a response, he or she would probably say they did. But that employee would never admit it in a group discussion with colleagues for fear of being shunted away from the fast track. And this helps explain why Rochester, New York-based Eastman Kodak—for which I did a year's worth of consulting work in the 1980s—filed for bankruptcy in 2012 because it could not offset the decline in traditional camera film sales by applying its silver-halide strategy—giving away a camera and film at low prices to make profit on developing prints—to build winning products for new customers in the digital imaging market.

Case Scenario

In 2011, I was amazed that Kodak had survived as long as it had. In the 1980s, my consulting work for the maker of the Brownie led me to believe that it was heading unstoppably to its end decades before—but it took longer than I had anticipated. When Kodak was founded in 1888, quality was its "fighting argument." It gladly gave away cameras in exchange for getting people hooked on paying to have their photos developed—yielding Kodak a highly profitable annuity siphoned from its 80% share of the market for the chemicals and paper used to develop and print those photos. Inside Kodak, this was known as the "silver halide" strategy—named after the chemical compounds in its film. Kodak had a fantastic success formula that keyed off of international distribution, mass production to lower unit costs, R&D investment to introduce better products, and extensive advertising to make sure consumers knew about Kodak's superior quality.

Unfortunately, competition came along and introduced ugly splotches all over this beautiful picture. Here are three examples:

- *Instant photography. A few days prior to Thanksgiving in 1948, a Massachusetts-based inventor, Edwin Land, offered consumers an instant camera that developed photos in 60 seconds. Instant photography threatened Kodak's profits from chemicals and film. Kodak responded by introducing its own instant photography products. Polaroid sued—alleging that between 1976 and 1986 Kodak stole its technology—asking for $12 billion in damages. In 1990, Polaroid won a mere $909 million and ultimately filed for bankruptcy in October 2001.*

- **Cut-rate film from Japan.** In the 1980s, Japan's Fuji started to sell rolls of film at a price way below the one that Kodak had been accustomed to charging. Fuji's willingness to cut prices was quite popular with the rapidly growing mass merchandisers like Wal-Mart that preferred to deal with suppliers who were willing to sell high volumes at ever-lower prices. And Fuji helped make consumers aware of its value by sponsoring big events—such as the 1984 Los Angeles Olympics. By 1999, Fuji's market share gains were so great that Kodak took a $1.2 billion charge along with 19,900 layoffs. Such layoffs persisted; for example, in January 2009, Kodak took a $350 million charge to dismiss 3,500 employees after a 24% drop in revenue.

- **Digital photography.** Digital photography offered consumers a better value but one that wiped out a decent way for Kodak to make money. After all, digital film—flash memory—was a low margin proposition even if you had the huge semiconductor fabrication facilities needed to produce it. And even though Kodak was number two in digital cameras by 1999, it lost $60 on each one it sold. In one of many bids to replicate its Silver Halide business model in digital photography, Kodak offered a Photo CD film-based digital imaging product—but since it was priced at $500 per player and $20 per disc, it did not attract many customers.

Another reason that Kodak failed in the digital photography market is that its primary customer for traditional film was women and digital camera buyers were predominantly men. Kodak created demand for traditional cameras by advertising "the need to preserve significant occasions such as family events and vacations. These were labeled Kodak moments, a concept that became entrenched in everyday life," according to the Wall Street Journal. Kodak's ad campaigns assigned women the role of preserving these Kodak moments. "As responsible and caring wives and mothers—they were morally obliged to keep a meticulous record of their family's history," according to the Journal.

When digital came along, the primary users of cameras became men. And digital images could be viewed on camera, phone, or a PC without any need for hard prints. The eliminated the role Kodak had ascribed to women of keeping the family archives by maintaining hard copy prints of a family's history. Men tended to take "transient" photographs and hence Kodak's strengths at marketing to women became irrelevant. Rather than accept that it needed to change the focus of its marketing strategy, Kodak "kept trying to recreate the photography universe of yesteryear, one based around sentimental images taken by women at family reunions and vacations," noted the Journal.

I had a personal encounter with another one of Kodak's strategic blunders. In January 1988, I was standing next to a fax machine on the executive floor of Kodak's Rochester, New York, headquarters. I watched in astonishment at a scrolling fax of a contract for Kodak to acquire Sterling Drug for $5.1 billion. Kodak thought this was a wise investment for two reasons: drugs had high margins and Kodak made chemicals. Unfortunately, those two facts were not sufficient to make this deal pay off for Kodak shareholders. To do that, Kodak would have needed capabilities that it lacked—such as the ability to come up with new, valuable, patented drugs or to make generic drugs at a rock-bottom cost. It only took six years for Kodak to realize that Sterling Drug was not a good fit for Kodak and sell it off in pieces.

One hope for returning to a decent business model might have been producing high quality personal printers for those digital images. Selling inkjet cartridges and papers might have yielded a nice profit stream for Kodak. But regrettably for Kodak, many other competitors—most notably Hewlett Packard had gotten there first. Since peaking in February 1999 at about $80 a share, Kodak shares suffered a steady tumble that wiped out 99% of their value—to 78 cents a share as of September 30, 2011. At the end of June 2011, Kodak's liabilities exceeded its assets by $1.4 billion. It then owed $1.4 billion and had $957 million in cash, down $847 million from the end of 2010. Its last CEO (since 2005), former Hewlett Packard executive Tony Perez, was unable to revive Kodak. In October 2011, it pulled $160 million from its credit line and hired restructuring advisor Jones Day even as Kodak denied that it was on the verge of filing for bankruptcy.

On January 19, 2012, the picture of Kodak's demise was fully developed—that's when it filed for bankruptcy. "As it watched digital dissolve its high-margin film business, Kodak had shed 47,000 employees since 2003, closing 13 factories that produced film, paper and chemicals, along with 130 photo laboratories," wrote Bloomberg.

Case Analysis

Kodak's bankruptcy reveals four fatal flaws that companies should seek to avoid if they want to grow from selling to new customers in their current market segments.

1. Too much success—particularly leading a company to a dominant position in its industry with little competition—can create a rigid culture that cannot adapt to change.

2. Rigid companies pick investments in growth opportunities that fit with what their top executives believe are the company's timeless strengths. If the executives' beliefs are not consistent with current and future marketplace realities, those investments are likely to consume resources that might have been allocated more effectively.

3. Developing new products without viewing them from the perspective of new customers is not likely to produce meaningful growth.

4. Large companies are in danger of failing to understand the unique requirements of winning new customers and introducing products that deliver superior value.

Comparing the success of Criteo and Kodak's failure reveal the importance of a basic insight when it comes to winning new customers. A large company is at risk of basing its growth strategy on internally important matters rather than what new customers demand. The Kodak case demonstrates that unless a company maintains what former Intel CEO Andrew Grove called "a healthy paranoia," it is in danger of flushing away its resources in a profitless quest to build a future on the foundation of its long-irrelevant old ways of running its business. By contrast, Criteo's success attracting middle-market customers reveals that its CEO maintained the right focus—on delivering a product that would offer new customers a competitively superior value proposition.

Principle Three Small companies seeking growth from current customers should pick customer groups with a high willingness to pay, deliver excellent service, and encourage them to recommend the company to members of their network.

Small companies have considerable advantages over big ones—the general rule for them is that they either grow or die. The Kodak case illustrates that big companies can die as well—but they have far more resources and can muddle along for decades as long as they don't borrow too much money or burn through their cash. Small companies must find growth if they hope to survive. After all, many of them—particularly technology start-ups—tend to sacrifice profits and cash flow for very rapid growth. If the small companies achieve the aggressive growth goals that investors set, they can raise more money and keep growing until they ultimately go public or get acquired. This pressure to get big fast small companies to focus on how to capture growth opportunities before they run out of cash.

In contrast to large, resource-rich corporations, their resource scarcity heightens the intensity of small company CEOs' efforts to craft and execute strategies to meet ambitious growth goals. To do this, small companies must do three things:

- Focus on the right customer groups—for example, ones with significant purchasing power and meaningful unmet needs.

- Co-develop products with early-adopter customers to satisfy those customers' unmet needs.

- Deliver new products that customers see as irresistibly superior to competing products.

If a small company has done this well, it is likely to have gained some market share. And one growth vector it can choose after that initial success is to seek to sell more of its current products to a larger share of the customer group it initially targeted. To do that well, small companies ought to turn their current customers into their best salespeople—by giving them products and support services that they perceive as excellent so they will enthusiastically recommend them to others in their social network.

Successful: Social Finance (SoFi)

Introduction

Between its founding in 2011 and May 2016, SoFi, a San Francisco-based consumer finance start-up in which I invested in December 2014, had made about $10 billion worth of loans. When I invested, SoFi was valued at $1 billion and by September 2015 it had raised an additional $1.4 billion in capital, valuing it at roughly $4 billion.

Case Scenario

SoFi's profits came from charging investors loan-servicing fees and by selling loans to investors for more than it cost to make the loans. It also kept some loans and collected interest payments. SoFi offered below-market-rate student loan refinancing, mortgages, and other consumer loans using funds obtained from institutional investors and wealthy individuals to whom it paid as much as 6.5% annual interest—depending on the borrower's rate of loan repayment. Of SoFi's 150,000 members, 100,000 joined between June 2015 and June 2016 when it originated $600 million to $700 million in loans every month (compared to about $200 million per month in the first quarter of 2015).

The inspiration for SoFi could be an event that left a deep impression on its CEO, Mike Cagney, when he was 11 years old. That's when he lived in Grosse Ile, Michigan, and his father lost his job as the manager of a steel-rolling plant. "We had to rely on a lot of community support during the two years he was looking for a job. The way people stood up and helped out, everything from our local banker to people bringing food, it left a lasting impact on me," he said. But SoFi — which has been profitable since 2014—has bigger ambitions. As Cagney told CNBC, "We actually are trying to change a fundamentally broken [banking] system." And with the new capital, Cagney planned to expand through "initiatives in wealth management, banking account alternatives—things that allow us to give a holistic solution [that will lead] people to leave their existing banking relationship and just work with SoFi," Cagney said.

To understand its success, SoFi enjoyed five competitive advantages over traditional banks—such as Bank of America.

- **Market segmentation.** Traditional banks were highly regulated and could not cherry-pick the best borrowers and ignoring the rest. SoFi—which did not take deposits and was regulated at the state level by the Consumer Financial Protection Bureau—had more strategic flexibility. SoFi prospered by targeting students at relatively selective schools—such as Stanford and Harvard—whose alumni tended to get high-paying jobs and to be financially responsible. Moreover, SoFi's original concept matched up wealthy alumni of those schools who in addition to providing the money to refinance those loans helped borrowers seeking career advice.

- **Lower loan rates.** SoFi estimated that it can save the typical student loan refinancing borrower about $14,000 and that its rates "started" at 3.50% fixed and variable rates start as low as 1.90% [annual percentage rate] APR (with AutoPay). Bank of America rival, Citizens Bank charged more—from 4.74% APR to 8.90% APR (with autopay) for fixed rate and 2.33% APR to 6.97% APR (with autopay) for a variable rate loan.

- **Higher deposit rates.** Like most traditional banks, Bank of America paid a barely detectable 0.03% interest rate to depositors—but it could go up as high as 0.08% for those with an account at its Merrill Lynch unit. SoFi did not take consumer deposits. However, individuals who qualified to provide cash to borrowers could earn much higher yields—up to 6.5% depending on the rate at which borrowers repay. To be sure, the people who provided capital to SoFi were taking a much bigger risk than a depositor at Bank of America. But with deposit rates near zero for the last eight years, SoFi offered a substantial reward to those willing to take that risk.

- **Better customer experience.** Bank of America was the second-largest U.S. lender but the leader when it came to customer dissatisfaction. According to an April 2015 J.D. Power survey of 80,000 bank customers on problem resolution, products, and fees, Bank of America ranked "last in four of 11 regions in 2015 including the Northwest and Southeast, compared with two in 2014." I could not find such a survey for SoFi, however, a comparison of SoFi's loan application process to Bank of America's revealed one reason why consumers might like SoFi more. SoFi offered to give a potential borrower a rate on their loan within two minutes based on the borrower's response to questions asked on its web site. Bank of

America's website let a potential borrower fill in an application but did not guarantee the time it would take to deliver the rate quote.

- **More rapid response to change.** Since I first wrote about SoFi in 2011, its business strategy evolved in response to market feedback, changing technology, and upstart competitors. It started off in student loan refinancing. SoFi broadened its sources of capital from wealthy alumni to others—such as securitizing and selling the loans to institutional investors. Then it expanded into mortgages. In 2016, 60% of SoFi's current loans were for student loan refinancing, but by the end of the year, new origination in mortgages and consumer loans [were expected to] top student debt refinancing, Cagney told Fortune.

SoFi planned to continue to adapt. As Cagney said, achieving his vision was "going to require us [to take] some chances. And those are things that are difficult to do as a public company, when you're on a quarterly reporting calendar." Having established itself with this initial strategy, SoFi pursued growth by seeking to gain a larger share of the well-educated borrowers it targeted initially. SoFi refered to its customers as members and it sponsored events that engaged those members with the company and with each other. Here are four ways SoFi does this:

- **Sponsor social events.** SoFi regularly invited members to gather for happy hours around the country. Cagney estimated that SoFi hosted two to three events per week, which in 2016 included a yoga class in New York; a dinner party in Richmond, Virginia; and a skydiving trip in San Francisco.

- **Help find a spouse.** SoFi sponsored events for its single members—for example, the skydiving outing held on Valentine's Day 2016, was specifically for singles. SoFi was developing a dating app that expected to launch in 2016.

- **Assist in starting a business.** SoFi invited members to apply for its entrepreneur program, a six-month, full-time boot camp that connected founders to accredited investors and venture capitalists. SoFi let entrepreneurs defer loan payments during the program.

- **Offer career counseling.** SoFi employed career counselors who coached members seeking to switch fields or achieve professional goals. The counselors also "led workshops on negotiating raises and mastering informational interviews."

"Once you have a relationship, no one is in a better position to deliver a second product than you are," said Cagney. "If it's based on trust and value and reciprocity, you should be able to scale that into a huge opportunity." In the spring of 2016, SoFi *faced a significant challenge when the CEO of one of its publicly traded rivals was fired—casting a dark shadow on the industry. In May 2016, Lending Club founder and CEO, "Renaud Laplanche was forced out after an internal investigation found that he had sold $22 million in loans to an institutional investor, despite knowing that the loans did not meet the investor's 'express' criteria."*

In a bid to restore confidence, SoFi sold a very high quality $280 million bundle of loans to investors—holding 5% of the loans on its books. In May 2016, Moody's "gave SoFi its first-ever triple-A debt rating [for that bundle], the highest available to a startup online lender." That move proved insufficient to restore a major growth challenge for SoFi—in the first quarter of 2016, it originated a mere $1.85 billion worth of new loans—well short of its $2.4 billion goal. While SoFi was in better shape than its rivals—at the end of April 2016, asset manager Hartford Funds put the same value on its SoFi shares as it had in October. LendingClub shares fell 44% in the same period.

However, by July 2016, Cagney was considering a variety of options for SoFi's growth strategy that were intended to shore up its need to raise capital for financing its loans:

- ***Becoming a Utah Bank.*** *In March 2016, SoFi told Utah officials it would create 400 jobs and invest $8 million in the state. Cagney said that its Utah operations would handle borrower phone calls but would also be useful if the company sought a bank charter in the state.*

- ***Partnering with JP Morgan.*** *In February 2016, Cagney met with J.P. Morgan CEO Jamie Dimon—in a meeting arranged by Arthur Levitt, a former Securities and Exchange Commission chairman who is an adviser to SoFi. Cagney and Dimon discussed their backgrounds and SoFi's goals but both companies wanted to control the customer relationship and they had not announced a partnership as of July 2016.*

These options were diametrically opposed to Cagney's anti-bank rhetoric from earlier in SoFi's history. But they demonstrated his willingness to adapt to rapidly changing business conditions in pursuit of SoFi's long-term vision.

Case Analysis

The SoFi case study reveals five critical lessons for small company executives seeking growth by gaining share among their current customers:

- **Participate in a huge market.** SoFi's initial market of student loans totals over $1 trillion and the other consumer loans it offers also represent markets larger than $1 trillion.

- **Segment the customers.** The key to SoFi's initial success was its recognition that students could be segmented by where they attended school. Moreover, SoFi realized that graduates of different schools had varying loan repayment rates.

- **Offer a better value to the most attractive segment.** SoFi recognized that it could offer lower interest rates to groups of students with the highest repayment rates—thus yielding a profitable portfolio of loans. Moreover, SoFi offered more responsive service to its customers than its rivals—large banks.

- **Turn customers into enthusiastic product promotors.** SoFi dubs its customers members and creates opportunities for them to interact with other members and to develop their careers with the intent of selling them more services and encouraging them to bring their peers into the SoFi club.

- **Adapt to rapid change.** SoFi stumbled in the first quarter of 2016 as rivals suffered even more significant challenges. It is noteworthy that as of April 2016, the $4 billion valuation at which it had raised capital in 2015 had held up. And SoFi was scrambling to develop new sources of funding to restore its rapid loan growth.

Unsuccessful: Homejoy

Introduction

A common prescription for start-up failure is to cut price to win customers and to focus so intently on getting new customers that you neglect current ones. This leads to a predictable doom loop. The customers that signed up with you because of the discount get terrible service so they are determined not to buy from you again. What's more they will refuse to recommend your service to members of their social network. This bad treatment of customers is often accompanied by similar mistreatment of the employees who you hired to deliver the service. Your unhappy employees find ways of letting customers know that they don't like the company. And employee turnover spikes. Now the firm is in a double-bind—it needs to spend more money to attract new customers and to hire enough people to serve the ones it has. Burning through cash, its executives realize that the company needs to raise more. But its underwhelming growth performance and prospects scare away potential investors. And the company shuts down.

Case Scenario

This seems to be what happened to San Francisco-based home cleaning service Homejoy that opened in 2012 and shut down on July 31, 2015—wiping out $40 million in investment. Homejoy targeted an estimated $400 billion global market by offering on-demand home-cleaning services. The company captured significant press attention "because it offered low-cost cleaning and was using software to automate the process of booking so it would be more efficient," according to Business Insider.

Founded by Adora Cheung and her brother Aaron—both computer science majors, Homejoy did not grow as fast as its competitor Handy, and customers complained after Homejoy raised prices. Before shuttering, Homejoy raised $40 million from Y Combinator, PayPal founder Max Levchin, First Round Capital, Redpoint Ventures, and Google Ventures. It operated in 35 cities in the United States, France, the United Kingdom, Canada, and Germany and had 100 employees and roughly 1,000 cleaning professionals," according to Re/code. Homejoy put most of the blame for its failure on four lawsuits it was fighting over whether its workers should be classified as employees or contractors—which Cheung said had made fundraising more difficult.

But perhaps Cheung was too uncomfortable to admit that Homejoy's failure was due to mismanagement. Indeed the culprit for Homejoy's collapse seems more likely to be "mounting losses, poor customer retention, a costly international expansion, run-of-the-mill execution problems, technical glitches and the steady leak of its best workers to direct employment arrangements with its own (now former) clients," according to Backchannel. Homejoy copied Handy's customer acquisition strategy—offering Groupons to attract first-time customers. Despite internal data that customers who accepted the Groupons did not use the service again, by mid-2014, "thousands of people" accepted the $19.99 cleaning offers.

This strategy was costly for Homejoy. Indeed a third-party analysis of its financial statements revealed that roughly 25% of its customers kept using the service after the first month and fewer than 10% used it after six months. Homejoy was losing money every time it cleaned a home. Daniel Hung, Homejoy's second full-time engineer, told Backchannel, "The key problem is that we weren't making enough money on our customers. We were spending a lot of money to acquire them, but not really retaining them." Moreover, in pursuit of geographic expansion, Homejoy cut its standard prices dramatically to attract customers in dozens of new cities.

At its peak, Homejoy operated in over 30 cities, including Los Angeles, London, Berlin, and New York. Between the spring of 2013 and the spring of 2015, Homejoy grew from 20 employees to over 100 including "city managers, customer support, and an enviable engineering team poached from giants like Facebook and Google." Homejoy could not attract enough customers or hire a sufficient number of professional cleaners in cities with more geographically dispersed populations such as Tampa Bay, Florida; or Atlanta, Georgia. And Homejoy's international expansion caused numerous problems. In Berlin it was difficult to meet the demand for cleaners and in London, American best practices for cleaning were of no value.

Basic supply chain and operations also failed. Homejoy's city managers spent too much money on cleaning supplies because they did not know which products worked best, they didn't track unused supplies, and they failed to negotiate low-priced supply deals. Homejoy's service quality was also poor. Many first-time customers were dissatisfied or suffered a last-minute cancellation. One problem was a flaw in its scheduling algorithm that only allotted 30 minutes for cleaners to cross Manhattan as they traveled from Brooklyn to New Jersey. Despite repeated requests from Homejoy's cleaners, it took months before Homejoy's engineers began fixing the algorithm.

Cleaners would arrive late and angry customers would demand discounts—furthering heightening Homejoy's cash burn rate. If the stress was not enough to make it hard to retain good cleaners, Homejoy's below-industry-average pay—$15 an hour that barely covered transportation costs and forced workers into very long hours to make ends meet—almost guaranteed high turnover. And after cleaners quit, Homejoy could not figure out how to distinguish in hiring between good and bad ones. Moreover, in order to comply with IRS regulations regarding contractors, Homejoy city managers could not require cleaners to attend training classes. And Homejoy could not control quality very well—it would simply stop sending jobs to cleaners who frequently canceled at the last minute or worked fewer than 30 hours a week. Homejoy did not require a dress code, uniform, or standard set of cleaning tasks.

Last-minute cancellations were particularly damaging to Homejoy's service quality ratings because it could only make up for the canceled appointment 15% to 20% of the time. This problem was particularly pronounced in cities where the demand for cleaners exceeded the supply. Homejoy's best cleaners would set up their own services so they could boost their pay. But only soon before it shuttered did Homejoy fulfill customer requests to work with the same cleaner. "We were trapped between being accountable to our customers and not being able to take much responsibility for quality of service. We couldn't properly train our cleaners to meet fixed standards without fear of a legal backlash," according to former Homejoy operations manager Anton Zietsman.

Case Analysis

Homejoy's failure is a result of five flawed assumptions that companies should avoid if they are seeking growth by gaining share among their current customers:

- **The CEO's strengths are the company's key to success.** Homejoy's top management acted as though building and operating a scheduling algorithm was the key to Homejoy's success. It was not until too late in the company's development before it realized that it needed to attract and retain the best cleaners and manage their customer relationships to achieve high levels of service.

- **Lower prices will always lure in new customers.** Homejoy assumed that the only way to get customers was to offer them cleaning at a discounted price. Homejoy failed to appreciate that a one-time customer who received poor service would not buy again. And Homejoy would then need to spend heavily on marketing to replace the lost customer.

- **The best way to beat a competitor is to copy its strategy.** Homejoy lacked insight into the needs of its potential customers and concluded that the only way to grow would be to imitate the strategy of a fast-growing rival. Homejoy's failure to listen to customers left it with little understanding of how it would be able to attract new customers, make them want to keep buying, and encourage them to recommend Homejoy to others in their social network.

- **Employee quality and satisfaction are not important.** Homejoy lacked standards for cleaners that it could use to screen out people who would provide poor quality cleaning service or cancel appointments at the last minute. Moreover, Homejoy paid its cleaners less than subsistence wages and was unable to assure that the training they needed to deliver high quality service.

- **Unprofitable services can be overcome with sufficient volume.** Finally, Homejoy pursued rapid geographic expansion to boost its revenue growth without considering in sufficient depth the capabilities it would need in order to sustain its business in those new locations. Moreover, despite losing money on each transaction, it lacked a strategy for becoming profitable and seemed to assume that another owner would take over the company and worry about that problem.

Principle Four Small companies seeking growth from new customers should conduct research to rank their purchase criteria, analyze competitor offerings, and deliver superior value.

When a small company seeks growth from a new customer group, the most important mistake to avoid is assuming that the strategy that worked for its current customers will also work for the new ones.

In this area, small companies are no different than large ones. The big difference for small companies is that due to their limited cash reserves, going after new customers could be the last bet the company will be able to make. Whereas a large company might fail in its efforts to target new customers, that failure is not as likely to be fatal. But if a small company seeks to grow by targeting new customers, it is more likely that the move could require investments that would divert the company from its core customers and ultimately lower its chances of surviving. Therefore, small companies must be particularly cautious when they seek growth from new customers. They should have very well-researched answers to questions such as the following:

- Are we earning sufficient profit from our core customers?
- If so, have we grown as much as we can from selling to them?
- Would a new group of customers be more profitable?
- If so, what product can we offer those new customers that they will eagerly purchase?
- What is the investment required to design, build, sell, and service the new product?
- Will that investment pay off before we run out of cash?

Small companies lack the resources to hire a big consulting firm to answer these questions, but they should find a way to get good answers before betting they can get growth by selling to new customers.

Semi-Successful: Actifio One Targets $580 Billion Small and Medium-Sized Business (SMB) Market

Introduction

In early 2015, Waltham, Massachusetts-based data management start-up Actifio announced that it would seek to grow by adding small- and medium-sized business customers to its original Fortune 1000 customer base. But by July 2016, Actifio had shifted its strategy and the results suggested a mixed picture for its future.

Case Scenario

Founded in 2009, Actifio made appliances that helped companies save money on data storage by reducing to one the many copies of corporate data that companies traditionally stored for various different purposes including backup and recovery, compliance, testing, and data analysis.

Companies bought Actifio's products because making and saving copies of their data—as many as 12 per company for uses like backup and application testing—was costly. Actifio saves companies money by letting them do all those things with a single "golden copy." This saved them money—for every dollar a company invested in Actifio's product, customers saved as much as $15. As of June 2016, Actifio had raised a total of $207.5 million from investors including Advanced Technology Ventures, Andreessen Horowitz, Technology Crossover Ventures, Tiger Global Management, Greylock Partners, and North Bridge Venture Partners. In its most recent funding round in March 2014, Actifio raised $100 million led by Tiger Global Management at a valuation of $1.1 billion. In an earlier round in 2013, Actifio had raised $50 million in a Series D round that valued the company at $500 million. As a private company, Actifio was under no obligation to disclose its financial results; however, in March 2014, Actifio revealed that its revenues for 2014 would be "well over" $40 million and that its average deal size was $388,000.

In 2012, Actifio thought it would be going public in 2014. But that did not happen. On February 2, 2015, I spoke with Actifio CEO Ash Ashutosh after which it become clearer why the company did not go public in 2014 and what it planned to do to get there. In previous years Actifio had been heavily dependent on large accounts—making its revenues and profits lumpy and thus not as appealing to public company investors. To remedy the lumpiness, Actifio wanted to provide a service to the Small- and Medium-Sized Enterprise (SME) market that it hoped would smooth out its financial results by adding many smaller accounts that paid regularly and more predictably. This was a clear change in strategy for Actifio, which in June 2014 was going for growth from big companies. "We keep reaching for bigger numbers. And we are executing—coming in every day and closing new business. We used to focus on Global 2000 companies, then Fortune 500. Now we are going to the Fortune 5. The transformation that we bring is so large that we are having an impact in the biggest companies," Ashutosh said. But in February 2015, Actifio announced that it would target small- and medium-sized businesses—a market amounting to $580 billion worth of IT spending—by launching Actifio One, a "business resiliency cloud" service that enabled small- and medium-sized businesses to store and retrieve their applications.

Until then, Actifio had been selling an appliance that combined commodity hardware and its own software that it called Actifio CDS. In 2014, Actifio launched Actifio Sky—what it referred to as "the next generation of our technology that required no third party hardware and ran on a virtual machine." An early customer—the Town of Banff, Alberta, suggested that Actifio One was competitive. Andrew Wheelhouse, IT coordinator for the Town of Banff said, "I was very impressed with the innovative Actifio One software service as well as the excellent technical assistance, ease of implementation and purchasing." His decision to buy boiled down to two factors—rapid data restoration and competitive price. "Actifio One is price competitive. But more importantly, if you need something to work, it needs to work. And while you are struggling with a long, slow restore process, you won't be congratulating yourself on saving a few dollars at the purchase," argued Wheelhouse.

Actifio's new strategy would require an investment in marketing and a simpler user interface. As Ashutosh said, "The go-to-market model is different, that's been the real investment here. This is a lower average order value, higher velocity, more channel-friendly offering. We're also making investments to simplify the software user interface and better enable customers to support themselves."

To be sure, Actifio saw itself as helping to solve customer problems rather than trying to take customers from rivals such as EMC. "That erosion will continue, sure. But we don't really focus on winning share from the old guard. It's all about solving customer problems for us, and [Actifio One] will most certainly do that," noted Ashutosh. Actifio did not expect the new service to generate significant revenue in the short run. After all, its SME customers paid an estimated $200,000 a year while larger companies spent as much as between $1.8 million and $2 million on Actifio subscriptions.

But it did expect Actifio One to help it tell a better story to public market investors. "As we begin telling our story to institutional investors in the public market, we recognize the importance of our business being both high growth and highly predictable, and we think offerings like this will play an important part," he said.

Things did not work out quite as Ashutosh had planned. As he told me on July 12, 2016, he thought that it would be much more efficient to sell to distribution partners who sold to SMEs. "With big companies, it takes us 83 days to convince them that we can generate business value. But it can take six to 14 months for their procurement departments to qualify us and pay us as a first-time supplier. Working with distribution partners who sell to SMEs, the procurement process is shorter—20 to 80 days."

He set up Actifio One along the lines that Clayton Christensen prescribed for disruptive technologies—as a separate subsidiary charged with killing the parent. "We spun out a separate group across the street. After one-and-a-half quarters we realized that the logic was right but the reality was that we had the organizational DNA of working closely with large enterprises—developing technology solutions to work with petabytes of data," said Ashutosh. Actifio then realized that it lacked the capabilities to succeed in selling to SMEs. "One of the biggest differences in working with SMEs was how we needed to run finance. Whereas big companies might make three to five big payments during a contract, SMEs would pay monthly. To bill and collect from them we needed to add 20 people and be PCI-compliant so we could accept credit cards from them. Also, we were uncomfortable not having a direct relationship with the end-users of our product," he said. Actifio decided to scrap its separate subsidiary and instead license its technology to bigger "service providers"—companies that deliver an array of IT services to SMEs. As Ashutosh explained, "We license our technology to five of the 10 largest service providers that deal with SMEs. Like large organizations, they make a smaller number of large payments. And they may have 100 to 600 SME customers within a region. To sell to them, we need to show that our technology will help their SME customers to cut capital expenditures and achieve operational excellence."

In 2012, Ashutosh told me that he wanted Actifio to go public in 2014. That did not happen. Nevertheless it continued to hold onto many well-known companies as customers. At the start of 2016, Actifio had nearly 600 customers—including Unilever, HBO, Netflix, IBM, SunGard, and Time Warner Cable's NaviSite—in 36 countries, double the number in 2014. And in June 2016, he told CRN that Actifio did not need to go public and its goal was to get cash flow positive in 2016. That was when Ashutosh reported that despite his 2015 call that an IPO was "the next big milestone" for Actifio, he expected that to be delayed until at least 2017—after the company was profitable for the first time—which he hoped to accomplish by the end of 2016.

Actifio cited Uber's ability to raise capital privately as a reason not to rush an IPO. "This fascination with being public is a little overrated and I think we're learning now, very quickly, that you can create Uber—a $67 billion company—being completely private, so why go public unless we have to?," he told CRN UK. How would Actifio become profitable by the end of 2016? "[First] you spend time building the core technology, then you spend time building the core business. The third stage is how do you scale up this business to be a large institution? That's the phase we're moving into," he told CRN UK. "We are focusing on getting to be a profitable business so we can create a sustaining institution. It's going to be growth balanced with getting to be a profitable company—that's going to be a big tipping point for us this year."

Case Analysis

The mixed outcome of Actifio's strategy to target a new customer group reveals four important lessons for small business leaders:

- **Pick a compelling mission.** Actifio had a clear reason for targeting SMEs—a desire to smooth out its lumpy cash collections to make its financial statements more compelling to public investors. While this may not be the most exalted of missions, it was clearly one that would help investors and employees realize their financial goals—therefore it had motivational power.

- **Understand the distinct requirements of the new customers.** Actifio did not make its shareholders the sole focus of its SME strategy. It also concentrated its attention on the specific requirements of potential SME customers—a desire for quick restoration of their IT systems after a business interruption and a low price.

- **Build a better product.** Actifio's customer, the Town of Banff, bought Actifio One because it satisfied those needs—it offered rapid recovery at a low price. Actifio's success here recognizes a fundamental condition for successful growth—new customers will only consider a small company's product if it delivers competitively superior features at a lower price.

- **Invest in a new strategy.** Actifio realized after about 16 weeks of trying that it had the wrong strategy for winning with SMBs. It should have realized ahead of time that competing for SMB business would involve different capabilities throughout the value chain—including sales and marketing, after-sales service, and billing and collection. Moreover, although Ashutosh hoped that channel partners would shorten the time to close deals, he should have seen that working with channel partners would be frustrating. After all before launching its SMB strategy, Actifio had valued working directly with its big company end users. By working with channel partners, Actifio lost its direct customer interaction.

Unsuccessful: Color Labs

Introduction

If a company tries to grow by serving one group of customers and fails, it should at least learn something that helps it succeed with the second group of customers it targets. The fundamental lesson that companies must learn if they seek growth from new customers is that they must offer them a product that the new customers see as an irresistible value. That perceived value could come in many bundles. Companies could deliver a good product at a very low price compared to competitors, or they could offer a much broader set of features at the same price. The most common reason small companies fail is that they burn through all their capital before they figure out a product that customers believe is an irresistible value—making them eager to pay a higher price than the company's costs to design, build, ship, and service it.

Case Scenario

That is what happened to Palo Alto, California-based photo-sharing app, Color Labs. It shut down in December 2012 after burning through much of the $41 million it raised. Color initially tried to sell a location-based social network—that failed and it "pivoted" to a photo and video sharing service that also failed. Color was cofounded by Bill Nguyen and Peter Pham on August 1, 2010. Despite his failure to build companies that lasted, Nguyen's previous track record of starting and selling companies—in 1998 Nguyen started a web-based fax service that he sold for $850 million two months before the dot com crash; and in 2009 Apple bought Lala, a cloud-based music service Nguyen started, for a reported $80 million—made him a venture capital magnet. By October 2012, Apple had acquired Color's 20-person technology team and some of its key intellectual property assets for $7 million and Color Labs ceased to operate at the end of 2012.

The intervening two years between Color's launch and its shutdown reveal some classic start-up errors. Nguyen's pulled the plug on his first idea—a game called Furr, in which "this furry creature would basically colonize the world everywhere you went physically with your phone, buildings would emerge"—after three months.

From there, Color Labs worked on a photo-sharing app that it launched in March 2011. The free app that let "people in close proximity to one another gain real-time access to photos, video, and text messages, simultaneously, from multiple smart-phones"—was launched on the Apple App Store and Android Market. The app's launch was overshadowed by news that Color Labs had raised $41 million "without any proof of concept, traction with the public, or revenue generated."

The day it was launched users rated the app a terrible "one or two stars out of five—nails in the coffin, given an oversaturated app market that was spawning more than 1,000 new apps a day. The problem was simple: In order for Color to work, many users had to be in a similar location, but since Color hadn't widely seeded the app prelaunch, users arrived to a social network that resembled a ghost town," according to Fast Company. A few months later, Pham was fired and by June 2011, it was clear that the app was not a winner. "Despite the company's riches, the app landed with a thud, attracting few users and many complaints from those who did try it. 'It would be pointless even if I managed to understand how it works,' one reviewer wrote in the Apple App Store," according to the New York Times.

In retrospect, it is clear that Color was beaten to the pot of gold at the end of the photo-sharing rainbow by a lean competitor, Instagram, which started with a mere $500,000, hired a small team, and raised capital as it achieved product success. In April 2012, Facebook acquired Instagram—whose 30 million registered users gener-ated no revenue—for $1 billion a few weeks after Instagram had raised $50 million at a $500 million valuation. Instagram may have sold too early—about three years later Instagram had 300 million users and two analysts valued the company—as if it were independent—at $37 billion. By contrast, Color was careless with its cash. It "spent $350,000 to buy the web address color.com, and an additional $75,000 to buy colour.com. It rents a cavernous office in downtown Palo Alto, where 38 employ-ees work in a space with room for 160, amid beanbag chairs, tents for napping and a hand-built half-pipe skateboard ramp," according to the Times.

Nguyen was bruised by the failure but decided to build a new service to "compete with Apple, Google, and Facebook by tying together group messaging, recommenda-tions, and local search, all while making money through advertising. He [planned] to build applications that will use data from Facebook to create temporary social networks, say at a conference or sporting event, to help users meet people who grew up in the same town or like the same band," reported the Times. He boasted that Color's new service would "literally turn your Facebook network from 500 people to 750 million people," according to the Times. Nguyen never launched the new service.

Part of this failure may have been due to his dismissive attitude toward offering a better product than what rivals are providing. "I have this other really bad trait. I never use anyone else's products but my own. I never do a competitive matrix ever. My entire life, I've never done it. I could care less what other people make. I have no interest whatsoever. I don't ever listen to any of it. I mean, I literally don't think there's anything to be learned from other people's stuff," he boasted to Fast Company.

Perhaps Nguyen convinced himself that if he aped Apple's late CEO Steve Jobs he could convince people that he was just as talented. "The fallback of the visionary is they say, 'I don't need to talk to people because there's no point in doing focus groups on revolutionary products.' But that's such a false dichotomy. No one is suggesting you make all of your decisions based on how people respond to surveys," Paul Kedrosky explained to Fast Company.

A few months before Color shut down, Nguyen stopped running the company on a day-to-day basis. Then reports trickled out that Color was winding down its operations and being bought by Apple. In November 2012, a post on Color's web site announced the end of the company: "We hope you've enjoyed sharing your stories via real-time video. Regretfully, the app will no longer be available after 12/31/2012."

How could Color have gotten a dime of funding? Color's failure reveals a fundamental flaw among Silicon Valley investors who combine a blind faith in an entrepreneur who has made money in the past with a fear of losing ground to rivals. As Kedrosky told Fast Company, "Color was just this magnificent confluence of everything the Valley likes to fund: It had pieces of what had made money for people before, which is to say mobile and photos; it had an experienced team; it had a multiple-success CEO; and it brought together some investors who were really eager to re-demonstrate their bona fides." "The unfortunate thing about Silicon Valley is that it isn't the best ideas that get funded, it's the people who do. I've been a beneficiary of that," Nguyen said to Fast Company.

Case Analysis

Color Labs's failure is a result of five flawed growth strategy assumptions that companies should avoid if they are seeking growth by gaining share among their current customers:

- **The CEO can dictate what the market will buy.** Nguyen acted as though he shared with Steve Jobs the visionary talents needed to persuade millions of potential customers to buy his products—regardless of what those potential customers needed. In fact, Jobs tended to attack large markets with a superior product rather than trying to create a new one as Nguyen attempted to do.

- **There is no need to analyze competitors while designing a new product.** Nguyen did not spend time examining competitors' products while designing the Color Labs apps. While he believed that this was a waste of time, in retrospect that could have helped Color Labs to succeed. For example, if Nguyen had noticed the rapid growth of Instagram, he might have learned why its service was so popular and might have been able to build a better product.

- **Getting customer feedback before launching is a waste of time.** Customer feedback immediately following the launch of its app in March 2012 indicated that Color Labs assumed that it would be popular without getting customer feedback. While Nguyen was clearly aping Jobs—who famously disdained market research, the app's poor customer ratings eloquently testify to Nguyen's overestimation of his entrepreneurial ability.

- **Employee retention is irrelevant.** Nguyen was able to hire a team of brand-name executives to build Color Labs. Those executives may have been hoping they would get rich quickly—but when Nguyen's initial product ideas failed, he was quick to blame his executive hires and manage them out of the company. The fundamental mistake Nguyen made here was to assume that he was the only one who mattered and the talented people he attracted were mere window dressing to attract investment.

- **Careful cash management is pointless.** Finally, Color Labs excelled at raising venture capital but Nguyen decided to spend significant amounts of cash on frills that did not contribute to the quality of its product or growth in its number of active users. Nguyen's out of control spending was based on a flawed assumption that he would always be able to get enough customer adoption to persuade another company to buy his company before it ran out of cash. While Nguyen excelled at raising capital, he was weak at using that capital to build a successful company.

The lessons from these cases have two critical implications for companies:

- **Boards** must assess whether the current CEO has the mindset and skills needed to conceive and execute an effective growth strategy from current or new customers. If not, the board may wish to replace the current CEO with one who can.

- **CEOs** should recognize that despite considerable over-laps, growth strategies for large and small companies vary depending on whether the company is targeting growth from current or new customer groups.

Applying the Principles of Growth through Current or New Customers

Leaders seeking to assess whether they apply these principles to their organizations should be able to answer Yes to these six questions:

- What percent of next year's growth will come from selling more to your current customers?

- How much of next year's growth do you expect to come from new customers?

- Are your revenues growing faster than your industry?

- If so, what makes your company's value proposition better than that of rivals?

- If not, why is your company growing more slowly than the industry?

- How does your company plan to improve the value it creates for current and/or new customers to accelerate its revenue growth?

Chapter 8: Growth Road Maps provides a detailed methodology for applying the principles of growth through new products.

Summary

Speeding up growth by selling to current or new customers is a relatively obvious strategy. The case studies we've reviewed in this chapter reveal that the biggest challenge in getting results from such a strategy may be the mind-set and skills of the CEO. If a CEO is intellectually humble enough to listen to customers, study competitors, and work with internal team members, then the company may be able to find and exploit growth opportunities either from selling to more members of its current customer segment or from gaining a significant share of a new customer segment.

In Chapter 3 we will explore how and why companies achieve faster growth by expanding within their current geographies and/or new ones. In so doing we will highlight the importance of gaining insights into the challenges of overcoming various forms of distance between the company's current geographies and potential new ones.

Growth via New or Current Geographies

In Chapter 2, we saw how companies get off the ground by finding and solving customer problems. Seeking growth, they sell that solution to customers who share important attributes with their original customers. Eventually, companies tap out the growth potential from their initial group of customers. In that case, leaders seek growth from new or current geographies. Quite often, the geographic expansion strategies depend heavily on whether the company is founded in a country with a large or small domestic market for its products.

A company started in a big domestic market—such as the United States—tends to delay geographic expansion until it has reached its market share limit among its core customer groups. Whereas a company started in a market with relatively few potential customers—such as Israel—might be born global. More specifically, companies whose founders hail from small countries sell globally from their inception—often co-locating in the small country and the big one right from the start.

While the idea that globalization means the death of distance is popular, the reality is that significant distances remain between the location where a company starts and the new geographies into which it seeks to expand. Companies

© Peter S. Cohan 2017
P. S. Cohan, *Disciplined Growth Strategies*, DOI 10.1007/978-1-4842-2448-9_3

should consider using the Cultural, Administrative, Geographic, and Economic (CAGE) framework to evaluate these distances before launching into new geographies.

This framework can help leaders to evaluate four key questions:

- **How wide is the cultural gap between our current geography and the future one?** The first dimension that companies should consider is cultural distance— measured by factors such as differences and similarities in language, work style, religion, and ethnic makeup.

- **How significant is the administrative gap between our current geography and the future one?** Companies should next analyze the administrative distance between the core and new geography—investigating factors such as the absence of colonial ties, shared currency, shared legal system, shared attitudes toward corruption, and common political aims.

- **How great is the physical distance between our current geography and the future one?** Companies should analyze how easy or difficult it is to bridge the physical distance between the core and new geography—studying factors such as the quality of roads and bridges, the robustness of air and ground transportation networks, the quality and breadth of communications networks, and how these factors might affect the quality of the company's product as it travels from the factory to customers in the new geography.

- **How big is the economic distance between our current geography and the future one?** Finally, companies should assess whether they can bridge the economic distance between the core and the new geography—analyzing factors such as differences in labor costs; customer price sensitivity; natural, financial, and human resources; and distribution systems.

Principles of Growth from Geography

What distinguishes the winners who search for growth from geographic expansion? In this chapter we'll see that successful geographic expansion depends on a combination the CEO's intellectual humility and a detailed understanding of the specific opportunities and risks inherent in geographic expansion. These general principles take different forms depending on whether a company is large or small.

Large companies seeking growth from current geography should be open to learning about how customer needs are evolving and develop a compelling product vision for satisfying those needs more effectively than competitors. Conversely, companies that fail to achieve growth goals assume that strategies that worked in the past will solve future challenges, they fail to apply their strengths to growth opportunities, they ignore changing customer needs and new competitors, and they allow internal departments to battle each other instead of coordinating them.

When large companies expand into new geographies, they ought initially to target countries with the smallest CAGE distance from their home geography. They should also strike a balance between the urge to tailor the product to each country and the efficiency benefits of a standardized one-world product. By contrast, large companies that fail at expanding into new geographies set unrealistically high goals, ignore CAGE distance, and fail to take appropriate action when it becomes clear that those goals are out of reach.

Small companies seeking growth from current geographies must assure that the operations in their current location works flawlessly before expanding. Such small companies should carefully eliminate flaws in current locations, research new locations rigorously, overestimate the capital and time to achieve success in new locations, and measure performance to fix problems and invest where growth is most promising. Conversely, small companies that fail in this endeavor tend to assume that strategies that worked for the CEO in the past will work again, they overinvest in growth at the market peak, and they ignore changing customer needs and the potential to learn from successful upstart strategies.

Small companies seeking growth from new geographies must apply intellectual humility in adapting the company's strengths to alleviate customer pain in new geographies with minimal CAGE distance, understand the pain of customers in those locations, and apply the company's strengths to relieving that pain. Similar to the other cases, failure tends to flow from executives who assume a strategy that worked for a previous market will yield success in the new one, ignore customer feedback, and disregard the strategies of successful rivals.

Case Studies

Let's examine pairs of case studies of successful and unsuccessful applications of four principles of growth from geography:

- **Large companies seeking growth from current geographies** should build and market products that beat competitors in customers' top-ranked purchase criteria.

- **Large companies seeking growth from new geographies** should target locations with the shortest CAGE distance from their core.

- **Small companies seeking growth from current geographies** should find and market to customers who value their products' superior attributes.

- **Small companies seeking growth from new geographies** should market to customers in new locations with low CAGE distance who value their product attributes.

Principle One   Large companies seeking growth from current geographies should build and market products that beat competitors in customers' top-ranked purchase criteria.

Companies seeking growth from within their current geography can reach their goal by understanding specifically what customers want and giving them more of those benefits than competitors do. While that sounds painfully obvious, many companies can't pull it off. That's because in order to achieve growth within a company's current market, companies must know more than their rivals about customers and technology and turn that superior insight into consistent actions that deliver customers a better outcome.

As we will explore later in this chapter, leaders can forge effective growth strategies for gaining share in their current geography by taking five steps:

- Listen to customers to understand the specific, ranked factors they use to compare among competing suppliers.

- Ask them to evaluate your company relative to competitors on each of those factors.

- Understand the level of performance your company would need to achieve for your company to gain market share.

- Build or enhance the skills—such as product development, marketing, and service—needed to deliver a competitively superior customer experience.

- Lead the design, manufacture, delivery, sales, and service of the new products your company introduces to achieve growth.

Doing these things is particularly difficult for a large company. That's because large companies are often slow to adapt and lock themselves into ways of working that make it more difficult for customers as executives struggle to beat out internal rivals for the next promotion. In some ways, seeking to expand within a company's current geography is easier because the company does not have to grabble with the CAGE distance that might exist between the company's core market and destination geography.

Successful: T-Mobile Wins U.S. Customers from Rivals

Introduction

Bellevue, Washington-based wireless carrier T-Mobile added nearly 33 million new customers in the United States due to a new bundle of services—dubbed Un-carrier because T-Mobile believed that traditional carriers such as AT&T would find it unprofitable to match its strategy. Specifically, T-Mobile's Un-carrier strategy offered consumers high network quality, responsive service, and competitive rates. T-Mobile's customer growth extended over a five-year period as its share of U.S. wireless subscriptions grew from 11% in the first quarter of 2011 to 16.3% in the first quarter of 2016. T-Mobile's increased market share was accompanied by a 24% compound annual growth in the number of customers. According to 451 Research, "From the end of 2012 through the end of 2015—the three-year period of Un-carrier—T-Mobile has grown from 33.4 million customers to 63.2 million customers. That growth has catapulted its market share from 10% to 17%, and enabled it to surpass Sprint to become the number-three US-based operator."

Case Scenario

T-Mobile's growth occurred at the same time that rivals were losing market share. For example, in April 2015, T-Mobile announced that it had added 1.8 million customers. During that same period, "Verizon Wireless reported disappointing subscriber growth, and while AT&T managed to reduce its rate of customer defections, its own subscriber growth is well short of the rate that T-Mobile was enjoying," according to CNET.

T-Mobile's U.S. growth resulted from Un-carrier—a bundle of services designed to eliminate wireless consumers' biggest annoyances with larger carriers. Between March 2013 and December 2015, Un-carrier consisted of a sequence of eight service changes:

- ***Offer opt-out contracts.*** *In March 2013, it eliminated longer-term contracts—replacing them with phone-leasing arrangements out of which customers could opt at any time—by giving up the phone or paying for the remaining balance.*

- ***Provide more frequent phone upgrades.*** *Its second major change was to replace two-year upgrade contracts with its JUMP program that enabled consumers to pay a slightly higher fee to obtain a newer model phone more frequently.*

- **Eliminate data roaming charges.** *T-Mobile's third change was to replace high international data roaming charges in 100 countries by letting consumers use data networks so they could send messages without incurring high roaming charges.*

- **Pay rivals' early termination fees to win new customers.** *The fourth Un-carrier tactic was to pay off the Early Termination Fees for Verizon, AT&T, or Sprint customers if they switched to T-Mobile.*

- **Boost network quality.** *Fifth, T-Mobile introduced a new wireless network technology that delivered better voice quality and data transfer.*

- **Deliver free music streaming.** *Sixth, after observing the large amounts of data that T-Mobile subscribers downloaded to play music on their smartphones, T-Mobile introduced Rhapsody unRadio—a free and advertising-less music streaming service.*

- **Expand Wi-Fi.** *Next T-Mobile expanded its Wi-Fi service to include connections in airplanes.*

- **Enable unused minutes roll over.** *Eighth, T-Mobile allowed customers to roll over their unused data into the next month— at no additional charge for all new and old subscribers.*

Each Un-carrier service introduction required T-Mobile to change its operations—for example, to boost network quality, T-Mobile invested in new network equipment and software. When it launched Un-carrier, T-Mobile's network was behind that of its rivals. However by the end of 2015, it had mostly caught up—covering 305 million points of presence with its (Long-Term Evolution) LTE technology and reaching 268 markets with its wideband LTE technology. In order to introduce Rhapsody unRadio, T-Mobile had to negotiate a partnership with the Rhapsody streaming service—to make this work the companies shared payment processes and technology.

T-Mobile's strategy was marred by one slightly unpleasant reality—it chose growth over high profitability. Between 2012 and 2015, its revenues soared at an 85% annual rate from $5.1 billion to $32.1 billion but its 2015 net margin was a mere 2%. Yet investors seemed to approve of its choice—between March 2014 when it introduced Un-carrier and July 8, 2016, its shares rose 130% from $19.60 to $45.

The architect of the Un-carrier strategy, T-Mobile CEO John Legere, had significant executive experience within and outside the telecommunications industry before he joined T-Mobile USA in September 2012 as president and CEO. His 34 years of industry experience included serving as CEO of Global Crossing, president of Dell's European operations, and president of AT&T's Asia-Pacific operations and global strategy. Though he had been in the telecommunications industry for many years before joining T-Mobile, he thought of wireless as very different. However, he became comfortable with the industry by listening in his first few months as CEO to T-Mobile's customer service calls. These calls revealed that customers disliked traditional wireless services providers. As Legere explained to Fast Company, "None of the [technology] mattered. There was this plethora of hatred for this industry and this never-ending list of things people wanted to change. They didn't want to know what I don't know. They don't care!"

Though T-Mobile had considered changing its strategy to respond to customer dissatisfaction, its managers had been afraid of following through. Legere's predecessor said, "We hate the rules of the industry, but we're tied to them. No one will be crazy enough to do anything about it." But Legere—who had previously taken Global Crossing out of bankruptcy and sold it for $3 billion in 2011—was not afraid. At the January 2013 Consumer Electronics Show early in his T-Mobile tenure—when employees were still discouraged after a failed takeover attempt by AT&T, the cumulative effect of listening to all those customer service calls gave him a strong desire to change the industry. "My head exploded and I just went on a rant about the wireless industry and how I didn't get it," Legere said. Then he started asking, "Why, why, why? People hate contracts. Let's not have them! 'You can't,' companies say. Why?," he concluded.

In addition to winning customers by removing industry practices that annoy customers, he also takes pleasure in beating competitors to market with good ideas. In December 2014, T-Mobile learned that Legere's former employer, AT&T, planned to introduce a new data-rollover plan. AT&T's plan was scheduled to launch a month ahead of the one that T-Mobile had in store. To beat AT&T, T-Mobile introduced its own offering a week later. Moreover, Legere kept coming up with new ways to delight customers and tweak its rivals. In July 2016, Pokemon GO—an augmented reality version of the Pokemon game for smart devices—became an instant hit following its July 8 launch.

On July 14, T-Mobile announced a promotion that would provide free data to Pokemon GO players. T-Mobile subscribers were offered a chance—between July 19 and August 9—to play the game without the resulting data usage applying to their data caps. The promotion lasted a year after subscribers claimed it and came with "one free Lyft ride up to $15 and a discount on battery packs to keep customers' phones powered up," according to the Washington Post.

Case Analysis

Legere's success at winning new customers within T-Mobile's current geography reveals four important lessons for leaders seeking to achieve similar success:

- **Pick a CEO with a growth mindset.** A common pattern of successful big company growth strategies is the selection of a CEO who has experience outside the company and is not afraid to think and act in ways that improve customer satisfaction with its products. This was true with McDonald's selection of Easterbrook and Legere at T-Mobile.

- **Listen to customers complain.** The wireless tele-communications industry provides an excellent example of how monopolies and oligopolies tend to put corporate interests ahead of customers'. This creates opportunities for a growth-minded CEO. Legere was wise to listen to customer service calls as a way to identify many sources of customer dissatisfaction.

- **Design, build, deliver, and service products that relieve their pain.** As this case reveals, the CEO with an inertial mindset will tend to ignore information that does not confirm that that CEO already believes. However, a CEO with a growth mindset will take ideas for improving the customer experience that are obvious to lower-level employees who listen to customers each day and implement them. Legere was clever in realizing that T-Mobile could offer new service features in a sequence over time that would relieve big sources of customer dissatisfaction.

- **Repeat the previous two steps.** Sadly for T-Mobile, competitors could often copy many of Legere's innovations but that did not discourage him. Instead he continued to listen to customers and to add new services that yielded rapid customer growth at the expense of competitors' market share.

Unsuccessful: Avon Products Loses Share in Developing Countries

Introduction

Founded in 1886, by July 2016 Avon Products had suffered 18 consecutive quarters of declining revenue as it lost customers—particularly due to its inability to retain sales representatives in developing countries such as China and Brazil which by 2010 had surpassed the United States as its largest market. After peaking in June 2004 under Andrea Jung—its CEO from November 1999 to April 2012—Avon's stock had since plummeted. Jung was replaced that April in the wake of a bribery scandal in China by Sheri McCoy—who rose to vice chairman at Johnson & Johnson before being passed over to succeed William Weldon as its CEO. Under McCoy, Avon's stock plummeted 91% to $3.94 by July 2016. Avon's financial performance cratered under McCoy—who had no prior direct sales or cosmetics experience. In 2011 Avon generated $11.3 billion in sales and $514 million in profit. But by the end of 2015, its revenues had plunged nearly in half to $6.2 billion and it posted a net loss of $1.1 billion.

Case Scenario

The story behind that plunge has much to do with the decline of this 130-year-old company's traditional business model of recruiting "Avon Ladies" to sell perfume door-to-door under the advertising tagline, "Ding-Dong Avon Calling." Jung acted as though she was embarrassed by Avon's door-to-door sales legacy. Instead, she tried to set Avon up as a competitor to more upscale brands such as Procter & Gamble and L'Oreal—not a surprising outcome given that Jung had previously worked at upscale brands Neiman Marcus and Bloomingdale's. Nevertheless, recruiting direct sellers was Avon's heritage and still a big part of its business. By 2012, Avon employed 6.4 million active representatives who marketed its lipsticks and lotions to consumers. The growing popularity of selling over the Internet created confusion within Avon. Should it try to sell more online and compete with its representatives? Or should it help its representatives to sell more using the Internet and social media?

Indeed, the Internet already seemed to be cutting into the profit contributions of its representatives. By 2012, operating profit per representative in the United States had plunged 75% over the past decade, according to an analysis by Sanford C. Bernstein. And Avon was clearly struggling to figure out the best answer to the second question. As Michele Risner, an Avon representative based in Gibson City, Illinois, told the Wall Street Journal, "I think [Avon is] still struggling with trying to figure out how it can help them. Some apps for smartphones would be something we could really benefit from."

Avon could not answer representatives' questions regard how the Web could help their business "The big struggle with people is, 'How do I make a Facebook fan page? How do I do this on Twitter? Is it really going to help?,'" said Risner. In addition to direct selling from the Internet in the United States, Avon was missing the rapid growth of direct selling in emerging markets such as Brazil. However, Avon did not participate in the growth because of Jung's lack of focus on its strength as a direct seller.

Between 2006 and 2011, the global market for direct selling grew 30% to $136 billion, according to Euromonitor International. Yet during those five years, Avon added a mere 1.1 percentage points to its 11.4% share of 2011's direct selling market. One reason for its failure to keep up with the growth of global direct selling was Avon's U.S. decline. Indeed by April 2015, Avon's U.S. business door-to-door sales force that had shrunk for the each of the previous 19 quarters—tumbling 18% in 2014 alone, according to Deutsche Bank. Avon's market share tumbled from 10.2% in 2007 when it led the United States among direct sellers down to 4.3% in 2014, according to Euromonitor International. Mary Kay took over the top spot in the United States in 2013.

Why did Avon lose in Brazil? It was not paying enough attention to its direct sellers there even as Brazil surpassed the United States in 2010 as its biggest market. Avon botched the introduction of an electronic invoicing system that the Brazilian government required. Problems with Avon's computer systems tripled the number of service issues for representatives. Those systems problems led to missed late orders, inaccurate demand forecasts, late-arriving products, unfilled orders, and delayed shipments to representatives. Moreover, Brazilian representatives sold other vendors' products—most notably Natura's—which *did not suffer the service interruptions that plagued Avon. It is remarkable that Avon did not lose all its business in Brazil—especially given that those sellers could make money by selling products of a rival that had better operations.*

McCoy was not helping to turn things around. By the first quarter of 2016, Avon's revenues had fallen nearly 16% and it lost $166 million—more money than the same quarter of 2015. This was the eighteenth straight quarter of declining revenues at Avon. And McCoy was struggling with how to bail out the rapidly sinking ship that Avon had become under her leadership. By December 2015, Avon was so hungry for cash that it agreed to give up control of its North American business to a New York hedge fund, Cerberus Capital Management. Cerberus paid Avon $170 million for 80.1% of its North American business—which represented 14% of Avon's 2015 revenues—and Cerberus coughed up another $435 million 16.6% of Avon's listed shares.

Word of this move put a further damper on its sales representatives' enthusiasm for the company. Elizabeth Balestracci, a successful Avon representative, was disillusioned by this move. She had allowed her "Avon business to dwindle when she moved to Myrtle Beach, South Carolina, in 2013 and started working full-time as a radio-show host. She was 'heartbroken' to learn that Avon planned to sell its North American business," according to the Wall Street Journal.

In June 2016, Moody's downgraded Avon's debt-paying ratings and gave its stock a negative ratings outlook. "The downgrade reflects the separation of the company's North American business, risk associated with executing the new transformational plan, exposure to high volatile emerging markets, and challenging economic conditions in its key regions," according to Market Realist. Members of Avon's board should have been asking themselves, Is McCoy the right leader for Avon? If not, what criteria should it use to pick Avon's next CEO? Will the Transformation Plan produce sufficient revenue and profit growth? If not, what should Avon do instead?

Case Analysis

Its slow and painful decline reflects five flaws that help explain why Avon lost ground within its current geographies:

- **Poor fit between CEO skills and strategic challenges.** Jung and McCoy—while quite accomplished in their previous endeavors—did not have the skills needed to sustain Avon's growth in the face of its many strategic challenges. Avon's board clearly failed in retrospect with these two CEO choices.

- **Failure to focus on strengths—in Avon's case its representatives.** Avon's competitive advantage was its direct selling channel—however, the company did not figure out how to harness the Internet and social media to make its representatives more successful at bringing in new consumers and encouraging old ones to keep buying.

- **Inattentiveness to changes affecting consumers.** Jung was so focused on her efforts to boost Avon's brand prestige that she failed to notice the growing importance of online sales to consumers' purchases of beauty products. A failure to track changes in consumers' spending and purchasing habits can be fatal for a company seeking to grow—especially within its current geography.

- **Failure to monitor competitors.** Jung seemed to want to transform Avon into a rival to upscale retailers—such as the ones where she had worked before. She was focusing on the wrong competitors—instead she should have been analyzing the strategies that caused Avon to lose market share in Brazil and China.

- **Lack of internal coordination among different business functions.** Finally, Avon was not good at coordinating its marketing and IT staffs to produce seamless services that helped its direct sales representatives to achieve better results. As we have seen in many of the case studies in Chapter 2, failed execution of a strategy flows from the failure to coordinate different functions to pursue a shared growth goal.

Principle Two Large companies seeking growth from new geographies should target locations with the shortest Cultural, Administrative, Geographic, and Economic (CAGE) distance from their core.

When it comes to expanding into new geographies, too many companies have made the mistake of confusing that country's population with its revenue potential for their products. A case in point is China—with a population of about 1.3 billion—which has drawn many U.S. companies seeking growth by selling their product to a population that is several times larger than their home market. Sadly for many of these companies, their efforts to generate profit growth in China resulted in ignominious retreats after years of struggling to break in.

In 2006, electronics retailer Best Buy bought Five Star, a China-based appliance and electronics retailer with 136 stores for $180 million. At the time, Five Star had $700 million in revenues and was growing at a 50% annual rate. Best Buy considered the deal to be a way for it to learn how to reach the Chinese electronics market that was expected to grow at a 10% annual rate through 2016 and to reach $100 billion by 2010. By June 2014—after struggling with cultural and economic differences, Best Buy wanted to sell Five Stars, which had expanded to 190 locations in the wake of a 10.5% decline in international revenue due in part to its inability to compete in China. By December 2014, it announced the sale of Five Stars for an undisclosed price to a Chinese real estate company.

How can leaders avoid such pitfalls and achieve faster growth in new geographies? They ought to follow a growth discipline that ranks new geographies based on four factors:

- The profit potential of the company's industry in that geography;

- The CAGE between the company's home market and the new geography;

- The company's potential competitive strength in the geography; and

- The investment required to gain a meaningful position in that market and the expected return on that investment.

In a nutshell, to achieve faster geographic growth companies should focus on new geographies with the most profit potential, the shortest CAGE distance, in which they are likely to occupy the strongest competitive position and earn the highest return on their investment.

Successful: Netflix Goes Global

Introduction

In January 2015, Netflix announced plans to operate in 200 countries by 2017—adding millions of new international customers in 2015 while deferring expected profits. By July 2016, Netflix had made significant progress—expanding from 50 to 130 countries and pursuing a risky strategy of offering a very similar product for different geographies—with the notable exception of China. In January 2015, Netflix stock rose 20% in the wake of beating expectations for international subscriber growth by 13% to 2.43 million. At the time, Netflix was already operating in 50 countries but set the goal of adding 150 new countries by 2017. But achieving that ambitious goal meant Netflix would need to overcome many challenges. Those included countries with limited broadband needed to watch video via mobile devices—in 2014 78% of developed market households had Internet access while only 31% of those in developing nations did, varying local regulations, and the cost of expanding licensing deals to new geographies. Another potential hurdle Netflix faced in adding 150 new countries in two years was that many of these smaller countries would receive a Netflix service with less local dubbing and less local content than Netflix had provided with its earlier international launches.

Case Scenario

Netflix was confident that it could overcome the hurdles to growth due to what it had learned from offering its service in 50 countries. As CEO Reed Hastings said, "We already offer Netflix in about 50 countries and have learned a great deal about the content people prefer, the marketing they respond to and how to best organize ourselves for steady improvement." Netflix also believed that it could overcome the cost of content licensing. Chief content officer Ted Sarandos explained that Netflix had been seeking worldwide distribution rights, for its original shows. Moreover, Sarandos anticipated that its original content would have an international audience. "It might be that there are some cultural barriers to U.S. content as we get into more exotic markets. But my guess is that we're going to continue to see our original programming travel and carry the Netflix brand around the world." Other challenges remained for Netflix—such as questions about whether it would need to provide tailored strategies in each country by catering to unique needs for product packaging, marketing, and delivery, conforming to country-specific regulations for privacy, and aligning with each country's unique billing and payment practices.

Netflix was poised to tread carefully in China. As Hastings explained, "For China, we are still exploring options—all of them modest. We'll learn a great deal if we can successfully operate a small service in China centered on our original and other globally licensed content. Moreover, Netflix needs to get a license to offer service in China, and it's not 100% clear we're going to be able to do that." By August 2015, Netflix had made considerable progress with its international expansion. It launched successfully in Australia and New Zealand in March 2015 and had scheduled launches in Japan in the third quarter of 2015; Spain, Italy, and Portugal in the fourth quarter of 2015; and China in 2016. In addition to offering its U.S.-developed content globally, Netflix also developed Spanish content including Club de Cuervos and Narcos.

Unfortunately, the financial effect of its international expansion was mixed. Its second quarter 2015 international revenue soared 48%; however its international net loss rose from $65 million to $92 million between the first and second quarters.

Investors were responding favorably, however—adding 100% to Netflix's market capitalization between August 2014 and August 2015—moreover its stock rose 55% between May and August.

A year after launching, Netflix was in 180 countries.

Netflix believed that offering the world a single, identical service would boost demand. As Elizabeth Bradley, Netflix's chief of content acquisition argued, "The global library opens up huge new markets for filmmakers. For example, if Anime fans in Japan like certain kinds of Hollywood blockbusters, we can figure out which Anime films would do well with Americans watching the same blockbusters."

Moreover, due to Netflix's recommendation algorithms, Netflix expected to find global demand for specific kinds of content for small audiences in many different countries who shared common tastes. As Netflix's chief product officer, Neil Hunt, said, "Every country has a wide range of taste. No one else is going to be able to find a niche audience that's not in Poland and is interested in a Polish story."

Netflix's second quarter 2016 financial report suggested that the company was struggling a bit in pursuit of its global growth goals. On July 18, Netflix posted a 33% increase in earnings and a 28% surge in revenues to $2.11 billion.

But investors were disappointed by the growth in its subscribers and subtracted about 13% from its stock market value the next day.

Netflix's international subscribers are likely to surpass its U.S. ones by 2020. Netflix eventually expects to have 60 million to 90 million customers in the United States while Nomura forecasts that Netflix will "claim 88.7 million subscribers outside the U.S. by 2020," according to Bloomberg.

But investors ignored that and focused on where Netflix fell short. In April 2016, Netflix predicted it would add two million overseas subscribers but reported 24% fewer than it had forecast. In a statement, Netflix also said it missed its projection of 500,000 new U.S. subscribers by a whopping 68%—bringing the company's total subscriber base to 83.2 million.

Some Netflix customers canceled their service. Hastings believes that those departing customers were upset when their bills increased by $1 or $2 a month.

But Hastings argued that "some members perceived the news as an impending new price increase rather than the completion of two years of grandfathering [in higher new rates for older subscribers]," according to the statement.

Netflix faced a few challenges in international markets. Many of them were already populated by rivals with lower prices and localized content. For example, in India, Japan, and Poland Netflix is "in the early days of learning the best ways to satisfy users," according to Bloomberg.

A cost of $7 or $8 a month was a high price to pay for many consumers in international markets, but Sarandos had been investing in movies and TV shows to appeal to local tastes.

One other challenge Netflix faced was the rapid rise in costs that accompanied its acquisition of new content for all these international markets. After all, Netflix's streaming content obligations rose from $10.1 billion to $13.2 in the second quarter of 2016 and its free cash flow was negative $254 million in the quarter, according to its statement.

Was its second quarter result a signal that its international strategy was failing or just a small speed bump on Netflix's way to a leading position in global online streaming?

By January 2017, Netflix's strong financial results suggested that its globalization strategy had been a success. It fourth quarter 2016 results featured 56% profit *growth and soaring subscriber counts—36% ahead of its forecasts—thanks to its successful expansion into 130 countries during 2016. And its stock price hit an all-time high.*[1]

Case Analysis

Netflix's rapid global expansion modifies traditional approaches to growth from new geographies. Specifically, its success in pursuing its goal of operating in 200 countries highlights four key principles:

- **Fit CEO skills with growth challenges.** Hastings and his executive team shared clearly articulated goals and were flexible about how best to achieve them. Moreover, their previous success in turning Netflix from a DVD-by-Mail service to an online streaming provider suggested that they were willing and able to reinvent the company to achieve growth goals.

- **Reduce the CAGE distance between core market and few bigger new ones.** Netflix was selling its internally developed shows around the world—including some Spanish-language programs that were intended for Latin American markets.

- **Accept wider CAGE distance between core market and many smaller new ones.** While tailoring the product to each country makes sense for markets with greater revenue potential, Netflix was also mindful of the marginal costs of such tailoring. To that end, it hoped to succeed in smaller markets that might be willing to accept English-language content with relatively minor amounts of tailoring to local culture.

- **Learn from success and failure and adapt.** Rather than spending months or years studying a potential strategy, Netflix is willing to try growth strategies for new geographies and assess their effectiveness. In so doing, it can learn what works and what does not and modify its approach to achieve its long-term goals.

---

[1]Peter Cohan, "Netflix Beats Subscriber Count Target By 36% As Growth Strategy Pays Off," Forbes, January 19, 2017, http://www.forbes.com/sites/petercohan/2017/01/19/netflix-beats-subscriber-count-target-by-36-as-growth-strategy-pays-off/

Unsuccessful: India Thwarts Apple's Used iPhone Initiative

Introduction

Apple has a strong presence in India—in fiscal 2015 that amounted to $1 billion in revenue (0.4% of its total), and India's government was seeking to encourage Apple's expansion there. However, in April 2016 an Apple initiative to boost iPhone sales there—by selling used iPhones in India at low prices—backfired badly. And the factors underlying that outcome are instructive about the dangers of seeking to grow in new geographies where there is a wide CAGE distance between a company's core geography and the new one.

Case Scenario

Apple's attempt to sell used iPhones in India was first rejected in 2015. So Apple tried again in 2016 only to meet the same fate. When Apple applied to sell used iPhones in 2015, India's environment ministry rejected Apple's application "without much fanfare," according to Bloomberg. However, by 2016 India had become more important to Apple thanks to a slowdown in China on which Apple had previously depended for most of its revenue growth. That left India, the second largest mobile market in the world, as "a vast untapped opportunity" in which Apple had "publicly talked up its prospects" and where it was "on course to get the green light to open its first retail stores," Bloomberg reported.

Sadly for Apple, its urgent need to seek growth by expanding its presence in India was met by even stronger opposition from India-based rivals who rallied around Prime Minister Narendra Modi's Make in India program to encourage local manufacturing. Those executives warned Modi that letting Apple sell used iPhones in India would "open the floodgates to electronic waste, jeopardize local players, and make a farce of [his] Make in India program." Sudhir Hasija, chairman of Karbonn Mobiles said his company sold about 1.7 million phones a month—giving him ample economic incentive to warn that letting Apple sell used iPhones would turn "Make in India into Dump in India."

Apple also faced opposition from India's Mobile and Communications Council (MCC)—a lobbyist for Indian phone brands that included Micromax, Intex, and Samsung. MCC's chairman Ravinder Zutshi told Bloomberg, "Why even consider allowing import of used phones when import of other used goods such as cars are precluded by 300 percent duty levies?" Apple's application went into a governmental process known as inter-ministerial discussion—the outcome of which was uncertain but seemed to favor the vocal Indian opposition to Apple.

The price competition for smart phones in India was intense. Eighty percent of such phones sold in India were priced no higher than $150—and branded smartphone prices could drop as low as $35.

At the time, Apple's market share in India was less than 2% and in March 2016, Apple introduced a lower priced phone—the iPhone SE with a starting price of $399—that was still too expensive to make a dent in the Indian market. Nevertheless, Apple enjoyed a whopping 76% rise in its Indian sales in the holiday quarter, which inspired CEO Tim Cook to comment on India's "incredibly exciting" prospects. Selling refurbished iPhones would likely enable Apple to drop its prices and earn a profit in India's smartphone market.

Yet local rivals were arguing ferociously to the Indian government that allowing Apple to pursue this strategy would lead to "a deluge of used electronics imports, making mince-meat of Modi's localization drive," noted Bloomberg. Apple rivals also criticized the company's refurbished phone strategy because it would create toxic waste—in the form of used batteries and LCD screens—which India would not be able to dispose of effectively.

In its application Apple offered to set up facilities to handle the toxic waste—it typically managed to collect and recycle 85 percent, by weight, of devices produced seven years earlier, according to Bloomberg. And its India refurbishment proposal would give Apple something to do with the roughly 15 million older U.S. iPhones that it expected to receive as part of a trade-in program it offered customers in exchange for a "small monthly fee." Sudhir Hasija, chairman of Karbonn Mobile, an Indian smartphone maker, believed that Apple represented a threat to its business even above the top-of-the-line-for-India-price of $150. "Even if the refurbished iPhones are priced a bit more than 10,000 rupees ($150), that will hurt our sales because Indians may choose Apple for its snob value," he told Bloomberg.

By July 2016, Apple's efforts to sell refurbished iPhones there were in limbo as were plans to set up Apple stores there. As for opening Apple stores in India, the government sent mixed signals. In June 2016, India approved Apple's application to operate stores in India. The seemingly good news was that since the Indian government appeared to consider that Apple sold "cutting-edge" products and "state-of-the-art: technology, it would be exempt from a so-called local content requirement for three years—after which Apple would need to sell products containing at least 30% so-called local content.

Apple's confusion was understandable—after all, under India's original rules, Apple had been invited to build its stores in India free of the local content requirement and it was unclear what was required to comply with that provision. Moreover, different parts of India's government came to different conclusions about whether Apple sold cutting-edge products—the Department of Industrial Policy & Promotion (DIPP) said it did, but the Foreign Investment Promotion Board disagreed. Apple did not want to invest until these issues were cleared up. A source told Economic Times, "There is a certain opaqueness regarding the rules. In addition, the company does not want to commit to complying with local sourcing requirements. It can only start manufacturing in or begin sourcing from India once it attains a certain scale of business which is difficult to estimate right now."

Case Analysis

While it remains to be seen whether Apple's efforts to gain market share in India will succeed or fail, its lack of progress in 2015 and 2016 reveal three reasons that large companies often fail when they seek faster growth from new geographies.

Unrealistically high expectations for successful market penetration. Apple was facing severe pressure from investors to maintain its thirteen-year streak of quarterly revenue growth. But it suffered a serious reversal due its excessive dependence on iPhone sales from China—which fell significantly and put pressure on Cook to find a new source of growth to replace its declining China revenues. Yet Apple's need to penetrate the Indian market quickly was incompatible with the realities of the Indian smartphone industry.

Superficial grasp of CAGE distance. Apple demonstrated that it had some understanding of how to apply for a license to enter the Indian market—both for Apple stores and for selling refurbished iPhones. Yet Apple appears not to have grasped that Indian smartphone companies would use their influence with the government to block Apple's efforts—or at least try to delay them considerably.

Unwillingness to take uncomfortable steps required to overcome challenges. Bribery is common in Indian business. An Ernst & Young survey found that 25% to 50% of respondents in the technology industry found that India was corrupt—meaning that bribery was part of doing business. The U.S. Securities and Exchange Commission (SEC) had extracted fines as high as in the tens of millions of dollars from a wide variety of companies for alleged violations of the Foreign Corrupt Practices Act (FCPA). Was Apple willing to find a way to do business in such a corrupt environment? If not, perhaps it should have considered a different country from which to seek growth.

Principle Three   Small companies seeking growth from current geographies should find and market to customers who value their products' superior attributes.

Small companies pursuing growth within their current geography should use different approaches depending on whether they sell to and service with their customers in person or via machine. If small companies interact in person with their customers, then success depends on picking new locations that will have the same characteristics as the stores where the company is currently enjoying the most profitability and growth. If the company interacts with customers online or wirelessly, it can expand geographically without investing in new physical locations.

In either case, small companies face unique challenges when they contemplate expanding within their current geography. Specifically, they ought to apply the following principles:

- **Work out the kinks in current geography before expanding.** Small companies must experiment with their current locations until they become successful—either profitable or at least cash-flow neutral—before seeking to expand. After all, a company could burn through its capital if it replicates a cash-flow consuming business model in more locations. Moreover, once the small company reaches that goal, it should understand the reasons for its success—such as competitively superior ways that the company markets, operates, and services customers.

- **Research new locations rigorously.** If the small company intends to expand into new locations, it should approach the process in a rigorous way. If the company offers a service to consumers, it should locate where many of those consumers are likely to find it convenient. The company ought to analyze the specific factors that make a location convenient for the consumers it wants to serve and pick locations that best fit with those factors.

- **Overestimate resources required to expand.** Unless a company's executive team has prior experience opening up new retail locations, it may be difficult to estimate the capital and management attention required to make new locations successful. Therefore, companies should consider doubling their initial estimate for the resources that will be required to expand into new locations.

- **Measure obsessively and respond to feedback in new locations.** Finally, once a company has opened new locations, it ought to measure their performance and adjust based on results. Companies might consider measuring factors such as customer traffic, customer wait times, and capacity utilization by hour and by day of the week in addition to the location's growth, profitability, and cash flow.

Successful: MiniLuxe Expands Nationally

Introduction

Boston-based nail salon chain, MiniLuxe, raised $25 million in 2015 to expand nationally thanks to the popularity of its higher-quality operations. At the core of MiniLuxe's success was a radical rethinking of how a nail salon might be operated in order to provide a better customer and employee experience that would boost prices, employee loyalty and productivity, and store cash flow. Moreover, MiniLuxe's geographic expansion flowed successfully from taking a rigorous approach to selecting new locations.

Case Scenario

The idea for MiniLuxe came from John Hamel, a general partner at Boston-based venture capital firm, CueBall. Hamel was no expert on manicures—but he had been given a challenge and he realized that nail salons could be a way to address it. In 2007, Cue Ball CEO, Tony Tjan, challenged his partners "to find a highly fragmented industry that could do what Starbucks did for the coffee shop: use a combination of smart design, systems and company culture to create a following," according to the New York Times. Hamel was driving through his hometown of Revere, Massachusetts, and noticed five nail salons near each other in the same strip mall.

When he first walked into a nail salon, Hamel—who had been a consultant with AnswerThink—was struck by the strong smell of nail polish. But the smell of acrylics was just one of many problems Hamel discovered with the typical nail salon. Hamel was most disturbed by the filth in the foot tubs used to provide pedicures. He learned that these tubs had jets that were impossible to clean. He also found many hygiene problems—manicurists reuse tools that are not properly sterilized and the people who perform the waxing double-dip the swabs they use to pull out hair. If that is not bad enough, scheduling was not done or not done reliably and the fluorescent lighting was unappealing.

CueBall also learned that nail salons mistreated their workers and wanted to create a company that would do better. How badly? According to a Nails Magazine survey, "35% of nail workers cannot remember the last time they had a vacation, and 12% earned less than $150 a week."

Hamel realized that Cue Ball could do to the U.S. nail salon industry—which consisted of 65,000 salons generating $10 billion in annual sales—what Starbucks had done to the coffee shop business.

Hamel and his partner Mats Lederhausen—who had been managing director of McDonald's Ventures and had overseen investments in Chipotle Mexican Grill, Boston Market, Pret a Manger, and Redbox DVD—were among CueBall executives who saw an opportunity to develop a "systems approach to nails," according to the New York Times. They rethought how a nail salon would operate—including activities like hiring and training, cleaning, product development, scheduling to match the supply of manicurists to customer demand, measuring store performance, and picking store locations.

MiniLuxe believed that happy employees made happy customers. So it invested in training, scheduling, and developing the careers of employees. By January 2015,

MiniLuxe had about 200 part- and full-time employees, all of whom had "company health insurance, paid time off, profit-sharing and a company 401(k)," according to the New York Times. MiniLuxe kept its tools cleaner than did the typical nail salon. As Tjan wrote, MiniLuxe "uses medical grade autoclaving equipment (a sterilization process for the instrumentation) and exposes that process through a glass 'clean lab' where clients can see the tools being sanitized and sterilized. That is a unique process and asset in the nail salon world." What's more, MiniLuxe's foot tubs were free of the jets that Hamel found impossible to clean. And in 2014, MiniLuxe introduced its own nearly toxin-free polish and uses it along with popular brands.

The higher quality made it possible for MiniLuxe to charge $20 for a manicure and $39 for a pedicure "slightly more than a typical strip-mall nail salon, but less than a spa for comparable services," according to the New York Times. MiniLuxe hired a data scientist to handle scheduling so that customers would not have to wait after they walked in to a salon and technicians would not be idle. A key insight was that walk-in traffic rises 5% for every 10-degree increase in temperature but rain does not reduce traffic. MiniLuxe also operated an always-on online booking service, introduced a mobile app to buzz users' phones when it was their turn for a service, and was testing apps to share scheduling and client preference details with employees. MiniLuxe had its own way of measuring how well its stores were doing. As Tjan explained, it used a "Net Promoter Score—a measure of how likely a client would be to recommend the service to another person; weekly sales growth compared to the previous year; time to positive cash flow in a new location; and sales per square foot." Finally, MiniLuxe had a rigorous process for picking locations that used data from its stores to map out suitable spots. But at the beginning, Hamel looked online at Massachusetts Starbucks locations, counted the number of nail salons within a half mile to one-and-a-half mile radius and sought space for MiniLuxe in whichever "had the most density," he told the New York Times.

By January 2015, MiniLuxe had eight locations in the Boston area, had $23 million in venture capital, and was preparing to expand nationally—including eight salons in and around Dallas. When MinLuxe moved to Dallas in February 2015, it told a local newspaper that it had picked the city due to the "Pedicure Index—the number of days above a certain temperature, and therefore sandal weather."

By July 2016, MiniLuxe had raised another $7.5 million from investors. With 15 stores it was planning to expand to Los Angeles. MiniLuxe's locations throughout Texas had done well and Tjan was looking for more locations where there was "a stronger cultural emphasis on grooming and warmer weather where open-toed shoes are more popular"—creating more demand for pedicures. Could MiniLuxe go national or would it be too difficult to provide consistently high quality service nationwide?

Case Analysis

The MiniLuxe case illustrates two useful principles for small company CEOs seeking to expand into new geographies:

- **Work out the kinks in the business model before expanding.** MiniLuxe had extraordinary patience in taking about seven years to build its presence in the Boston area before raising capital for expansion to Dallas in 2015 and a planned move to Los Angeles in 2017. The apparent success of its Dallas expansion suggests that MiniLuxe's patience was wise.

- **Make sure the strategy from your current location works in new ones.** Consumers were willing to pay a higher price because MiniLuxe performed key activities—including human resources management, cleaning, scheduling, performance measurement, and choosing locations—in a competitively superior manner. This strategy worked in Boston and Dallas—and MiniLuxe was hoping it would translate well to Los Angeles.

Unsuccessful: Pacific Sunwear's Slow Motion Wipeout

Introduction

Anaheim, California-based surf retailer, Pacific Sunwear of California (PacSun), filed for bankruptcy in April 2016 after 36 years. Its failure flowed from a poorly conceived and executed 2005 plan to expand by 40% its U.S. store count and its lack of responsiveness to changing fashion trends.

By 2016, its shareholders were wiped out as its revenues plunged 40% from their $1.4 billion high. Its shares fell 96% in the year ending April 8, 2016.

Case Scenario

In retrospect PacSun's problems started when the demand for products related to surfing and extreme sports was at its peak. In 2005, brands such as Quiksilver, Billabong, and PacSun—whose Roxy and Hurley labels were popular with mall-going teens—were flying high and PacSun's shares peaked. That year, it operated nearly 1,000 stores across America and PacSun executives announced plans to boost that number by 400 within three years—many of these stores ended up underperforming and had rent costs that were above market price. That 40% increase in store count coincided with turmoil at the top for PacSun.

The executive behind that increase in store count was Seth Johnson—a Yale graduate with an MBA from the University of Chicago—who had been chief operating officer at Abercrombie & Fitch where he helped launch Abercrombie's popular Hollister stores in 2000. Johnson was brought in as PacSun's COO in 2004 by then-CEO Greg Weaver and was promoted to CEO in April 2005. And Johnson's geographic expansion plans were indeed very ambitious. In February 2006, PacSun planned

- *To open 600 to 800 One Thousand Steps shoe stores for 18- to 24-year-olds (noting that Weaver "thought we could have a great [shoe store] business");*

- *To expand from 907 to 1,000 the number of PacSun stores— that sold surf and skate clothing and accessories store targeting shoppers ages 12 to 18; and*

- *Increase from 198 to 400 the number of d.e.m.o. stores— which sold hip-hop clothing and accessories store targeting shoppers aged 16 to 24.*

Johnson appeared very confident of the success of his strategy for geographic expansion based on his belief that PacSun could expand into big malls. "There's no reason for us to do a new concept unless it can be in a lot of malls. We're a big business now, and to add meaningful growth, we do have to be able to contribute a lot of volume and profit," he said. Johnson also wanted to build bigger stores. "The Galleria at Tyler store is 9,000 square feet. It was a little over 5,000 before. We added some home products, accessories and shoes. Our average store today is 3,600 square feet. We could easily have several hundred stores that could be 5,000 to 6,000," he continued. Johnson believed that PacSun was successful and did not need fixing. But under Johnson, total company same-store sales for the third quarter of 2006 declined 2.4%, PacSun sales were down 1.2%, and d.e.m.o. same-store sales plunged 9.4%.

In October 2006, PacSun's board allowed Johnson to "resign to pursue other interests" and installed Sally Frame Kasaks, former CEO of Abercrombie & Fitch, Ann Taylor, and Talbots to "win back teens lost to such stores as Hollister and Zumiez," according to Bloomberg. Kasaks's plan—to shut money-losing stores and transform PacSun to a destination for "Southern California cool-girls" with private-label clothes and rival surf brands—flopped due to its plethora of money-losing stores.

In 2009, former Vans CEO Gary Shoenfeld replaced Kasak. In 2011, Shoenfeld began closing 200 stores and in 2012 tried to get girls excited about its stores by signing Kendall and Kylie Jenner to sell fashion for juniors. This strategy also failed. With foot traffic in malls down, PacSun had closed 40% of its stores—leaving it with 593 stores and 2,000 full time employees—and its revenue had fallen 40% from its 2005 peak to $800 million by the end of 2015.

In April 2016, San Francisco private equity firm Golden Gate Capital took over PacSun by converting most of its 65% share of PacSun debt into equity. Josh Olshansky, managing director at Golden Gate Capital, sounded (perhaps unrealistically) optimistic about PacSun's future. "PacSun has successfully transitioned beyond its historical base of action sports brands to what we believe is the most relevant and coveted mix of brands celebrating the California lifestyle," Olshansky said in a statement.

Beachside brands Quiksilver and Wet Seal also overexpanded and filed for bankruptcy. They cut their retail store count and tried to boost revenues by selling their more popular brands online. PacSun—still with Schoenfeld as CEO—may follow suit—shifting from surf brands—which were out of favor with teens to "California casual gear, such labels as Brandy Melville, LA Hearts, and Kendall + Kylie," noted Bloomberg.

Case Analysis

PacSun's bankruptcy highlights important principles about what to avoid in seeking growth by expanding within a company's current geography. Specifically, PacSun's geographic expansion resulted from three failure principles:

- **Follow in the previous CEO's footprints.** A new CEO may feel gratitude toward his predecessor. And that gratitude might encourage the new CEO to pursue a strategy set in motion before he arrived there. Johnson seems to have taken this approach in launching a shoe store chain at PacSun. Most industries change rapidly and basing strategies on what a retired CEO did could lead to investments that do not generate a return.

- **Invest heavily at the market's peak.** PacSun's geographic expansion came at what was in retrospect the peak of the surf-wear trend—which was boosting demand for all the leading industry participants. PacSun's ambitious expansion strategy was based more on a fear of falling behind competitors rather than an objective assessment of whether its investment in additional supply would be met with a greater increase in demand.

- **Ignore changing competitive landscape and consumer trends.** PacSun's expansion took place under the direction of a new CEO whose previous success building Hollister may have caused the company to avoid looking for reasons not to do what he wanted. As a result, PacSun invested in expansion before conducting objective analysis of the changing competitive landscape and evolving fashion trends among its customers. As a result, PacSun expanded geographically with a business strategy that appealed to an ever-shrinking group of customers.

Principle Four   Small companies seeking growth from new geographies should market to customers in new locations with low CAGE distance who value their superior product attributes.

The risk of geographic expansion is highest for small companies that open shop in new countries. How can small company CEOs make a compelling case to their investors that the benefits of such geographic expansion are comfortably greater than the risks? The cases that follow suggest that small company CEOs can boost their odds that expanding into new geographies will lead to faster revenue growth if they follow four principles:

- **Be humble.** As we first discussed in Chapter 1, a company whose CEO seeks to impose his world view on customers will rarely succeed. To develop and implement a successful growth strategy, a company's CEO must be intellectually humble—that means a willingness to assume that what has worked in the past will not help in the future. Intellectual humility means that the CEO will form a hypothesis, gather data, and use the analysis of the data to make a better strategy.

- **Minimize CAGE distance.** Such as CEO should start off by narrowing down the countries to which the company ought to expand. Potential countries could be ranked based on factors such as their potential revenue for your industry, their CAGE distance from your home country, the investment required to begin selling there, and how long it might take to generate revenues.

- **Find customer pain in those countries.** Next, the CEO should meet with potential customers in new countries and ask them what factors the use to evaluated competing suppliers of the product, how well they think those suppliers perform on the factors, and whether they have unmet needs that the company could satisfy.

- **Apply your strengths to alleviate customer pain.** If many of those customers indicate interest in your product, let them try it out for a while—or if that's not possible, encourage them to speak with current satisfied customers in your company's home country. After the product trials or conversations with reference customers, ask the potential customer what they think about the product. If the customer finds the product interesting—it's bad news for expanding to the country. If the customer asks how soon you can deliver, there is reason for optimism.

Successful: Critical Software Goes International

Introduction

Coimbra, Portugal-based software provider Critical Software (CS) used internally generated capital to expand from Portugal to Brazil and Mozambique. Even as Portugal was in the midst of an IMF bailout in 2011, CS was expecting to boost its hiring by 40% in 2012 to satisfy the needs of customers in new countries where it was expanding.

Case Scenario

CS helps companies alleviate a major source of pain—their technology cannot adapt quickly enough to changes in their business. For example, a company wants to get a new product to market quickly to keep up with a more aggressive competitor, but it cannot get its IT department to build the systems needed to support that new product as quickly as it can design and produce the new product.

CEO Goncalo Quadros explained to me in 2011 that CS alleviates that client pain. According to Quadros, CS clients want "Partners capable of delivering reliable solutions, taking proper advantage of state-of-the-art technology, within the right time-frame, at the right cost. That's what we deliver."

CS works with companies and with governments. One of the more interesting CS projects was its work improving the Portuguese Emergency Management System (people dial 112 to get the service there). Before CS's involvement, the 112 system merely took calls and forwarded them. To that, CS added enhancements—closing the loop from reporting to managing the resolution of the emergency.

CS was founded in 1998 by three PhD students from the University of Coimbra, a few hours north of Portugal's capital Lisbon. Their research work aimed at reducing the development cost of mission critical systems by combining software technologies with commercial off-the-shelf components.

While mission critical systems were typically only found in very critical domains, such as aerospace and defense, they thought there would be an opportunity to use that approach to address the problems of business critical applications in other industries such as manufacturing, finance, health care, and energy.

CS had ambitious goals. Between 2011 and 2014 it wanted to operate seven companies in the group generating $120 million in sales and pretax profit of $24 million. And it sought to increase its employee base from 250 to 350 and establish new subsidiaries, in addition to its existing units in the United States, United Kingdom, Brazil, Angola, and Mozambique.

CS was in Mozambique—a Portuguese trading partner and colony from 1498 to 1975—as far back as 2008. In October 2008, CS signed three contracts with companies in Mozambique—two with its telecommunications company, Telecomunicações de Moçambique; and one with a government agency, the Maputo Municipal Council.

By July 2015, CS's presence in Mozambique continued to generate compelling growth opportunities. Certainly, CS's people appreciated the country's culture. According to CS, "In Maputo, the capital city of Mozambique, life is colorful. Not only do CS employees enjoy a buzzing metropolis, beautiful scenery and exciting food, we are also challenged with interesting, high-profile projects across a broad range of industries." These projects included helping the government build an "off-grid photovoltaic power generation" capability and an IT training program for bank employees. In 2011, revenue increased 15% to about $20 million—with most of the growth coming from international expansion—in 2011 CS's operations in the United Kingdom, Brazil, the United States, and Mozambique grew by roughly 45%.

Between 2011 and 2016, CS underwent some turmoil at the top but ended up achieving significant growth as it expanded globally. In January 2012, CS appointed Marco Costa—who started as an intern at CS in 2000 and earned a MSc in Computer Engineering, and an MBA from the INSEAD—as its new CEO with Quadros becoming CS's chairman.

Quadros was excited about the change represented by Costa's appointment. "Change is an essential pillar in CS's culture—it brings us plurality, ambition and determination, but also intelligence, demand and merit. Marco is an extremely capable manager, in whom we place all our trust and he can depend on all the human capital, knowledge and experience that makes CS what it is today," Quadros explained.

But Costa appears to have fallen short of CS's expectations. About 30 months later, Quadros returned as CS's CEO and Costa was gone. Quadros's reinstatement resulted from "a year-long analysis carried out by the Board of Directors, taking into account the company's strategic, organizational and cultural goals." CS's board concluded that Quadros had "the necessary charisma, energy, experience and knowledge of the organization required to successfully implement" an ambitious strategy to boost the company's growth. Quadros's return as CEO contributed to a record year for CS. In 2015, the company "grew its annual global turnover by 12% to €26 million for the year. Most impressively, as a measure of profitability, year-on-year [earnings before interest, taxes, depreciation, and amortization] EBITDA grew by 77% to €3.9m, and [earnings before taxes] EBT rose to €2.5m, up 178% on the previous year's results." The strong financial performance flowed from "further growth in European and North American markets, while growth in "energy, financial services and space—which increased threefold," were also important contributors.

Case Analysis

CS's continued growth—despite the limited capital markets in Portugal—reflected the application of its strengths to customers in geographies with relatively narrow CAGE distance from Coimbra, Portugal. Key principles for CS's successful expansion into new geographies include the following:

- **Minimize CAGE distance.** CS chose new geographies that were culturally, if not geographically, close to Portugal. Although much of its growth came from providing services to customers in the United States and the United Kingdom—with slightly more cultural distance from Coimbra—its decision to target Brazil and Mozambique suggest that it realized that as former Portuguese colonies, these countries had even shorter CAGE distance.

- **Match your strengths against unmet customer needs.** Due to CS's expertise in building systems that support critical operations in specific industries, it was able to win contracts among customers who had those problems in new geographies. Its geographic expansion strategy was built on a two-phased growth trajectory— first develop world-class expertise in solving specific problems, the solution of which customers are willing to pay a high price and then find new geographies where customers are seeking such solutions.

Unsuccessful: Sweden's Rdio Loses to Spotify

Introduction

Rdio, a San Francisco-based music streaming service started by the found- ers of Skype in August 2008, launched its service to the U.S. market in 2011, raised nearly $126 million in capital in six rounds, went bankrupt in 2015 and was acquired by Pandora Media for $75 million that December. Although it enjoyed a year head start over Stockholm, Sweden-based Spotify, Rdio suf- fered significant competitive disadvantages and ultimately stumbled to its demise. One simple reason Rdio failed was that it charged users a monthly fee whereas Spotify let users stream music for free when it launched in the United States in 2012.

Case Scenario

Rdio was founded by Skype's cofounders Janus Friis and Niklas Zennstroem. Friis was the most directly involved and "was thought to have invested more than $200 million in Rdio. In 2013, Rdio struck a deal with U.S. radio giant Cumulus, trading 15% of its equity for $75 million in radio advertising, that valued the company at $500 million In early November 2015, Cumulus revealed to investors that it had taken a $19.4 million write-down on its equity in Rdio," according to Variety.

But Rdio's most significant competitive disadvantage was that its CEO did not appre- ciate the importance of marketing whereas Spotify's CEO was a marketing whiz. Rdio felt an urgent need to become profitable before it had become a dominant supplier. Spotify invested heavily in getting to be the biggest fast.

The result was a huge market share advantage for Spotify. Rdio was the first modern music streaming service to arrive in America. In August 2010, Rdio offered a $5 Web-only streaming service because smartphones were not ubiquitous. Rdio offered 7 million songs, which was far fewer than the 30 million that its rivals provided by November 2015. Between its care in designing a user interface—including features such as a "calming blue-and-white design and a simple grid of album artwork"—and its negotiations of content deals, Rdio took two years to launch its service, according to The Verge.

Rdio tried to grow through social networking—the idea that friends would listen to the songs that their friends liked the most. Chris Becherer, Rdio's head of product told The Verge, "The founding premise was the best music recommendations come from the people you know. That was the whole idea." Rdio lost because that strategy was less effective than that of Spotify, "a cunning and well-financed competitor that excelled at generating buzz—and using that buzz to acquire paid subscribers."

Spotify's buzz started just as Rdio was gaining early customers from San Franciscans who appreciated Rdio's design. Sadly for Rdio, Spotify was generating much more enthusiasm as Americans saw its free-with-advertising business model as "free iTunes." While Spotify launched and gained many users quickly, Rdio struggled to explain why people should pay for the service and it lacked marketing leadership— unable to retain a chief marketing officer for more than a few months.

Rdio also spent R&D funds on features that did not boost its market share. For example, Rdio took too long refining what it called its queue—where users could store music for later listening. The problem was that customers did not care about this feature as much as others, which Rdio neglected to develop.

By 2013, a year after launching, Spotify had 24 million users, 6 million of whom paid. Rdio was unable to grow and sold an equity stake to Cumulus Media, which operated 525 terrestrial radio stations, which began selling advertisements for Rdio. Rdio was five years behind Spotify—which had been offering a free-advertising-supported service since 2008. Rdio CEO Drew Larner resigned in June 2013 right before the Cumulus deal was announced. Rdio's survival also was threatened by its inability to fix the inherently low profitability of the streaming music industry. Record labels leave only a sliver of revenue for the streaming services. Spotify raised $1 billion under the premise that it could spend heavily to add subscribers with the hope that it would be able to generate enough advertising revenue to become profitable.

By November 2015, Spotify had over 75 million users and 20 million paid users, yet it remained unprofitable. Rdio built finely crafted apps for a small group of "snobby album purists" who were not willing to pay a high enough price to keep it in business. Rdio's collapse reflects a common pattern of failure. A founding team tries to apply the same skills that led to its initial success when it starts a different business. The skills that made the first business a success do not help the new business succeed. But the company founders ignore what customers want and dismiss the strategies of faster-growing rivals. The key to Skype is that it is free and the marginal cost of production is zero. Skype runs directory servers that connect users who then communicate peer-to-peer. Unlike a phone company, Skype does not carry the traffic from point a to point b. This strategy did not work with Rdio because there was a marginal cost of service delivery—the royalty to the artist. The founders wanted to fund this with a subscription model, which stunted Rdio's growth. Spotify chose an advertising based model with an upgrade to an ad-free subscription-based model. Despite the growth, they did not achieve sufficient economies of scale to lower their costs below their revenues.

Case Analysis

Here are three principles that lead to failure when a small company expands into a new geography:

- **Failure to analyze differences between core and new geography.** Rdio's cofounders built Skype into the dominant voice-over-Internet-protocol service. At the core of its success was technical excellence that yielded near-global scope and good quality using a freemium pricing model. However, when Rdio opened a music streaming service, it failed to realize that technical skills would not make the difference between winning and perishing.

- **Not listening to customers.** Rdio built a service that would appeal to its founders—who assumed that if they liked it, the vast American audience would share their passion for the product. Since Rdio's founders did not listen to American consumers, they did not realize that a free service would appear to be an irresistible value.

- **Unwillingness to learn from more successful competitors.** Though Rdio had a year head start over Spotify, it quickly fell behind because of its failure to recognize that consumers preferred its rival's free-with-advertising business model. Rdio was five years too late in replicating Spotify's service. That was too late to survive.

Applying the Principles of Growth through Geography

Leaders seeking to assess whether they apply these principles to their organizations should address these six questions:

- How much has your company saturated the growth potential of its current geographies?

- Which new geographies have the most growth potential for your company?

- Can your company manage the challenges presented by the CAGE distance between its current geographies and the new ones?

- Does your company understand how it will provide more value to customers than competitors do in these new geographies?

- Has your company contracted profitable arrangements for manufacturing and distributing your product in these new geographies?

- Have you appointed effective executives to lead your expansion into new geographies?

Chapter 8: Growth Road Maps provides a detailed methodology for applying the principles of growth through new products.

Summary

Speeding up growth by selling to current or new geographies is a very common source of growth. The cases we've analyzed in this chapter reveal that success in geographic expansion strategies depends on providing potential customers with a better value than competitors do. We also saw that a common error among companies expanding into new geographies is to equate a country's population with its attractiveness as a market for the company. To avoid that mistake, CEOs need to consider different factors—including the potential revenues for the company and its peers, whether those revenues will grow and why, whether the company can offer such a compelling value to customers that it will be able to grow faster than the market, and whether the CAGE distance is short enough between that country and the company's home market.

In the next chapter, we explore a third growth vector—building or acquiring new products—which forces leaders to confront a different set of challenges.

Growth via Building or Acquiring New Products

In Chapter 1, we introduced the concept of S-curves. If a company finds itself too dependent on a downward sloping S-Curve, its hope for resuming growth depends on getting itself onto a new S-Curve that is just beginning to slope upwards. To accomplish that aim, companies can either build or acquire new products.

Principles Of Growth from New Products

In this chapter we will explore the principles that distinguish the successful builders or acquirers from their peers. In both cases, CEOs who are open-minded and who make decisions based on analysis of data prevail over those who assume that approaches that worked for them in the past will work equally well for the immediate challenges they must face.

© Peter S. Cohan 2017
P. S. Cohan, *Disciplined Growth Strategies*, DOI 10.1007/978-1-4842-2448-9_4

CEOs who build or acquire new products successfully start the process by identifying customers who are likely to buy the new products. Such CEOs listen to those customers to understand their pain—and to focus on a vision for a product that would relieve that customer pain more effectively than competing products do.

There are some key differences that distinguish successful new product builders from new product acquirers. CEOs who lead the development of successful new products are good at managing the process of building rapid prototypes of new products and sharing them with potential customers to get their feedback on what works, what does not work, and what is missing from the prototype. Through such learning, CEOs improve the prototype and identify the need to add new skills to the company—in areas such as sales, technology, purchasing, distribution, or manufacturing—so it can win and keep new customers of the new product.

Less successful product builders focus on building what the CEO believes customers want and pushing to complete the product development quickly and without feedback from customers. This approach depletes a company's resources by building a product that customers are reluctant to buy. When small companies take this approach, they often run out of money and cease operations or find an acquirer.

CEOs who achieve growth through acquiring new products realize that they must manage the acquisition of a company—not just a product. In so doing, those CEOs must do two things well:

- Analyze whether the acquisition makes sense, and
- Manage the integration of the two companies well.

Picking the right company to acquire hinges on analyzing whether the company participates in a fast-growing, profitable industry; whether the combined companies will have the products and skills needed to gain market share; whether the price the acquirer pays is low enough to ensure an adequate return on the investment; and whether it will be possible to integrate the two companies so that customers of the acquired company do not suffer once the deal closes.

CEOs who manage the integration well start off by running their companies with a clearly defined culture. Such a culture has specific and well-articulated values and puts those values into practice when they hire, promote, and manage people out of the company. Such CEOs also spend time with the key people in the target company to make sure they fit with their company's culture; work closely with those key people to knit together the two companies' products and skills; and tie the awarding of stock to achievement of specific milestones that will boost the value of the combined company.

CEOs who fail at acquiring for growth make up their minds about doing a deal, skimp on analyzing whether it makes sense, speed through the due diligence, and lose interest after the deal is done—delegating the integration to subordinates and mentally checking out of the process thereafter.

In the remainder of this chapter, we examine case studies to illustrate four principles of growth through new products:

- **Large companies seeking growth from designing new products** should create, market, and service products that beat competitors on customers' top-ranked purchase criteria.

- **Large companies seeking growth from acquiring new products** should make acquisitions that pass industry attractiveness, better off, NPV > 0, and integration tests.

- **Small companies seeking growth from designing new products** should extend product features to gain a larger share of their customer's wallets.

- **Small companies seeking growth from acquiring new products** should only invest in products that uniquely relieve "customers' pain points" when combined with the acquirer's capabilities at a price that does not capitalize future gains.

Principle One   Large companies seeking growth from designing new products should create, market, and improve products that beat competitors on customers' top-ranked purchase criteria.

Case Studies

There are many ways to think about how to manage a large company. It is common for large companies—especially publicly traded ones—to hire CEOs with strong financial skills who focus on winning at the popular Wall Street game I call Beat and Raise. The rules of this game are simple to describe— each quarter a company should exceed Wall Street expectations for revenue and profit growth while boosting its forecast for the next quarter. To win at Beat and Raise, CEOs seek to milk as much growth as they can from current products while avoiding expensive bets in the future that might take the company off the quarterly path to Beat and Raise victory.

Another way to run a large company is to think of it as a start-up with more resources. In this model, the CEO is an entrepreneur with a passion for seeing the future and getting there ahead of rivals. In so doing, the CEO pays close attention to what is bothering customers, analyzes the strategies of faster-growing rivals, and invests in new products that will create new growth opportunities while solving the problems bothering customers.

In this section, we examine how a large company—Amazon—used this entrepreneurial approach to generate significant growth by creating a new S-Curve—through its AWS cloud service.

Successful: Amazon Creates and Dominates the Cloud

Introduction

Amazon, the $107 billion (2015 revenue) company that grew 28% in the first quarter of 2016, was founded in 1994 by its current CEO Jeff Bezos.

Amazon started off selling books online to consumers. But its most profitable and fastest growing service is not for consumers—it's AWS, a computer service for large companies that Amazon started in 2006. AWS has maintained its lead in the cloud services industry despite efforts by some of the largest companies in the world—Microsoft, Google, and IBM—to dethrone it.

Case Scenario

What is AWS and why is it doing so well?

AWS rented computer access to companies. The market for such cloud infrastructure services totaled $23 billion in 2015—a market that grew 52% from the year before. AWS was the market leader in 2015 with a 31% market share and it grew at 63% in the fourth quarter of 2015. The second largest competitor, Microsoft, had 9% of the market—but grew much faster, at a 124% annual rate.

AWS sustained its market leadership—in 2016 it had over a million business customers—due to five competitive advantages:

- *More services. AWS could meet more business computing needs than could its competitors—these included "cloud native applications, e-business hosting, general business applications, enterprise applications, development environments and batch computing."*

- *More different kinds of software. AWS had a large group of software providers that used AWS to deliver their software to companies as a service.*

- **Large group of application development partners.**
  AWS had many partnerships with application development companies, managed service, and professional service
  providers.

- **Most technical features.** AWS offered the most features
  within its Infrastructure as a Service (IaaS) and Platform as a
  Service (PaaS) offerings.

- **Fastest rate of innovation.** AWS introduced new service
  offerings and expanded its more advanced services at a faster
  rate than did rivals.

AWS's sheer scale also provided Amazon with important cost advantages and a
global scope that gave it access to a large population of potential customers. Its data
centers made AWS services available in 33 zones within 12 regions worldwide. Each
availability zone had up to 6 data centers and redundant power to keep customers
from losing their service. Each data center operated between 50,000 and 80,000
servers and could handle enormous volumes of data—102 terabytes per second
worth of bandwidth.

While these advantages shed some light on AWS's market leadership, a few interviews with AWS customers offered a clearer picture of why AWS had so many customers.
Here are four examples of businesses that used AWS because it met their specific needs:

- **Large AWS capacity lets businesses add computing
  quickly as their needs change.** Pfizer used AWS to operate a system that analyzed data for pharmaceutical research.
  As Dr. Michael Miller, Pfizer's head of R&D High Performance
  Computing said "Research can be unpredictable, especially
  as the on-going science raises new questions." AWS enables
  Pfizer to add to its computing capacity quickly when needed.

- **Match computing supply with peak demand without
  building excess capacity.** Online travel company Expedia
  received 240 requests per second from travel service providers.
  AWS enabled Expedia to meet demand surges without adding
  permanent extra computing capacity. As Murari Gopalan, technology director of Expedia, said, "The advantage of AWS is that
  we can use Auto Scaling to match load demand instead of having
  to maintain capacity for peak load in traditional data centers."

- **Ability to add storage quickly to keep up with
  demand,** Music streaming service Spotify had 16 million
  licensed songs in March 2016 and was adding more than
  20,000 new ones daily. AWS's S3 enabled Spotify to add to
  its storage just in time to keep up demand growth—rather
  than struggling with long lead times to add that extra capacity.

How did AWS get started and grow?

Amazon created AWS to manage the high volumes of data needed to operate its e-commerce and others' services. However, when AWS was first getting started, Bezos urged AWS developers to build the service in anticipation of making it available to outside businesses.

As former Amazon employee Steve Yegge recalled, Bezos "issued a mandate [in 2002] that was so out there, so huge and eye-bulgingly ponderous, that it made all of his other mandates look like unsolicited peer bonuses."

Bezos deliberately wanted AWS to be built to benefit customers. And after perfecting AWS to meet its own needs, Amazon wanted to profit from it.

But it was head of global infrastructure Chris Pinkham, who first came up with the idea of building a business around "Infrastructure of the World." Working with website engineering manager Benjamin Black, Pinkham envisioned an infrastructure using a new technology for Amazon at the time—Internet Protocol —that would be so standardized that AWS customers could demand and get more computing capacity just in the nick of time at a very low price.

By 2005 Amazon was offering AWS to some customers under nondisclosure agreements—officially launching it in the summer of 2006. As Pinkham said, "Amazon is a very strong believer in moving very aggressively. [Amazon scaled AWS very quickly and set its prices slightly above costs to] lock the door for competitors."

In 2015, Amazon finally let the world know just how successful AWS had become—it generated $6 billion in revenue and $1 billion in operating income—and by March 2016, AWS had generated $2.6 billion in quarterly revenue growing at 64% with a 23% operating margin—far above Amazon's 2.1% average.

Case Analysis

AWS's success— growing from scratch to nearly $10 billion in revenues in a decade— highlights the effectiveness of three principles that large companies should follow to achieve faster growth by introducing new products:

- **Appoint CEO with a start-up mindset.** Bezos is the only public company CEO who started his company and was still leading it very successfully nearly 23 years later as of January 2017. While this makes him exceptional, in theory other large companies could appoint CEOs who are focused intently on creating new products that deliver better benefits to customers— with a long-term focus that delays short-term profitability in exchange for gaining market share and achieving lower costs due to scale.

- **Create ever-better value for customers**. AWS's initial success was likely a result of its having been built for one of the most demanding computing environments in the world with the idea that it would be turned into a service that could be sold to businesses. Moreover, Amazon understood why companies would find AWS valuable— it had the potential to enable companies to rent increments of computing power when they needed it— thus lowering their fixed costs while enabling them to respond faster to changing customer demands.

- **Persistently innovate without fear of failure.** Amazon not only started off ahead, but it has continued to stay ahead in the highly competitive cloud services industry. AWS was likely guided by the insights about evolving corporate needs for cloud services because Bezos applied pressure on his people to keep its existing customers happy. Moreover, AWS's leaders also understood the requirements of a particularly demanding customer—its own e-commerce operations.

Unsuccessful: ESPN's New Programming Can't Stop the Bleeding

Introduction

In contrast to Amazon's success with AWS, ESPN was unable to create a new S-Curve because it defied this principle— creating a new program that it thought would offset the hemorrhaging of customers who failed to renew their cable subscriptions.

Between 2013 and 2015, ESPN lost $1 billion in revenue due to so-called cord-cutting—customers bypassing cable networks to access its service—despite efforts to offset the loss by adding new programs—such as one covering college basketball.

Case Scenario

ESPN's woes reveal a common strategic challenge that faces many large, successful companies: upstarts offer customers a way to bypass their high prices and the incumbents respond by hoping the upstarts will fail and when that does not work, the incumbents try to invest in strategies that worked in the past.

Simply put, many large companies store their executives in a bubble that is isolated from the world of consumers and competitors who vie for their money and attention. In that bubble, lieutenants compete with each other to be most like the person with the power to promote them—rather than creating new products that will boost the company's revenue growth rate.

ESPN's problem was cord-cutting—that is, consumers who get access to TV programs without paying cable or satellite broadcasters for the privilege. Instead, they access the content through so-called Over the Top (OTT) or mobile services.

Cord-cutting is painful for companies like ESPN. In 2015, 1.13 million U.S. TV households cut the cord—that was four times the cord-cutting pace of 2014. Moreover, another 1.11 million were expected to cut the cord in 2016.

The good news for broadcasters was that TV revenue rose—3% to $105 billion in 2015 and was expected to rise another 2% in 2016. The bad news was that OTT services were expected to grow much faster—up 29% to $5.1 billion in 2015 with another 30% growth forecast for 2016.

For consumers, the logic of cutting the cord was compelling. Rather than pay about $100 a month for a 200-channel cable bundle, consumers could watch smaller bundles containing the most popular sports and entertainment channels for $40 to $50 monthly from the likes of Amazon, YouTube, and Hulu. Moreover, so-called skinny bundles were available on the web for $25 a month.

Some of the cord-cutters were former ESPN subscribers—between 2013 and November 2015 they had cost the sports cable network about $1 billion since 2013.

The loss of revenue came from two sources—falling affiliate fees and declining advertising—both of which were due to a drop in the number of ESPN subscribers. Between 2013 and 2015, ESPN's subscriber count fell about 7% from 99 million to 92 million.

That meant cable companies and satellite broadcasters paid $650 million less in affiliate fees—which hedge fund manager Eric Jackson considered pure profit—and lost $250 million in advertising as a result of the declining subscriber count.

ESPN responded late to the cord-cutting trend. Former ESPN commentator Bill Simmons said in a 2015 podcast that ESPN executives did not start talking about cord-cutting concerns until 2014.

And its reaction was to invest in more programming and an upgrade to its TV set rather than to offer its own cord-cutting service. In 2014, ESPN added a new network called [Southeastern Conference] SEC Network, which focuses on college sports in the Southeastern United States, and it spent $125 million to revamp its Sports Center set.

ESPN's efforts did nothing to stanch the outflow of subscribers. By May 2016, ESPN had lost even more subscribers— to about 89.5 million—representing a daily cancellation rate of 10,400. At $80 per subscriber, that meant ESPN was pulling in $7.1 billion in revenue to cover its $6 billion in annual fees to sports leagues for the rights to broadcast their games.

By July 2016, ESPN was contemplating offering its own streaming live TV package directly to consumers. The new package would be sold to people who did not currently subscribe to pay TV and would exclude professional basketball or football, but included "niche leagues" and possibly some college sports.

While clearly designed to avoid cannibalizing ESPN's ever-declining base of cable subscribers, it was unlikely that subscribers to ESPN's new live streaming package would generate sufficient revenue to stop the loss of cable subscription revenue.

ESPN's three-year revenue decline highlights the way that big companies tie themselves in knots as they try to preserve their old way of making money in the face of rivals who are taking their customers with better value propositions enabled by new technology.

Case Analysis

More specifically, ESPN's failure to offer new products that boosted its revenue growth highlight three failure principles:

- **Executives in the bubble.** ESPN executives acted as though they hoped that cord-cutting would go away as long as they did nothing about it. ESPN executives may have been more concerned about not rocking the boat than on responding to rivals offering skinny bundles at big discounts.

- **Solving new problems with old strategies.** ESPN's 2014 launch of SEC Network and its $125 million investment in modernizing its broadcasting studio might have worked to boost subscribers before cutting the cord was costing ESPN over a million subscribers a year. But those tactics failed to slow the loss of subscribers because they did not solve the fundamental problem—consumers were paying too much for a 200-channel bundle, most of which they did not want to buy.

- **Focus on short-term revenues rather than creating superior value for customers**. After two years of accelerating declines in the number of subscribers, ESPN finally began to talk about responding directly to these skinny bundles that were persuading consumers to cut the cord. However, ESPN's proposed skinny bundle excluded the most popular programming—a move clearly designed to avoid cannibalizing regular subscribers—rather than to win back those who had cancelled their subscriptions.

Principle Two   Large companies seeking growth from acquiring new products should make acquisitions that pass industry attractiveness, better off, NPV > 0, and integration tests.

Most acquisitions fail. The reasons for the failures are often one or a combination of four causes:

- **Unattractive industry.** The industry in which the acquired company competes is inherently unprofitable or less profitable than the industry in which the acquirer participates;

- **Worse off.** The combined companies are worse off when it comes to creating products that customers want to buy and/or at performing the critical activities needed to grow;

- **Overpay.** They pay so much for the acquisition that the price capitalizes all the future gains; and/or

- **Inability to integrate.** They fail to manage the integration of the acquired company effectively.

Therefore, companies seeking growth from acquisition of new products should evaluate whether the acquired company can pass four tests designed to screen out failed deals before they close. To that end, when considering potential acquisitions, companies should apply the four tests mentioned above.

Successful: Facebook Earns 35-Fold Return on Instagram Acquisition in Under Three Years

Introduction

A month before its May 2012, initial public offering, Facebook paid $1 billion for a photo app—which connects photographers and people who love photos—with 50 million users and no revenues.

By December 2014, Citigroup valued that app at a whopping $35 billion—accounting for 16% of its $221 billion market capitalization.

Facebook— which in 2011 had 845 million users and $3.1 billion in revenues— acquired Instagram because it concluded that it would be better to buy a photo app than to build it.

Case Scenario

In 2014, TechCrunch obtained documents describing a stand-alone Facebook mobile photo sharing app. However, Facebook decided that a better way to add a photo sharing service would be to acquire Instagram and allow it to operate as a stand-alone app that would eventually connect to Facebook.

Perhaps one reason that Facebook bought Instagram—beyond taking out a potential competitor— was its tremendous popularity and its potential to grow. In April 2012, Instagram had 27 million registered Apple iOS users and after getting a million Android users within a week after its April 2012 launch, Instagram was expected to end up with 50 million registered users.

Instagram—founded in October 2010 by Stanford graduates Kevin Systrom and Mike Krieger and operated with 12 employees—would also have the potential to benefit from the acquisition by maintaining its company culture and getting access to Facebook's much greater design and engineering resources.

Facebook CEO Mark Zuckerberg argued at the time that its users would be most comfortable with the service if it continued to operate mostly as it had before the acquisition—enabling users to share photos on social networks other than Facebook. "We think the fact that Instagram is connected to other services beyond Facebook is an important part of the experience. We plan on keeping features like the ability to post to other social networks, the ability to not share your Instagrams on Facebook if you want, and the ability to have followers and follow people separately from your friends on Facebook," said Zuckerberg.

Indeed the merger with Facebook contributed to Instagram's growth. After all it began with 25,000 users, on its first day and by October 2015 it had 400 million monthly users. Systrom—interviewed at Instagram's own building within the dispersed Facebook campus— attributed this growth to Facebook's skills with sales, advertising, and targeting and relevance algorithms. That growth translated into considerable revenues. eMarketer estimated Instagram's advertising revenues hit $600 million in 2015 and expected that figure to rise at a 116% annual rate to $2.81 billion in 2017. And Wall Street had little difficulty estimating how much that growth contributed to Instagram's worth. At the end of 2014, Citigroup estimated that Instagram had 300 million users—contributed to its estimate that it would be valued at $35 billion—about 16% of Facebook's roughly $221 billion market capitalization.

Instagram appears to be better off as a result of its merger with Facebook. As Systrom explained, "There are fun parts of running a startup and not-so-fun parts, and Facebook handles the not-so-fun parts, like infrastructure, spam, sales. The real questions are, how big can Instagram get? Is it 400 million, or bigger? Can it be a viable business if it is that big? These are at the top of the list for everyone in Silicon Valley."

By July 2016, Instagram's user count had soared to 500 million. Assuming Citigroup was to use the same valuation per user ratio, by July 2016, Instagram would have been worth a whopping $58.3 billion—a 58x return on Facebook's April 2012 investment.

Case Analysis

The success of Facebook's acquisition of Instagram highlights the power of passing the four tests as a means of achieving new product growth through acquisition:

- **Attractive industry.** Instagram participated in a two-sided market, as Facebook did, in which the aim was to attract millions of users who did not pay so that companies would pay to advertise to the users. The mobile advertising industry has proven to be large— growing at a 25.7% annual rate from $19.2 billion in 2014 to $60.2 billion in 2019 and earning high net profit margins of 21%.

- **Better off.** The combined companies are clearly better off as evidenced by the rapid growth in Instagram users and revenues. This growth would not have occurred without Facebook's skills in sales, advertising, and relevance algorithms. Facebook clearly benefited to the extent that Instagram's growth contributes to its revenues and stock market valuations.

- **NPV > 0.** Given the 58-fold return that Instagram has generated in about four years—using Citigroup's assumptions—Facebook's purchase price was enormously profitable for Facebook.

- **Ability to integrate**. Zuckerberg kept his promise to Systrom—letting him run Instagram as a separate company with its own offices. Systrom's feeling of confidence in the future and acknowledgments of the benefits of the merger are compelling evidence of the success of the integration process.

Unsuccessful: AOL/Time Warner Merger Destroys $228 Billion in Value over 15 Years

Introduction

On January 10, 2000, Internet service provider AOL announced plans to merge with magazine publisher and cable network, Time Warner, at a price of $182 billion—including stock and debt. The proposed deal would create AOL

Time Warner, a new company—55% owned by AOL and 45% owned by Time Warner—valued at $350 billion.

Fifteen and a half years later, the companies that entered history's largest merger were worth about $122 billion—wiping out $228 billion in shareholder value or 65% of the deal's original value.

Case Scenario

What was AOL?

AOL—with a stock market value of roughly $163 billion before the deal was announced—provided access to the Internet to over 20 million consumers with PCs and dial-up modems through its AOL and Compuserve Internet services. In 1999, AOL generated $4.8 billion in sales, $748 million in net income, and employed 12,100.

What was Time Warner?

Time Warner, with $83 billion in stock market value before the deal's announcement, owned media outlets—including Warner Bros. Studios, HBO, CNN, Warner Music, Time magazine—and a cable network with 320,000 high-speed broadband subscribers and 13 million cable subscribers. Time Warner's 1999 sales were $14.6 billion; it earned $168 million in profit, and had 67,500 employees.

Why did they merge?

The deal made then Time Warner CEO Gerald Levin the CEO of the new company while Steve Case, then-AOL CEO, became chairman.

The two companies merged because AOL CEO Steve Case was able to persuade Levin that such a merger would be great for his legacy.

To be sure, AOL thought it would boost its market share by gaining access to 13 million Time Warner's cable subscribers via Time Warner's high-speed broadband network. While Time Warner's pre-deal stock market value immediately doubled.

Case viewed the deal as creating a historically significant portfolio of brands. "I don't think this is too much to say this really is a historic merger; a time when we've transformed the landscape of media and the Internet. AOL Time Warner will offer an incomparable portfolio of global brands that encompass the full spectrum of media and content," he said.

Levin said that the deal was the best way for Time Warner to build a service that would enable it to provide Internet access for its subscribers to its content. As Levin said, "I saw the power of that combination and as I looked around at other companies and other opportunities, I concluded that either we would do something with AOL or we would build ourselves, but this is infinitely preferable."

The deal destroyed $228 billion in shareholder value.

Two companies were spun out of the original as publicly traded companies and were acquired by others.

AOL was spun out of Time Warner in December 2009—at a value of $2.5 billion—and Verizon acquired it for $4.4 billion in June 2015. Time Warner Cable became an independent company in Match 2009—valued at $9.25 billion—which Charter acquired in May 2016 for about $60 billion.

Two independent companies are still publicly traded: Time Warner—which operates a TV and pay cable network and produces films, was valued at $60 billion and Time, which owns magazines was valued at $1.7 billion—both on August 1, 2016.

But by October 2016, Time Warner's independence was imperiled when AT&T offered to acquire it for $85 billion—a deal that looked like it might not gain regulatory approval.

In hindsight, it is obvious that AOL suffered the most precipitous fall in value—$159.6 billion in lost value or 97% of AOL's pre-deal valuation—between the time the deal was announced and its ultimate acquisition by Verizon.

One reason for the drop in AOL's value was the plunge in the value of dot-com stocks between the announcement of the merger and its completion.

The merger destroyed shareholder value for two overarching reasons. AOL's value was vastly overinflated by the dot-com bubble that peaked two months after the merger was announced. In the year that elapsed between the merger's announcement and its closing, the NASDAQ had lost about a third of its value—falling from 4,070 at the end of December 1999 to 2,781 in January 2001—and the market value of the deal had also lost a third of its value.

Secondly, the merger was poorly conceived and executed—starting with the absence of rigorous due diligence prior to closing the merger, which would have highlighted the many reasons not to do the deal in the first place.

At the core of the problem was Levin who acted alone—deliberately ignoring the advice of his subordinates who did not want to do the deal—because Levin was determined to leave Time Warner with a memorable legacy. According to Fools Rush In, Levin as he turned sixty wanted to be remembered for "integrity . . . high moral principles; and wisdom."

As a result of his determination to leave behind a lofty legacy through the merger, Levin forced the deal to close without considering objectively its potential risks. This failure to brook opposition left all but a small number of Time Warner executives in the dark about the pending deal until hours before it was announced. Moreover, even fewer Time Warner executives supported the proposal.

Levin allocated only three days to due diligence for the $165 billion merger and many top managers' sale of large chunks of stock—including Case who sold shares worth $100 million—shortly after the deal closed.

Despite this, Time Warner could have gotten out of the deal in the year that elapsed after the January 2000 announcement of the deal. During this year, the dot-com crash deflated AOL's stock price and the government investigated AOL's flawed accounting.

Moreover, AOL and Time Warner cultures clashed during that year. AOL executives dominated their Time Warner counterparts, who felt they were being acquired by brash, young interlopers with inflated dollars. AOL's culture was aggressive, and Time Warner executives—used to more genteel business practices—rebelled. In the midst of clashing cultures and conflicting management styles, AOL's business slowed and then stalled.

Furthermore, AOL came under government scrutiny, and when AOL conducted its own internal investigation, it admitted that it had improperly booked at least $190 million in revenue. If Levin had any second thoughts about the deal, this signifi-cant accounting fraud would have given Time Warner the Material Adverse Change it needed to legally withdraw from the deal. But Levin bulldozed ahead—leaving behind a legacy, for sure, but not one of integrity, principle, or wisdom.

About 14 years after the deal closed, 97% of AOL pre-deal value had been wiped out.

Case Analysis

Why did the merger fail? Here are three reasons that would have become quite clear had the two companies' CEOs not jammed the deal through so quickly:

- **Overpaying**. The dot-com collapse began a few months after the deal was announced. As noted above, the stock of the two companies declined so much during 2000 that it could have represented a legitimate justification for calling off the deal or at least renegotiating its terms. Nevertheless, the deal went through and dot-com stocks continued to tumble. AOL was thus forced to write-down the value of its assets. In particular it incurred a total goodwill write-down for 2002 of $99 billion, reflecting the difference between the high price AOL paid for Time Warner and the 2002 market value of these assets. This reduced its net worth by two-thirds to $53 billion and nearly caused it to violate the terms of its debt contracts.

- **Decline in Internet advertising.** Online advertising was thought to be a significant source of revenue from the combined firm. Time Warner thought that the AOL merger would lead to a huge boost in revenue. However, by the time the deal closed in 2001, the economy was slowing down and Internet advertising was decelerating. An example of this trend is Yahoo, which at the time derived most of its revenue from Internet advertising. In January 2001, Yahoo announced that its revenue growth would decelerate sharply from 88% to about 18% causing a 20% tumble in Yahoo shares. Yahoo attributed the poor revenue growth to the sharp slowdown in Internet advertising and a continuation of 2001's general economic slowdown. The result was that an anticipated source of new revenue from the combined companies did not materialize.

- **Cultural clash.** While Levin and Case sold the deal, in part, on the expectation that cash flow resulting from integration of AOL and Time Warner would grow 30% in the year following the deal's closure, the reality was less impressive. In fact, AOL Time Warner's Earnings before Interest Taxes Depreciation and Amortization (EBITDA) rose 17% in that first year—far short of expectations. A big reason for this shortfall was a cultural clash that impeded efforts at integration—plans for which had been neglected during the merger negotiations. According to *The Times*, this cultural clash was a major factor leading Robert Pittman to quit in frustration in mid-2002. Until then Pittman had been the AOL executive in charge of trying to achieve synergies, such as increasing AOL members' spending from $20 a month to $150 by selling magazines and other media to them and getting $200 a month out of cable users then spending $60, by selling them other AOL Time Warner products. Pittman failed in part due to cultural differences between AOL and Time Warner. There was a very ingrained culture at Time Warner and people there looked down at what they saw as a "gun-slinging culture" at AOL. They were suspicious of the dot-com world, intimidated by the high-tech nature of the medium and unconvinced by its value. And to Time Warner, Pittman epitomized everything that its old guard found intolerable about new media. He was seen as brash and overconfident. They called him "the Pitchman" for his excellent skills in marketing, but the salesmanship and unbridled enthusiasm that had been so valuable to a dot-com start-up led Time Warner executives to bristle.

In retrospect it seems clear that had Levin been less determined to leave a legacy, he might have negotiated a mutually profitable deal that would have enabled AOL to use Time Warner's high-speed cable network to replace its poky dial-up network. This would have given AOL a broadband channel over which to distribute Time Warner's rich content, which would have attracted Internet advertising. And it would have given Time Warner a significant revenue stream for its cable network. Ultimately Time Warner might have worked with AOL to digitize its content and share the resulting advertising revenues. Such an evolving partnership would have generated real value that might have withstood the dot-com stock collapse.

As Ted Turner, who founded CNN, which he sold to Time Warner, said on the tenth anniversary of the deal. "I'd like to forget it. That's what goes through my mind. I almost didn't do this interview because I didn't want to dig it up again. Let it pass into history. The Time Warner-AOL merger should pass into history like the Vietnam War and the Iraq and Afghanistan wars. It's one of the biggest disasters that have occurred to our country."

The failure of the AOL Time Warner merger illustrates why leaders should make sure that a proposed merger to boost revenues by acquiring new products passes the four tests of a successful acquisitions. To the extent that the AOL Time Warner merger failed each of the tests, it provides an excellent example of what CEOs should avoid in such mergers:

- **Unattractive industries.** The combined companies participated in several different industries—many of which were unprofitable. Specifically, magazines and Internet service providers were inherently unprofitable industries that were getting less attractive. Meanwhile, cable networks and video content production were moderately attractive industries.

- **Worse off.** The combined companies were clearly worse off as a result of the merger. It became increasingly clear that Time Warner's broadband network could provide better Internet access than AOL. Moreover, Time Warner's weekend of due diligence was insufficient to discover AOL's accounting problems.

- **Negative NPV.** In destroying $228 billion in shareholder value, the AOL Time Warner deal appears to have had one of history's most negative net present values. AOL overpaid tremendously—and the two companies should have used the 33% drop in the value of AOL's stock during the year that elapsed between the deal's announcement and its closing that the merger would destroy value.

- **Inability to integrate.** The two companies were not well integrated and the goals of the merger were not achieved. This failure to integrate the companies was evidenced by Bob Pittman's inability to encourage consumers to spend more on the combined companies' content and his ultimate resignation.

Principle Three   Small companies seeking growth from designing new products should extend product features to gain a larger share of their customer's wallets.

Many of the same principles apply to small companies as to large ones when it comes to designing new products to achieve revenue growth.

In general small companies have more limited resources than large ones so they take a different approach to designing new products. Small companies that achieve faster growth through new products follow five principles:

- **Listen to customers.** Small companies must listen to customers, observe how they use a company's product, and learn how they are planning to spend their budgets. Such observations can yield insights into whether customers might cut their spending on a company's products or increase that spending and why. Companies might also identify opportunities for new products based on different product categories where customers plan to increase their spending.

- **Identify new services that will boost the company's share of the customer's spending.** Companies should consider whether they have the skills required to build a compelling addition to such new product categories. To make this decision, companies should ask customers why they are increasing their budgets for those new product categories, what factors they use to decide among competing suppliers of those new products, whether customers might be dissatisfied with those offerings, and whether the company could develop a new product that customers would find more compelling.

- **Assess whether the company has the needed capabilities.** If companies believe that they can design such a product, they should make sure that they have or can create the manufacturing, distribution, sales, marketing, and service skills need to turn the idea into a profitable line of business.

- **Build prototypes of the new services.** Given their limited resources, small companies should not spend too much time and money developing an elaborate version of their product before introducing it to customers. Instead, they should build a quick, inexpensive version of the product's most important features and give it to potential customers.

- **Use customer feedback to improve the product.** Companies should observe how those customers use the product; ask them for ideas on what is missing, what should be improved, and what should be removed. The company should use this feedback to build ever-improved versions of the product.

Successful: New Relic's Six-Year Journey from Start-Up to Public Company with Five Products

Introduction

Lew Cirne started and ran Wily Technology, a web-performance monitoring company that he sold in 2006 for $375 million to CA Technologies. By 2008, he had started a new company—New Relic—that offers software to monitor the status and responsiveness of a company's digital operations.

By December 2014, New Relic—which raised over $214 million in venture capital—sold stock to the public and by August 2016 it had a stock market capitalization of $1.7 billion with revenues coming from five different products; 30% of its growth came from four new products introduced two years earlier.

Case Scenario

As Cirne explained in a December 2011 interview, in 2008, he started New Relic to undo all the mistakes he had made when he ran 260-employee Wily and sold it in 2006 to CA Technologies for $375 million. Cirne spent 2007 playing with his one-year-old daughter while thinking about what his next start-up would do. And one of the biggest things that bothered him about Wily was that only 15 of his 260 employees were writing the code that customers used. Most of the remaining employees participated in lengthy selling campaigns to convince Wily's 500 to 600 customers to pay some $10,000 per central processing unit per month to run its software.

When Cirne started New Relic in 2008, he decided to run it with a far leaner sales and marketing staff. But to do that, he needed to rethink the customer's experience. Instead of taking company executives on dinners and golf outings, New Relic built a product that sold itself. How so? It gave companies detailed information about, say, how many seconds it takes a consumer visiting their website to open their web page on a browser. New Relic's software was extremely easy to use and—for most users—free. Needless to say, such a combination of an easy-to-use product at no cost was a far easier one to sell. This is not to say that no customers pay for New Relic's product or that it has no sales force. But both of these are powerfully tamped down. By offering its software-as-a-service (SaaS) with a so-called freemium strategy, within three years of its launch, New Relic had signed up 14,000 customers—5,000 of whom paid for a premium version (up to a $199 per month maximum) either directly or through a New Relic partner. The reason customers used New Relic was that it generated useful information and could be up and running quickly at no charge. As Spotify engineer Jade Rubick, said, "It is a sort of aha moment when you use it, like, oh my god, how did I ever live without this information. A lot of things you used to guess about are immediately obvious. . . . You can build this yourself or use a tool that takes a few minutes to install and does it all for you, and gives you more info than you would ever build."

And New Relic did have a sales force but the sales people took calls from customers who had tried the product online and were seeking advice on whether they could satisfy their need for performance monitoring with the free version or whether they needed the premium one. Each of New Relic's telephone sales people closed around 40 to 50 deals a quarter. New Relic also focused on a particularly influential group of users—programmers who wrote in a language called Ruby on Rails—who had very high-quality standards and would advocate on behalf of vendors who satisfied them. "Rails developers are known for adopting the latest technologies, and passionately supporting products that rock, while brutally and vocally criticizing products don't meet their high standards. We were not the first product to target the Rails market, but we believe we had a strong product that immediately earned the support from thought leaders in the rails community," said Cirne.

Satisfied customers tended to buy more from New Relic—a concept dubbed negative churn. Specifically, each New Relic customer spent 14% more than the previous year because over time, as companies used the service they needed more servers to operate it. So despite steadily adding about 750 customers per quarter, its revenues grew.

While the $15 billion IT management software market was barely growing, the SaaS segment was exploding. According to Cirne, that growth translated into 200% annual growth. But given the compelling value proposition for customers, this growth is not a big surprise.

Cirne's goal was to reach at least 30,000 customers by the end of 2012. And for that, he would need to hire people to augment his staff of 70. Ironically, many of the people he would hire would be in sales and marketing — as well as R&D. But Cirne pointed out that his sales people were much more productive than those at Wily were.

These investments had clearly paid off by the end of New Relic's fiscal year 2016, which ended in March 2016. At that point, New Relic reported a 64% increase in annual revenues to $181.3 million. These revenues included 90% more large transactions—over $1 million—coming from 1,500 large-company customers such as Cisco Systems, Dunkin' Brands, LinkedIn, Norwegian Cruise Lines, Rakuten, and Unilever. New Relic also had many mid-market customers.

By that point, New Relic had introduced five paid products—each of which sold more than it had the year before. Moreover, 30% of New Relic's growth came from products other than its original one—application performance management (APM). This represented a significant improvement from New Relic's fiscal 2014 during which only 5% of its growth came from non-APM products.

The most successful of these new products was called Insights, which enabled companies to understand what was causing performance problems for customers who were using their digital platforms. New Relic found that many large companies chose to purchase all of New Relic's products due to the power of its Insights product.

New Relic cited an example of an Insight customer in the travel business. "They use Insight to look at ticketing activity second by second in real time, seeing how many tickets are flowing through the site, and in the same dashboard, they're showing how fast the page [moves] are and how fast the server time is. And they've proven beyond a shadow of a doubt that for their business, a slowdown in their application dramatically impacts their business in terms of ticket sales," explained Cirne.

New Relic's product development approach started with understanding the pressures facing its end users—IT operations workers. New Relic built new products that would relieve customers' pressures based on New Relic's view of which new technologies would be most effective a few years into the future.

A key part of New Relic's product development path was based on the idea of collecting more types of data about its customer's operations and analyzing that data to gain insights into what was slowing down their operations.

As Cirne said, "We're going to be smarter about the data we collect and we're going to collect more types of data. Imagine if all the data we are collecting from software is married with all the data by about what's going on in the server, such as who logged into a server just prior to that server having a problem? What was the thing they changed on that server?"

New Relic envisioned that its new products would help IT operations people to manage very large computing environments. "We want to service the needs of the operations people who have these enormous environments. They're busy, they're overwhelmed, and they don't have time to do anything but barely keep everything running. We want to make it easier for them to manage enormous environments by taking on the burden of doing more with the data that we collect for them," he said.

Ultimately, New Relic aspired to support companies that were rethinking how they work with customers based on what new technologies can do rather than automating their old business processes.

As he said, such companies use software as an offensive weapon. "The better you are at playing offense with software, at creating a great customer experience to drive the growth of your core business, the brighter your prospects are. If not, then you're going to get Ubered. There's going to be another company that will do your vertical what Uber is doing to taxis."

New Relic was seen by one industry observer as an industry leader.

IT researcher Gartner put New Relic in its so-called magic quadrant in the APM market between 2011 and 2015 due to the strength of its vision and the effectiveness of its execution.

In its December 2015 report, Gartner projected that "by 2020, 60% of APM buyers will reside outside of IT operations organizations, up from less than 35% today. New Relic identified this trend early on and designed its solutions to deliver software analytics data to bridge multiple functions across an organization."

Case Analysis

New Relic's success illustrates the way the four principles described above contribute to a small company's growth through new products:

- **Listen to customers.** In general, New Relic developed new products with two ideas in mind. First, by listening to its customers New Relic was able to understand the pressures that made their jobs difficult. Secondly, it understood where technology was headed and built products using such technologies to help customers manage these pressures.

- **Identify new services that will boost the company's share of the customer's spending.** New Relic broadened its product portfolio to include offerings—such as Insight—that enabled its customers to identify and solve problems with their digital operations. The value they saw in Insight encouraged companies to buy all of New Relic's products, thus boosting its share of their budgets. Moreover, New Relic's value encouraged customers to spend more on its products each year.

- **Assess whether the company has the needed capabilities.** New Relic's new products relied substantially on the capabilities it used to build and sell its initial product. Specifically, New Relic's strengths in engineering, product development, sales, and service were as useful for its new products as they were for its existing ones.

- **Build prototypes of the new services.** New Relic used a series of rough—but increasingly refined—versions of new products to test its new product ideas before selling them more broadly. This process enabled New Relic to get its products to market in a form that worked for its customers. As a result, between 2014 and 2016, New Relic was able to boost the portion of its revenue growth from new products from 5% to 30%.

- **Use customer feedback to improve the product.** New Relic's CEO listened to customers discuss their business challenges and their experiences with the company's products. If he identified customers pain—either in unmet needs or flaws with its products—Cirne would invest to add products and/or improve those in New Relic's current product portfolio to relieve that pain.

Unsuccessful: Imercive Is Shuttered after Initial and New Products Fail

The vast majority of start-ups fail. A common reason is that people who found companies lack a basic understanding of how to create a product that people will pay to use. So it comes as no surprise that when such founders realize that their first product idea is not working, they run out of money before their second product gains sufficient traction.

Introduction

Start-ups that fail due to a mismatch between their products and what customers need follow specific failure principles:

- Company believes market will embrace its first product.

- Company builds first product before getting customer feedback.

- Company realizes customers will not use or pay for product after spending most of its capital.

- Company decides on a new product based on CEO's vision.

- Company runs out of capital before it can build second product and shuts down.

Imercive—"a social media marketing company that provided a first-of-its-kind instant messaging marketing solution to help brands create new channels for consumer engagement"—followed these five steps to start-up failure.

Case Scenario

Imercive was founded in September 2006 by Keith Nowak, a 2006 Boston University graduate with a BA in Philosophy. Imercive raised $500,000 in seed capital from angel investors, hired three software developers and two sales people, launched applications for Moviefone and Hershey's, and shut down in December 2009.

In Nowak's view, the problem with Imercive was its failure to stop building its first product fast enough and to work on its second one instead.

As he said, "We stuck with the wrong strategy for too long. I think this was partly because it was hard to admit the idea wasn't as good as I originally thought or that we couldn't make it work. If we had been honest with ourselves earlier on we may have been able to pivot sooner and have enough capital left to properly execute the new strategy. I believe the biggest mistake I made as CEO of Imercive was failing to pivot sooner." Nowak described Imercive's first concept as a way for advertisers to reach people via branded instant messaging. Nowak believed that consumers would add advertisers as "IM buddies" so that consumers could access information, receive updates, and make purchases of the advertiser's product. Novak's idea was that consumers would not want to see advertisements on their IM but would want use IM to chat with advertisers.

Before running out of capital, Nowak said that Imercive was "able to make some good progress" but could not "generate enough traction before running out of capital." Nowak concluded that Imercive failed because it "got caught mid-pivot"—in other words it ran out of money before its second product became successful.

Imercive's first product—which it piloted with 20 Boston area restaurants—was an IM service that let customers order food from restaurants. The pilot program failed— taking longer and costing more than expected—after a year. In 2006, Nowak said he "began thinking bigger about my vision and the technology." To that end, Imercive "pivoted," offering a new product that would "provide IM apps to any brand looking to create further engagement with their consumers." Imercive was unable to raise new capital and ran out of money before it could build the new product.

Case Analysis

Nowak blamed Imercive's failure on eight causes:

- It did not build quick prototypes of the product and get customer feedback.

- It spent too much money and time on its restaurant product before admitting it was a failure.

- It used a contract programmer to build the product who took too long to complete his work.

- It did not talk to restaurants about what they needed before building the product.

- It lacked sufficient capital to cover operating losses during the long process of selling to large companies.

- It took too long to realize that the lack of competition did not mean that Imercive was targeting a large untapped market opportunity—it meant there was insufficient demand for its product.

- It waited too long before trying to build relationships with new investors to raise new capital.

- Its new strategy depended on obtaining revenues from marketing agencies that were cutting their budgets due to the financial crisis.

Imercive's collapse highlights a critical source of start-up failure—a CEO who does not listen to customers before building a new product. Imercive might have survived had it spent a few hours on a presentation with images of the app screens, shown them to potential customers, and asked for feedback.

If Nowak had been willing to accept such rapid feedback, Imercive might have realized that its first idea was not going to result in significant revenues. He might also have used this approach to test his second idea, and perhaps others, before running out of capital or possibly finding some success.

Principle Four   Small companies seeking growth from acquiring new products should only invest in products that uniquely relieve "customers' pain points" when combined with the acquirer's capabilities at a price that does not capitalize future gains.

It is amazing that anyone would buy anything from a start-up company.

After all, most start-ups fail. I estimate that only one in five million unfunded start-ups end up being worth over a $1 billion.

Yet if a start-up is able to offer a product that satisfies customers' unmet needs in such a way that customers are willing to pay more than the cost to produce the product, it may end up winning many customers.

But eventually, growth from a company's original products decelerates. And that leaves the company with two options for adding new products to boost its growth rate: building the product or acquiring it.

Given their limited resources, it is surprising that start-ups can afford to acquire other start-ups. However, such acquisition opportunities do arise when another start-up has run out of cash—and can't raise more capital—before it has launched its product.

When such acquisitions do occur, the amount of cash paid to acquire the company is generally very small while most of the consideration is in the form of equity or possibly revenue or profit sharing.

Target companies in these dire straits are generally willing to consider such terms, particularly if the acquiring company has a growing customer base, ample capital, and a bright future.

In that case, they would be happy to receive some cash and perhaps stock in the acquiring company, particularly if that acquirer's stock was highly valued and rising. But since small companies are usually privately held, the value of that stock may be difficult to assess.

Yet some small companies have acquired companies that added to their product portfolio. And of those few successful acquisitions, five success principles emerge:

- **High customer willingness to pay.** The combined companies will win a larger share of customers' budgets and they are willing to pay a price for those product that exceed their cost to the company.

- **Attractive market.** The acquired product will provide access to a market that is small but likely to get big fast with significant profit potential.

- **Better off together.** The acquiring company has skills that when combined with the target will yield a significant share of that market.

- **NPV > 0.** The acquiring company does not overpay for the target.

- **Excellent integration.** Such integration consists of three components:

- **Cultural fit of key people**. The acquiring company has a well-defined culture and invests time before discussing financial terms to assess whether the target's key people will fit within that culture.

- **Seamless-to-customer merging of products and capabilities.** Having passed that test, the acquirer and target must agree on how they will combine their products and capabilities to gain market share.

- **Link equity to accomplishment.** Finally, in order to retain key people, the acquirer should give out equity over time linked to accomplishments such as a new product launch.

- **Building acquisition capability.** The acquirer must view each acquisition as a learning opportunity—looking at successful mergers as sources of best practices and failed ones as opportunities to learn how to avoid similar mistakes in future deals.

Successful: Microsoft Acquires Seattle Computing for $75,000

Introduction

One of the single best acquisitions in history took place in 1981. A then-small company, Microsoft, was in discussions with IBM—which was seeking an operating system (OS) for its personal computer.

How so? In 1980, when IBM decided to enter the PC business, it was in a hurry. So instead of building a closed system for which IBM would supply all the hardware, software, and peripherals, IBM forged an open one to encourage other companies to develop OS software, microprocessors, displays, printers, and other parts.

Case Scenario

In 1980, IBM approached Gary Killdall's Pacific Grove California-based Digital Research, which had developed an OS called CP/M at the suggestion of Microsoft CEO Bill Gates. But when IBM came calling, Killdall chose not to come to the door— instead asking his wife to handle IBM. She refused to sign the nondisclosure agreement from Big Blue.

So IBM came back to Bill Gates, asking him if he could provide the operating system IBM was seeking.

Microsoft did not have one, so Gates—with a net worth of $78.3 billion by August 2016—decided to buy a company that did. On July 27, 1981, Microsoft paid $75,000 to acquire a 16-bit OS—QDOS (AKA 86-DOS)—from Seattle Computer Products. Soon after, the duo hired its programmer Tim Paterson and spent $50,000 for all rights to 86-DOS, which became Windows. This was the foundation on which Gates's fortune rested.

Had Gates merely acquired this technology and licensed it to IBM, he would not have achieved his phenomenal success.

What made the difference were the terms on which he structured the license.

Gates started with two basic insights. He understood that IBM—based on decades of dominance of business computing technology waves from desk calculators to mainframes to data storage—believed that its entry into the PC market would confer on it instant legitimacy. Moreover, IBM believed that its heritage of marketing excellence would let it prevail over any PC rivals.

IBM met with Microsoft, which in 1980 had developed BASIC programming software for small hobbyist computers such as the Altair. Unfortunately, Gates had no OS available for IBM, but was quick to perceive the huge opportunity with IBM.

So he acquired QDOS—neglecting to mention the IBM licensing deal to Seattle Computer Products. Gates sold IBM the rights to the OS for use on IBM PCs for a pittance. He just asked for one thing: unfettered rights to license the OS to potential clones of the IBM PC. IBM, assuming that no PC-clone market would emerge quickly, was happy to grant Gates's wish. IBM had convinced itself that Gates was naïve about the emergence of PC clones. If Gates was right, IBM reasoned, then IBM was no longer the marketing powerhouse it believed itself to be.

IBM was initially correct about its decision. Between 1981 when it introduced its first PC and 1983, IBM's market share climbed to 42%. But by setting the standard in this rapidly growing market, IBM attracted competitors like Compaq—whose low-priced portable clones enabled it in 1982 to reach $100 million in sales during its first year, making it the fastest growing company in U.S. history. Dell entered the market in 1984 and Hewlett Packard shifted from a proprietary architecture to IBM's standard. By 1985, IBM's share had fallen to 37% and four years later IBM controlled a mere 16.9% of the PC market. Finally in 2005 IBM sold its money-losing PC business to Lenovo Group Ltd.

Microsoft's acquisition of Seattle Computing, coupled with Gates's clever licensing deal with IBM led to the success of Windows. While the success on which Gates's fortune is based came from many other decisions and products, it is difficult to imagine that history will ever witness a better-spent $75,000 for an acquisition.

Case Analysis

More broadly, the success of this acquisition reveals the power of four of the principles outlined above.

- **High customer willingness to pay.** IBM was willing to pay a small amount for the OS—but Microsoft was able to extract higher prices from IBM clone makers.

- **Attractive market.** Gates realized that IBM would legitimize the PC market, thus expanding its size very quickly.

- **Better off together.** Seattle Computing clearly lacked Gates's insights into how best to negotiate with IBM. This resulted in Microsoft's successful licensing deal with IBM and assured that Microsoft received the lion's share of the benefit.

- **NPV > 0.** Microsoft's very low purchase price and the speed at which the deal closed—along with Gates's good fortune that Digital Research refused to deal with IBM—contributed to the high NPV of this acquisition.

Successful: Localytics Acquires Splitforce

Introduction

A second success case for small company acquisitions reveals deeper insights into how an effective acquirer integrates a small start-up.

In April 2015, I spoke with Raj Aggarwal, CEO of Boston-based app marketer, Localytics. Aggarwal was a Bain consultant before he started Localytics—which raised $35 million in March 2015 and its clients included ESPN, eBay, Hulu, and Rue La La.

Case Scenario

In March 2015, Localytics acquired six-employee Splitforce—which was billed as "an automated A/B testing and predictive analytics tool for mobile." Aggarwal did not disclose the terms of the deal. But he gave Splitforce's key people Localytics stock.

Here are five principles he follows to grow by acquiring new products.

1. Get to know the people well.

In most cases, the value of a start-up rests with its people. If the target does not even have revenues—but has a product with a fast-growing user base—then the key to making that acquisition pay off will be getting to know its key people.

Aggarwal explained how he got to know Splitforce's key people. "We worked together as partners since we had common customers. We were amazed that they shared our vision of using data for predictive purposes."

2. Make sure the acquirer and target share the same values.

The acquirer of a small start-up must be confident that those potential employees share the acquirer's values.

Aggarwal believed that it was important to get to know people in a less formal setting. "It is helpful if you can go out to dinner and have some drinks to get to know people better. We like to make fun of each other and if they were easily offended by our joking, we probably would have concluded that it would not have worked," he said.

The acquirer and target must also agree on what it takes to be successful in the market. Both companies shared a view of applying data science to solve business problems. Said Aggarwal, "We both agreed that data science is not just something in your head—it has to be useful to solve real world issues."

3. Know why the combined companies will be better off.

An acquirer and target must see how their products fit together on behalf of current and potential customers. And they must each have different strengths that when combined lead to greater market share.

Localytics was good at app marketing but it needed the ability to figure out which marketing techniques would work best for its customers. As Aggarwal explained, "20% of app customers never come back. By combining Splitforce's predictive intelligence horsepower with Localytics' suite of mobile app marketing and analytics tools we will be better able to spot when someone's about to quit using the app or identify new ways to reach them".

And Localytics also brought another skill—the ability to get and keep customers. "Splitforce's development people combined with our sales, marketing, and customer success organizations would help them to realize their vision for the future and boost the value of the combined company," said Aggarwal.

4. Set clear milestones for success and distribute equity based on their achievement.

As an acquirer and target are approaching agreement, it becomes crucial to define easily understood milestones for success on which to base equity distributions to the target's key employees.

As Aggarwal said, "We did not want to overcomplicate it. We had a timeline for when the beta version of the product would be ready to go and when we could ship the combined product. If we don't meet the goals, we will have to decide what to do next."

Equity for key people should be tied to achieving corporate goals. Aggarwal pointed out that in the deal with Splitforce, the vesting schedule for stock was tied to achieving the milestones.

5. Build up your acquisition capability.

Finally, many companies with strong marketing and sales skills find it faster sometimes to acquire companies with needed technical skills instead of doing all the development in-house.

So they need to improve their ability to make acquisitions that pay off. "We want to do lots of small acquisitions so we can strengthen our acquisition capability," concluded Aggarwal.

Case Analysis

Absent a detailed small company acquisition failure case in this chapter, it is worth considering that the opposite of Aggarwal's success principles could be thought of as primary sources of failure in small company acquisitions:

- **Neglect to understand target's key people.** When start-ups acquire other start-ups, there is a big risk of infecting the combined company with one or two people who do not fit. In that case, the rest of the company will be distracted from working on key priorities. This could hamper productivity or cause worse outcomes;

- **Fail to create a strong culture and to acquire companies with shared values.** Many start-up CEOs believe that culture and people are less important than building the product. Failure to create a strong culture with clearly defined values can contribute to acquiring key people who do not fit, creating similarly bad outcomes;

- **Ignore how the combined companies' products and capabilities will yield market share gain.** A merger should be made with the customer in mind. If an acquirer does not have a clear vision of how the combined companies will be able to take a larger share of a customer's budget because it offers the customer more value—in product variety and key capabilities—it is likely to be money poorly spent;

- **Give out equity to key people when the deal closes.** If an acquirer gives out equity to key target company employees up front, there is a risk that those people will lose their motivation and either stop working or leave; and

- **Don't learn from previous acquisition success and failure.** Failure to learn from previous acquisition successes and failures could boost the odds that future acquisitions would either repeat previous mistakes or fail to capture the benefits of learning from previous successes.

Applying the Principles of Growth through New Products

Leaders seeking to assess whether they apply these principles to their organizations should be able to answer Yes to these six questions:

- Do at least half of your company's revenues come from products introduced in the last five years?

- Do you spend at least 20 percent of your time listening to customers and analyzing the strategies of fast-growing rivals to envision new products?

- When you consider new products, do you determine whether the market opportunity they will target is large enough to justify the investment?

- In building products, does your company use customer feedback on quickly developed prototypes to improve on new products before you launch them?

- If your company grows by acquiring companies that make new products, does it apply the four tests of a successful acquisition?

- Has your company improved the way it builds or acquires new products based on analyzing its prior successes and failures?

Chapter 8: Growth Road Maps provides a detailed methodology for applying the principles of growth through new products.

Summary

Speeding up growth by building or acquiring new products is a particularly challenging way to accelerate a company's top line. Developing new products creates a tension within the organization with those who support the old ones. And acquiring a company can be quite risky unless the acquired company is managed properly. However, growth leaders overcome these challenges. Companies that create successful new products start with deep insights into unmet customer needs, and they deliver products that better satisfy those needs than do rival products. And companies that grow through acquisition target superior capabilities at large and growing markets.

In the next chapter we take a deeper look at how companies achieve growth through capabilities—exploring how the most successful companies are able to match their capabilities with new growth opportunities and adapt those strengths to exceed the requirements needed to capture them.

Growth from Current or New Capabilities

In the last three chapters we explored growth opportunities that come from looking outside a company and trying to boost sales by matching what is inside the company with outside opportunities.

In Chapter 2, we looked at how to grow by selling more to current or new customers; in Chapter 3 we examined how to boost sales by expanding geographically; and in Chapter 4 we examined how companies can build or acquire new products that will add to a company's revenue.

However, in Chapters 5 and 6, we look at how things inside a company can be aimed at new market opportunities to yield revenue growth—examining how a company's capabilities can be applied to new market opportunities to gain share. And in Chapter 6 we will examine how a company's culture can be used to accelerate its growth.

© Peter S. Cohan 2017
P. S. Cohan, *Disciplined Growth Strategies*, DOI 10.1007/978-1-4842-2448-9_5

What Are Capabilities?

It is easier to start with what capabilities are not. I have found that many technology executives think that capabilities are the features of a specific product—such as a smartphone's screen size or battery life. I would call these product features—which are most useful if those features produce benefits that boost customers' willingness to buy. Capabilities are repeatable business processes—such as new product development, purchasing, human resource management, manufacturing, shipping, marketing and sales, and customer service—which a company performs to win and keep customers.

Such capabilities vary by industry. But as we will see later in this chapter, the right capabilities are the ones that a company can coordinate to provide customers with competitively superior value. More specifically, a company might sell customers a better product for which they are willing to pay a price premium by exercising superior capabilities—such as new product development, manufacturing, marketing, and customer service. Or companies might grow faster than the industry by selling a product of adequate quality at a much lower-than-industry-average price.

Small companies evolve their capabilities very quickly as they grow. Initially, the cofounders might split up tasks such as sales, hiring, finance, and product development. Once a company reaches, say, 50 to 75 employees, its capabilities might be the primary responsibilities of executives hired specifically to run them. Simply put, rather than the CEO doing the selling, hiring, and product development—those capabilities would be the full-time job of specific vice presidents for each of those functions.

As long as a company's evolving capabilities deliver competitively superior value to customers, the company is likely to keep growing. However, if the CEO does not monitor the changing external environment, such a winning collection of capabilities might evolve into a competitive strait jacket that impedes a company's ability to adapt to changing customer needs, upstart competitors, or new technologies. Simply put, success can give undue corporate power to the people in charge of a company's key capabilities. And those executives may put their own parochial interests ahead of what makes sense for the company and its customers. Such an internal focus is likely to create an opening for rivals who are more focused on how to boost market share by offering customers a better value proposition than these now-self-defeating incumbents. On the other hand some companies have built up capabilities that—with minor modifications—can enable them to generate meaningful new growth in a sequence of large markets.

Principles of Growth from Capabilities

To achieve growth—whether for large or small companies using current or new capabilities—companies ought to give customers a product that delivers more value to customers than competitors by using their capabilities to satisfy the unmet needs of customers in the market from which they hope to take share. Leaders ought to start by listening closely to the people to whom they want to sell their product to identify and rank potential customers' unsatisfied needs; inventory their current capabilities and evaluate which ones they can use to design, deliver, and service new products that potential customers will be eager to buy; and decide whether to hire, partner, or acquire to close key capability gaps.

Large companies seeking growth from current capabilities apply this principle from the inside out; whereas large companies seeking growth from new ones do so from the outside in. More specifically, big companies look for new markets where their strongest capabilities will enable them to win—as Apple did when it went from its iPod success to introducing the iPhone. We contrast this success case by the exploration of how GM's 2009 bankruptcy might have been fended off if the capabilities of its Saturn subsidiary had spread throughout the company—rather than being homogenized just a few years after it took the lead from Toyota and Nissan in the small car segment a few years after it launched. As we will explore in the case of News Corp's purchase of Myspace, a large company can also destroy the value of a promising start-up it acquires unless the large company's capabilities help that start-up to grow.

The danger with the inside-out approach is that the company does not perceive changes in its competitive environment and thus preserves capabilities of increasingly limited competitive value. Companies that follow the outside-in approach enjoy the advantage of listening to customers with a more open mind since they are willing to change their capabilities to satisfy the unmet needs they discover. The risk of the outside-in approach, however, is that the cost of creating new capabilities is so high that the return—in the form of profitable growth—must be much higher to justify the investment. Ultimately, the two meet in the middle—the inside-out companies modify their current capabilities and the outside-in ones reuse many of their current ones—so that the resulting bundle of capabilities generates rapid growth.

For small companies, the same principles apply. However, in most cases small companies face a more binary set of outcomes. Rather than muddling along if their capabilities are not the best in their industry, small companies are more likely to perish if they can't assemble the capabilities needed to satisfy unmet customer needs. In this chapter, we review the case of SailPoint, an information security company that enjoys rapid growth by crafting its capabilities—such as product development; human resource management, and customer service—to deliver a service that customers perceive as far superior to that of rivals such as IBM. And in exploring a failure case—HealthSpot, a maker of kiosks for virtual meetings between doctors and patients—we see how a small company can easily run out of capital because its capabilities are so weak that an insufficient number of customers are willing to pay for its product.

Let's examine growth from current capabilities by examining pairs of case studies of successful and unsuccessful applications of four principles:

- **Large companies seeking growth from *current* capabilities** should identify and attack large untapped markets where their unique capabilities will enable them to gain significant market share.

- **Large companies seeking growth from *new* capabilities** should build or acquire the capabilities needed to gain a significant share of new markets created by changing technology and evolving customer needs.

- **Small companies seeking growth from *current* capabilities** should identify and attack untapped markets where their unique capabilities will enable them to gain significant market share.

- **Small companies seeking growth from *new* capabilities** should envision new market opportunities and build, partner, or acquire the skills need to gain share.

Principle One Large companies seeking growth from current capabilities should identify and attack large untapped markets where their unique capabilities will enable them to gain significant market share.

If a large company can assemble the right capabilities and use them to attack large markets, they can grow substantially. However, CEOs must gather data from customers and about competitors to gain sufficient assurance that their companies' capabilities will yield market share gains.

Success in applying current capabilities to new markets hinges on four principles:

- **Identify unmet customer needs.** A CEO must listen to customers with an ear toward whether they are satisfied with current products or whether they might be unhappy with current offerings. If unhappy, the CEO must identify specific unmet needs and try to assess whether the company can satisfy those needs profitably.

- **Analyze capabilities needed to satisfy those unmet needs.** To answer that question, the first step is to figure out what capabilities a company would need in order to satisfy those unmet customer needs. For example, if a customer was looking for a device that would enable her to access mail wirelessly and watch videos, a company might need to develop partnerships with wireless service providers and video producers—in addition to managing hardware designers, manufacturing, procurement, and shipping capabilities.

- **Assess the company's ability to outperform rivals in these key capabilities.** If a company can't perform the key capabilities better than rivals then it may not be able to take customers from them. And if it can't win customers, it will fall short of its growth goals. Therefore, a CEO should hire an objective outsider to assess how well the company performs those key capabilities relative to competitors—based on customer and industry research.

- **If the company has the right capabilities—or can assemble them—it should develop a strategy for the new market.** Based on the foregoing analysis, a CEO ought to conclude whether the company has or can assemble—through partnerships, key hires, or acquisition—the capabilities needed to succeed in satisfying customers' unmet needs. If the evidence suggests the answer is yes, the CEO should develop a strategy—including choices of target customers, product features, pricing, key capabilities, and investment—to apply its capabilities to the new opportunity.

Case Studies

Successful: Apple Captures $150 Billion in Smartphone Profit

Introduction

In 2007, Apple tapped its then-current capabilities of hardware design, ecosystem building, supply chain, and marketing to introduce a new kind of cell phone—the iPhone. The result was a product that had sold a billion copies between 2007 and August 2016, generated $155 billion in operating profit for Apple in 2015 alone—which represented 92% of the industry's 2015 profits—and accounted for 66% of Apple's 2015 revenue.

Indeed the iPhone has accounted for an extraordinary amount of profit during its life. According to Strategy Analytics, a research firm, "from 2007 through Q2 2016, the iPhone generated operating profit of [nearly] $214 billion with an operating profit margin of 34.5%."

Case Scenario

How did Apple achieve these exceptional results? In a nutshell, it is better than its 1,000 smartphone rivals in critical capabilities. More specifically, Apple outcompetes its rivals in four critical areas:

- **Product design.** *Apple decided to sell the iPhone to people who were using cell phones—already a huge market. But the superior design of its hardware—and its much broader set of product features—encouraged many people to swap their cell phones for iPhones.*

- **Marketing.** *Apple's advertising campaigns, its carefully crafted launch presentations by former CEO Steve Jobs, and its network of Apple Stores—stocked with so-called genius bars that gave consumers technical help all contributed to a significant consumer fever to own iPhones. Indeed Apple's marketing contributed to its ability to charge a higher price than do its rivals—in 2014, Apple's iPhone sold for a global average of $624, compared with $185 for smartphones running Android.*

- **Third-party partnerships.** *Apple needed to make sure that the iPhone could make consumers' lives better. To that end, it created opportunities for independent application developers to sell their wares to consumers on its App Store—in its first 18 months, consumers download four billion Apps that were either free or priced at 99 cents apiece of which Apple kept 30%. In addition, the iPhone relied on Apple's previous success creating iTunes—the first legal online music store for which consumers paid 99 cents per song. And Apple partnered with wireless service providers to provide iPhone customers with voice and data services.*

- **Supply chain.** *While the first three capabilities were essential to create demand for the iPhone, Apple would not have generated so much profit were it not able to supply millions of iPhones to satisfy that demand. Moreover, Apple shareholders would only benefit from its ability to match demand and supply if customers were willing to pay a much higher price for an iPhone than its cost to Apple. Due to Apple's contracts with*

> suppliers such as Foxconn, Apple was able to manufacture
> iPhones and deliver them to Apple stores at a unit cost that
> was well below its price.

In developing the iPhone, Apple was targeting capabilities that it had developed at different levels during its history. For example, its ability to design and market consumer-pleasing hardware had been around for decades.

Among these skills was the ability to entice potential customers for a new product through compelling demonstration delivered by Apple's late CEO, Steve Jobs.

His iPhone demo was extremely effective. Jobs kicked off its January 9, 2007, iPhone demonstration by saying, "This is a day I have been looking forward to for two and a half years." From there he told stories about why consumers disliked their cell phones and then showed listeners why the iPhone would replace their cell phone hate with iPhone love. To that end, Jobs showed them how the iPhone could play music and watch a movie clip, how it could make a phone call, operate an address book and voicemail, send a text or email, look at photos, browse news sites, and use Google Maps to find a nearby Starbucks.

But when it came to designing the iPhone hardware, building a supply chain and partnering with third parties, Apple had to extend its capabilities to meet the requirements of making the iPhone a success.

For example, Apple had never needed to build a device that contained a small antenna to connect it to a wireless network nor had it ever created a touch screen that could implement gestures like the one required to expand the size of a photo or select letter from an onscreen keyboard.

Apple—which spent about $150 million building the iPhone—was on a mix of solid and shaky engineering ground in the years leading up to its launch. Apple's hardware engineers had spent about a year working on touchscreen technology for a tablet PC and thought they could build a similar interface for a phone. Moreover, a new semiconductor, the ARM11 chip, made cell phones sufficiently fast and efficient to power the combined functionality of a phone, a computer, and an iPod.

However, Apple's engineers had some huge technical challenges to overcome. They had no prior experience in antenna design (a small but powerful one was needed), radio-frequency radiation (the iPhone needed to be safe when close to customers' brains), network simulations (the pathway for voice and data needed to be solid), and in building a glass screen that would not scratch and be touch sensitive.

After intense struggles within Apple, the company managed to build hardware that excited consumers. Engineers expected to be building a small version of the Macintosh but ended up building three different early versions of the iPhone in 2005 and 2006. Ultimately Apple made six "fully working prototypes of the device it ultimately sold—each with its own set of hardware, software and design tweaks," according to the New York Times.

Apple's partnership with AT&T was a tour-de-force by Jobs who tipped the bargaining power in favor of handset suppliers and away from wireless service providers.

Following 18 months of secret meetings, Jobs negotiated a five-year deal with AT&T's wireless division that would give it exclusive rights to service the iPhone in exchange for about 10% of iPhone sales in AT&T stores and a small share of Apple iTunes revenue. The deal granted Apple about $10 a month from every iPhone customer's bill; granted Apple design, manufacturing, and marketing control over the iPhone; and obliged AT&T to invest millions in a new service—visual voicemail along with streamlining its in-store sign-up process.

Within six months of its June 2007 launch, Apple's deal with AT&T had clearly made both parties better off. While AT&T attracted many new customers—40% of iPhone buyers had never used AT&T before, Apple sold an estimated three million iPhones at $399—generating $80 in profit per unit and another $240 from its share of customers' two-year iPhone contracts with AT&T.

And the supply chain that Apple built to satisfy iPhone demand helped to lock in those enormous profits. For example, by April 2016, Apple enjoyed a 60% gross margin on its iPhone SE. Customers paid $399 for the device that cost Apple $160 to manufacture. Apple was able to satisfy demand for the iPhone so profitably in part because of its global supply chain, which sourced parts from different countries, manufactured and assembled them in others, and operated warehouses to meet local demand for reliable and quick order fulfillment. Its 200 suppliers included displays made in Japan by Japan Display and Sharp, Touch ID sensors made in Taiwan by Taiwan Semiconductor Manufacturing Company and Xintec, transmitter and amplification modules from Skyworks and Qorvo in the United States, and screen glass from Corning and GT Advanced Technologies.

Five years after taking over as CEO, Tim Cook had not demonstrated the ability to apply Apple's capabilities to a new product category as it did for the MP3 player with the iPod or the tablet with the iPad.

As a result, despite introducing a highly touted new product—the Apple Watch—the company suffered two quarters of consecutive revenue and profit decline. By December 2016, it remained to be seen whether Apple would be able to continue to do what led to the iPhone's tremendous growth—apply current capabilities to a large existing market by building a superior product.

Case Analysis

The iPhone case highlights five key success factors in applying this principle:

- **Target the right market.** One of the most obvious realities for a large company is that meaningful growth can only come from targeting new markets that are big enough to make a difference in the company's revenue growth rate. For example, assuming that a new entrant may eventually be able to gain 10% of a market, a company with $100 billion in revenue would need to target a market of at least $200 billion in total sales in order to achieve 20% revenue growth from that market. There are very few markets that large—and the number of those markets that are relevant to a large company is limited by the company's capabilities. The cellphone market turned out to be big enough to make a difference to Apple's growth rate for years.

- **Identify significant customer pain**. If a large company can find a large enough market, there can only be an opportunity to win a meaningful share of that market if customers are not satisfied with the product offerings of incumbent competitors. As we saw in this case, Apple clearly understood that there were many ways in which cell phone customers were dissatisfied with the available products. In the absence of such customer pain, it may be difficult for a new entrant to use its skills to gain sufficient market share to warrant the investment.

- **Assess whether the company's current capabilities can yield rapid market share gain.** Every industry has customers with unique needs and the companies that satisfy the customer demand do so through the exercise of unique capabilities. For example, if customers demand the lowest prices and the fastest delivery for a product, companies seeking to gain market share will need strong capabilities in purchasing raw materials at very low prices, manufacturing products at the lowest cost in the industry, and operating warehouse and delivery networks that fulfill customer orders more efficiently than rivals. When Apple targeted the cell phone market, it realized that customers wanted to replace their cell phones and iPods with a single device that would make their lives more efficient. Apple also realized that the capabilities it had developed to succeed in the MP3 player market with the iPod would help Apple succeed with the iPhone.

- **If so, adapt current capabilities to requirements of the new market.** In order to be a source of growth, a CEO must adapt a company's capabilities so they can yield enough value in the eyes of customers to persuade them to buy the company's new products. To that end, the CEO will need to rethink all of the company's capabilities—and adapt each of them to the requirements for winning in the new market. Apple was able to use many of its capabilities—such as advertising, retailing, and product supply—with little alteration between the iPod and the iPhone. Yet when it came to hardware design and partnerships, Apple needed to enhance its capabilities. To that end, Apple enhanced its antenna and touch screen engineering skills and built new partnerships with wireless service providers. Unless a company adapts its capabilities to the competitive requirements of new markets, the capabilities will no longer contribute to growth—and may even impede the company's ability to capture new markets.

- **Look for new opportunities to achieve growth from the firm's capabilities.** Thanks to the ever-evolving nature of markets, companies must pay attention to new technologies, upstart competitors, and changing customer needs. The best CEOs work simultaneously at adapting the firm's capabilities to the company's core markets, the next new growth opportunity, and the ones thereafter. In the years between his 1997 return to Apple until his tragic death, Steve Jobs was able to continue to invest in growth opportunities and think about where Apple would look for more growth once those opportunities had matured. In the absence of such leadership, a firm's capabilities can atrophy and become an end in themselves. Such atrophy can ultimately lead a formerly successful company to slow down and ultimately give up its leadership position.

Unsuccessful: After 101 Years, GM Files for Bankruptcy

Introduction

In 2009, General Motors—which at its peak in the 1950s controlled over half of the automobile market—filed for bankruptcy. While the reasons for its bankruptcy filing were many—one factor that seems particularly significant was its failure to adapt to competition from Toyota and Nissan in the market for small, fuel efficient vehicles.

What is most noteworthy about this failure is that a former GM CEO had forged a path to success in this rivalry. In the 1980s, then-CEO Roger Smith tried to refresh the way GM designed, manufactured, and sold cars so it could compete with these overseas rivals. His efforts worked very well—creating a new line of cars that outperformed in customer satisfaction and quality a mere four years after launch.

Sadly for GM, Smith's successor killed the effort to rejuvenate GM based on the success it achieved with Saturn.

This failure to adapt its capabilities to tap new markets left GM vulnerable—making it harder to avoid bankruptcy.

Case Scenario

Why GM failed

General Motors was founded in September 1908. On June 1, 2009, at 8 a.m.—almost 101 years later—it ceased to exist, and control was handed over to turn-around executive Al Koch. Thanks to $19.4 billion in loans and $30.1 billion more in debtor-in-possession financing, a huge amount of effort by the U.S. government and GM's management, unions, dealers, suppliers and bondholders, the effects of that failure was terrible, but not catastrophic.

The United States took on 60% of the new GM, which included Chevy, Buick, GMC, and Cadillac. Canada took 12% after lending GM $9.5 billion, the United Auto Workers (UAW) received 17.5% (as payment for $9.4 billion of its $20 billion in health care obligations) with warrants to buy 2.5% more, the bondholders received 10% to as high as 25% through warrants, and old GM common shareholders received approximately nothing. Twelve to 20 more GM factories were slated to close, 21,000 union workers would be fired, and 2,400 GM dealers would shut down.

Three factors contributed to GM's bankruptcy:

- **Bad financial policies.** GM had posted a negative net worth for nearly three years before it went bankrupt. Moreover, thanks to two CEOs—Rick Wagoner and Fritz Henderson—who had risen up from its finance department, GM turned vehicles into a loss leader for car loans The 2008 financial crisis exposed the truth that GM had made too many bad loans.

- **Failure to adapt to competition.** GM had been ignoring competition—with a brief interruption (Saturn in the 1980s)—for about 50 years. At its peak, in 1954, GM controlled 54% of the North American vehicle market. By 2008, that figure had tumbled to 19%. Toyota and its peers took over that market share. Compared to its toughest competitors—GM's cars were poorly designed and built; took too long to manufacture at costs that were too high; and as a result, fewer people bought them, leaving GM with excess production capacity.

- **Managing in the bubble.** GM managers got promoted by toeing the CEO's line and ignoring external changes. What looked stupid from the perspective of customer and competitors

> was smart for those bucking for promotions. At the core of this
> managing in the bubble was confirmation bias—the tendency
> of managers to filter out information that does not match up
> with their preconceived notions. Confirmation bias kept GM from
> viewing the threat from Toyota as significant, contributed to its
> decision to pull its electric car off the market, and led it to ignore
> the impact of higher gas prices and a collapse in credit markets
> on consumers' willingness to buy profitable gas guzzlers like the
> Hummer or tricked-out Escalades and SUVs.

The reason it was so difficult for GM managers to break out of this bubble was that
it was created in response to a competitive threat from Ford in the 1920s. And that
response proved effective for another four decades.

After all, Ford dominated the market then. In the early 1920s, its Model T— offered
only in black— controlled 60% of the U.S. automobile market and half of the industry worldwide.

Between 1908 and 1920, GM's founder Bill Durant acquired 39 companies including Cadillac, Pontiac, Oldsmobile, Chevrolet, and several parts-makers— but ran
them as separate units. In 1923, GM nearly went bankrupt and it took on a new
CEO—Alfred Sloan, a ball-bearing entrepreneur who imposed tight financial controls.
Under Sloan GM expanded internationally—establishing factories in 15 countries
and buying Vauxhall in Britain and Opel in Germany.

Most important, Sloan and other executives developed a strategy to wrest control of
the industry from Ford based on the idea that as workers ascended the corporate
ladder, they could purchase ever more prestigious vehicles to celebrate their progress. GM would build cars that American consumers wanted—offering them different
makes and models at different prices. Moreover, GM created an organizational structure and culture to support the strategy—yielding substantial market share gains.
By the mid-1930s, GM controlled 42% of the market while Ford's share fell to 21%.

By the early 1960s, with its market share at over 50%, its bosses were more wor-
ried about avoiding antitrust action and a possible breakup than cost reduction
or improving GM's slow decision-making process. In the 1970s, GM responded to
government standards requiring automakers to boost fuel efficiency by making
dull-looking, unreliable vehicles that were less compelling to American consumers—
customers reported that American vehicles had 20% to 40% more defects than
equivalent Japanese models.

Saturn

GM went back to the principles that Sloan had put in place in the 1920s to take
back market share from Japanese rivals. In January 1985, GM's CEO Roger Smith
announced plans to create Saturn—a new division located in Spring Hill, Tennessee,
specifically to take market back market share from Toyota and Nissan in the lower-
priced, fuel efficient segment of the automobile market that accounted for about

25% of the market. By 1993, Saturn—financed with $3.5 billion from GM—had grown rapidly and led its Japanese rivals in dealer and customer satisfaction, quality, and reliability according to customer surveys.

Saturn achieved this success by conducting critical capabilities—product development, marketing, selling, service, and human resources—more effectively than the rest of GM. And in so doing, GM sought to create loyal customers boost long-term dealer profitability, ease the customer buying process, produce better quality cars, and boost employee engagement.

More specifically, Saturn's success offered GM compelling examples of ways that it could increase its market share by performing eight critical capabilities in new ways:

- **Product development.** Rather than engineers working in isolation from buyers, Saturn designed new products by working with customers and cross-functional teams—including engineering, purchasing, manufacturing, marketing, sales, and finance—and driving competitors' vehicles to design and build competitively superior products that were more fuel efficient—due to a lighter engine and frame—and easier to repair—as a result of using plastic as a bumper material.

- **Advertising.** Saturn produce memorable TV ads such as one featuring a customer in Alaska that needed service—rather than ask the customer to go to the dealer, the ad featured a helicopter flying technicians to her house.

- **Selling.** Saturn hired college-educated sales people who were not paid on commission. The salespeople asked customers about their transportation needs, provided information about no-haggle pricing set at 90% of rivals', and were motivated to build high levels of customer satisfaction—50% of Saturn customers referred others to the company.

- **Retailing.** Unlike other care companies, Saturn offered franchisees larger territories—340 retail sites with 2 sites per franchisee—contracting with managers who took a long-term view and had a track record of creating long-term customer satisfaction and a willingness to invest in Saturn's long-term success. Boost dealer territory size, and introduce no-haggle pricing to boost consumer satisfaction with the buying process.

- **Engaging workers in operational decisions.** Saturn's approach to human resources was to reduce the number of formal job classifications from about 200 to 2; provide workers with salaries, rather than hourly wages; tie 10% of pay to achieving profit targets—which was aided by access to detailed information about vehicle costs; decentralized teams; and extensive training.

By 1993, two-thirds of Saturn owners said that they would purchase a new vehicle; the company generated $3 billion in revenue and had earned a profit of $100 million. One of the goals of Saturn had been to transfer best practices—more specifically its more effective approach to product development, advertising, selling, retailing, and human resources—to the rest of GM.

However, Smith left the CEO's slot in 1990 and by 1991, his successor Jack Smith, was not committed to that goal. Indeed Smith insisted on stripping away Saturn's uniqueness, insisting on managing all its divisions centrally with a tight fist and demanding that Saturn management and its union align with GM's traditional ways of doing things.

If he had been, perhaps GM would have been revived as it was under Sloan—rather than being forced into a 2009 government bailout.

Case Analysis

GM's bankruptcy highlights three key failure principles that CEOs seeking growth from existing capabilities should avoid:

- **Appoint a CEO committed to preserving old ways of operating.** While Roger Smith used his tenure to innovate in many ways—including creating Saturn from a "clean sheet of paper," its success created jealousy throughout GM. Rather than trying to learn from Saturn's success, the other divisions sought to stamp it out and when Jack Smith became CEO, they had their champion who pushed Saturn to toe the traditional GM line.

- **Ignore the consumer.** Whereas Saturn enjoyed its initial success by listening to customers, learning from more successful rivals, and empowering workers, once Saturn was forced to give up control to GM's centralized control, it lost touch with the consumer. That lack of responsiveness doomed Saturn's future and its potential to improve GM's competitiveness.

- **Assume your competition is irrelevant.** Initially, Saturn's leaders wanted to understand the options that customers weighed when they were shopping for a new car. This ability to view car buying through the customers' eyes yielded insights for improvement in key capabilities including product design, advertising, selling, retailing, manufacturing, and human resources management. Once GM lost Roger Smith, understanding and learning from Saturn's competition became far less important than doing things the old GM way. And that way led to bankruptcy.

Principle Two   Large companies seeking growth from new capabilities should build or acquire the capabilities needed to gain a significant share of new markets created by changing technology and evolving customer needs.

As we saw in the Apple and GM cases, companies seeking to take advantage of growth opportunities often need to modify their current capabilities. However, in many cases capturing new opportunities requires a company to create entirely new capabilities and even siphon away resources from their existing capabilities to finance the new ones.

Few CEOs have the mentality required to accomplish this transformation. Indeed, since most public company CEOs are incented to exceed quarterly revenue and earnings targets, they tend to resist any strategic move—such as the one required to change the company's capabilities—that would put the company's stock price—and annual executive bonuses at risk. And this transformation is virtually guaranteed to interrupt a company's ability to beat expectations and raise guidance because it will cause the company to spend more money while cutting into revenue from the market opportunity that has contributed to its current success.

Sadly there is no easy way to solve this problem—and that is why large companies, hamstrung by their commitment to earnings per share targets—tend to underinvest in changing their capabilities to attack new market opportunities. A case in point is IBM which by the second quarter of 2016 had reported 17 consecutive quarters of declining revenue. This was due to the fact that its revenues from old products were declining far faster than its so-called strategic initiatives—such as those targeted at the cloud—could take up the slack. Indeed between 2011 and 2015, IBM suffered a $16 billion growth gap between the $13.8 billion revenues it added from "strategic imperatives" and the $29.7 billion it lost from a decline in its core revenues.

The CEOs who have pulled off the transition to building new capabilities that take advantage of new growth opportunities are either the company founders or have prior experience transforming other companies. CEOs who achieve growth from new capabilities follow four principles:

- **Stay alert to changing technologies, evolving customer needs, and upstart rivals.** A CEO must recognize that a company's current success is not guaranteed to persist—in fact success could impede the company's ability to adapt to new opportunities created by these changes. CEOs must have this mindset to sacrifice short-term financial success for faster longer-term growth.

- **Target growth opportunities.** Such longer-term growth will only occur for the company if it targets a market that is currently small but will grow large quickly. Such markets are difficult to quantify so CEOs who target these opportunities based on limited data.

- **Develop and defend product vision to capture market share.** Having identified an attractive market to target, the CEO must envision how to capture a significant share. To that end, CEOs must listen to customers to identify unmet needs, evaluate how well competing products satisfy those needs, envision a product that customers will be eager to purchase, and estimate the investment required to realize that vision along with the potential profit the company might earn from placing that bet.

- **Reinvent capabilities to realize the product vision.** Ultimately, such CEOs close the gap between their product vision and its realization. To do that, they evaluate objectively—a difficult emotional challenge—the new capabilities the company must add in order to achieve its growth goals. If the company lacks these capabilities, the CEO must decide whether to build them internally—by hiring experts or acquiring companies that excel in these capabilities—or outsourcing the capabilities. Reinventing the company's capabilities may also require phasing out the company's current capabilities to help finance the new ones.

Successful: Netflix Transitions from DVD-by-Mail to Online Streaming

Introduction

After success replacing video stores like Blockbuster Video with its DVD-by-Mail service, Netflix created an online streaming service built on a new set of capabilities—including content production and partnering with broadband service providers.

Case Scenario

Netflix got its start in the world by offering consumers an alternative to driving to a retail store to rent VCRs and DVDs. That alternative—dubbed DVD-by-Mail— enabled consumers to order DVDs online, take delivery of their DVDs at their mailboxes, and return the DVDs by mail—without the annoying late fees charged by the likes of Blockbuster Video. Netflix's DVD-by-Mail service became so popular that by March 2007, Netflix was the world's largest online movie rental subscription service with 6.3 million subscribers to a library of over 70,000 movie, television, and other filmed entertainment titles on DVD who paid monthly subscription fees starting at $4.99. Between 2002 and 2006, Netflix's revenues soared at a 59% annual rate to $997 million on which it earned $49 million in profit.

Netflix engineered its operations to win the battle for DVD-by-Mail market supremacy. Netflix was able to buy the DVDs in a retail store (copyright law allowed it to rent out those DVDs) and deliver them in a way that was more convenient for consumers than the immediate gratification they got from picking up DVDs at a video store.

In 2007, Apple launched its iPhone, which made Netflix CEO, Reed Hastings, realize that people would no longer be content to watch DVDs while sitting on the couch in front of their TVs. Instead, Hastings envisioned a world in which consumers would watch videos on their smartphones and other handheld devices.

Netflix struggled with how to survive the transition of customers who wanted to dump its DVD-by-Mail service and watch streaming videos instead. This struggle led to its highly controversial July 2011 pricing policy of raising prices as much as 60%. The new deal made customers pay $16 a month for one DVD out at a time plus Internet streaming—up from $10 a month for the combined package before the new rate went into effect for existing subscribers at the beginning of September 2011. Netflix stock plunged.

Unfortunately for shareholders, the capabilities required to win in the online streaming business were very different from the requirements for success in DVD-by-Mail. That's because Netflix was in a much weaker bargaining position with the owners of the digital videos—it had to engage in painful negotiations with studios and they had no incentive to cut Netflix a break—especially after watching Netflix's success with DVD-by-Mail. These higher costs showed up in Netflix's financial statements. For example, by the end of June 2011, Netflix's accounts payable had climbed 218% from $137 million at the end of 2010 to $435 million.

To its credit, Netflix did not give up with its online streaming efforts. Since studios declined to license online content on attractive terms, Netflix entered the studios' business of creating content—referred to as backward integration. In February 2013, Ted Sarandos, Netflix's chief content officer, told GQ, "the goal is to become HBO faster than HBO can become us."

And that strategy paid off. Netflix's first quarter 2013 results were much better than analysts expected. On April 22, 2013, its stock soared 24% in after-hours trading to $215.40—it announced that it had gained two million new U.S. customers in the first three months of 2013—reaching 29.2 million — which was 200,000 more than the average of seven estimates compiled by Bloomberg. At the core of Netflix's success was its creation of a new capability—content creation that yielded its own popular series including House of Cards and Orange Is the New Black.

Netflix built its content creation capability slowly over a decade. Initially, it licensed movies from two premium movie channels, Starz and Epix. However, Netflix had to wait a year after the movies had played in theaters before it could get access to them and that lasted for 12 to 18 months. So it began licensing TV programs like AMC's Mad Men and Breaking Bad for consumers who binge-watched the popular series. This was good for the networks since it generated revenues that partially offset their declining cable fees resulting from the rise of cord-cutters. And in 2012 networks began seeing the threat from Netflix, which decided to start creating its own content. Using data about what content its users liked—David Fincher directed drama and actor Kevin Spacey, Netflix decided to buy House of Cards. Fincher agreed to a $100 million deal for 26 episodes. The show became an instant hit when it launched in February 2013.

Netflix also added the ability to partner effectively with broadband services providers such as Comcast—which was critical to the company's growth since at peak hours, Netflix accounted for as much as 37% of total bandwidth consumption. In 2011 engineers set up Netflix's own 1,000- server content-delivery network. Using data on what shows users watch at what times and how long they watch the shows, Netflix can personalize its service—presenting users with content that is most likely to appeal to them.

Netflix achieved notable success with its streaming service while taking market share from cable service providers. Between its 2007 debut and July 2016, Netflix's streaming service enjoyed a six-fold revenue increase to $6.8 billion from 81 million subscribers who paid $8 to $12 per month. And Netflix's gain was cable's pain— during that time cable television lost 6.7 million subscribers. Moreover, in 2015, consumers spent 3% less time watching cable TV—and half of that drop was directly attributable to Netflix.

Case Analysis

While Netflix faces challenges ahead as it seeks to expand geographically, its success in achieving rapid growth through new capabilities reveals five principles that Netflix used as did Adobe Systems, a supplier of software as a service to creative professionals:

- **Solve the right problem.** The first step in reinventing a big company is for top management to focus on solving the right problem. For Netflix, the problem was that more of its customers were watching videos on handheld devices. And for Adobe, it was the high cost of finding new customers each time it introduced a new version of its software. As Mark Garrett, Adobe's chief financial officer, told the *Wall Street Journal*, "First is you can read the tea leaves, understand a problem you are trying to solve. Our problem was, if you go back to the 2008 recession, we only had 5% of recurring revenue in 2007. Following its change to a software-as-a-service strategy, Adobe seemed to be getting customers to renew more frequently. Explained Garrett, "Now we are well over 60%. That is a huge, positive change for us."

- **Rethink the entire business.** In order to solve the right problem, top management must follow the advice of my MIT professor, the late Michael Hammer, and start with a clean sheet of paper to rethink the entire business. Adobe did this when it changed to a subscription-based offering. As Garrett said, "Start with a clean slate. Rethink the whole business. What's the whole new strategy? What's the product line? It's not, 'Do I buy the car or lease the car?' That's just math. We had a completely [different] offering. That's the only way this works."

- **Transform operations.** A new strategy requires a change in operations. Netflix added new capabilities to implement its new strategy. And so did Adobe—building up its back office to give customers constant access to its service and changing how it measured those operations. As Garrett described the transformation, "A subscription-based business model needs to be up 24/7. It needs to be built up. It's different from shipping a shrink-wrapped CD. That requires a lot of back office work." In so doing, Adobe changed its systems, engineering, and key financial indicators. Noted Garrett, We needed to "rethink how [we ran] IT, how [we ran] engineering, [and] the metrics of the business from a traditional [profit and loss] business to whole new metrics to explain to Wall Street what the health of the business was."

- **Burn the boats.** As a company implements the new strategy, it must explain the change to its customers and employees. And if the employees do not agree with the change, they must go elsewhere. As Garrett argued, companies that change their capabilities must "burn the boats. At some point along the way, you have to say this is the right answer and a new strategy. You can't go back." Adobe educated its customers about the change, offered them the new service, and then began to withdraw the old product. To educate customers, Adobe recognized that they would resist the change. Argued Garrett," From a customer perspective, they are like anybody. They like doing things the way they've always been done. At first, you give them a choice of buying the old and new way.

A lot will fall back and not move to a subscription model. But you have got to get to the point where you say to the customer, we're not updating a perpetual product. It's a major milestone." With employees, Adobe was more direct in requiring them to get on board. "From an employee point of view, there will be some who resist change. They have to get onboard or leave, because frankly we are focused on this and this is the new direction," said Garrett.

- **Be transparent.** Finally, Wall Street will be willing to give a publicly traded company a chance to reinvent itself if the company discloses the transformation clearly and then exceeds new performance targets. Adobe did this—describing how the new strategy would hurt its income statement in the short run and boost it in the longer run. As Garrett said, "It was complicated for Wall Street to understand that you've got a perpetual model that's going to fall off. The faster the P&L goes down, the better you are as an investor because more people [were becoming] subscribers and over the long term" Adobe would be better off. Adobe gave Wall Street a new set of performance targets and exceeded them. "Give them some long-term benchmarks to see if you are doing what you said you were going to do. Knocking these things as you go builds up credibility," advised Garrett.

Unsuccessful: News Corp. Acquires Myspace

Introduction

In 2005, News Corp. paid $580 million to acquire Myspace—then a fast-growing social network that provided teenagers early access to music they loved. By June 2011, the romance was over—News Corp sold Myspace to Specific Media, a digital media group advised by Justin Timberlake for $35 million.

Case Scenario

News Corp. bought Myspace because it saw opportunity in digital advertising and it lacked the capabilities to take a significant share of that business. With Myspace's then rapid growth—which accelerated soon after the deal closed—it appeared that News Corp. had made a brilliant move.

However, Myspace was not the only social network competing for those online advertising revenues. Myspace peaked in December at 75.9 million monthly unique visitors in the United States, according to comScore. By May 2011, that number had dropped to 34.8 million—having lost about a million users per month in the prior 24 months. The decline in users led to a drop in advertising revenue from $470 million in 2009 to $184 million in 2011 according to an estimate from EMarketer.

Underlying this collapse was News Corp.'s approach to managing Myspace, which put the company at a serious competitive disadvantage in four critical capabilities—goal setting, product development, attracting and motivating talent, and marketing strategy.

Goal setting

Setting goals is the crucial starting point for strategy and there was a wide gap between the goals that News Corp. set for Myspace and what it needed to focus on to maintain its social networking lead. As a public company, News Corp. announced quarterly revenue targets to investors—and CEO Rupert Murdoch set and changed those goals without consulting with Myspace executives. Higher revenue goals placed a premium on boosting page views, which impeded efforts to streamline user navigation on the site.

For example, in early 2007, Murdoch predicted that Myspace would generate $1 billion in revenue in 2008. This panicked two former executives, according to Reuters. As one said, "It was a big blunder to say that to the Street. When you looked at how Myspace's numbers had been trending it was possible—but it was a stretch. After that moment it was basically like all the tentacles of News Corp got involved in a bid to make that target, so getting anything done became near impossible."

By contrast, Facebook avoided advertising and focused on accelerating user growth—which it was able to achieve—soon surpassing Myspace. As venture capitalist Sean Percival explained, Myspace expanded into many specific industry segments such as celebrity, fashion, sports and books—to boost advertising revenue—doing many things badly. By contrast, Facebook focused on making the site the best at a small number of things that appealed to users and boosted growth.

Meanwhile, in 2007 Murdoch lost interest in Myspace—which had been his primary focus for a few years—when he turned his attention to acquiring Dow Jones. This pursuit culminated in News Corp.'s 2009 acquisition for $5 billion of the parent of the Wall Street Journal. As one executive told the Financial Times, "Rupert took his eye off the ball on the internet. He got obsessed with Dow Jones and stopped paying attention to Myspace. That's when all the trouble really started."

The June 2009 departure of Murdoch's deputy, Peter Chernin, sealed the fate of Myspace's formerly prized executives—such as its CEO Chris DeWolfe—since Chernin was no longer in place to protect them from Murdoch who hired former AOL CEO Jonathan Miller who replaced Myspace's founders. In the year that followed his departure, Myspace lost ground to Facebook and suffered management changes, restructurings, and layoffs under News Corp.'s new chief digital officer; next year, the company would struggle through sweeping management changes, restructuring and layoffs, while losing more ground to Facebook.

Product development

Product development plays a large role in determining whether a site grows or shrinks. While Facebook's service was easy to use, lacked spam and seedy content, added a popular timeline, and a feature that made it easy for new users to add their email contacts to Facebook, Myspace was overwhelmed with content that repelled advertisers and users and it added too many new features—many of which further cluttered the site without attracting more users.

With the pressure to boost revenues to meet Murdoch's financial goal, Myspace added "a dizzying number of features: communication tools such as instant messaging, a classifieds program, a video player, a music player, a virtual karaoke machine, a self-serve advertising platform, profile-editing tools, security systems, privacy filters, Myspace book lists, and on and on," according to the Financial Times. That put Myspace at a competitive disadvantage to Facebook, which was creating "a robust platform that allowed outside developers to build new applications."

Attracting and motivating talent

The best talent is critical for winning the battle for market leadership. Myspace was originally located in Santa Monica and it moved to Beverly Hills after a few years. This move made it even more difficult for Myspace to compete for engineering talent—which was scarce in Southern California. Meanwhile, Facebook's location in Silicon Valley—coupled with its ability to offer stock options in what looked like a high potential company—enabled it to bring in the world's best talent.

While geographic location certainly put Myspace at a competitive disadvantage in recruiting, what really made the difference was that Myspace's cachet had long ago expired while Facebook's was rising. As The Guardian reported, "The baggage was too much. Users had too many bad experiences. They would go on there and they'd get hit with spam. There'd be all this weird stuff. On Facebook you were your real name, you were yourself. On Myspace you were like 420princessxxx, you're all these weird pseudonyms."

Marketing strategy

Soon after closing the deal to acquire Myspace, News Corp. signed a long-term advertising deal with Google valued at $900 million—but in order to receive the payments, Myspace needed to meet very challenging page view goals. At the same time, News Corp was opening Myspace offices around the world as a way to boost the number of users. Meanwhile, Facebook signed advertising deals that did not hinge on such page view goals and it was growing globally without the added cost of opening physical offices in new countries.

The Google agreement more than covered the price that News Corp. had paid for Myspace; however, the strings attached to the agreement put Myspace at a long-term disadvantage to Facebook. In order for Google to pay $300 million a year for three years, Myspace was required to generate a predetermined number of user visits. That reduced Myspace's ability to experiment with its site since the *experiments might fail and let Google off the hook. News Corp's Fox Interactive group—to which Myspace reported—pushed to meet quarterly revenue targets. "We were incentivized to keep page views very high and ended up having too many ads plus too many pages, making the site less easy to use than a site like Facebook," according to Reuters.*

Facebook was also able to take advantage of its relatively advertiser-friendly content to appeal to advertisers. While Facebook was introducing better tools for users to communicate with their friends through a clean interface, Myspace was unable to block spam—thus reinforcing its seedy image and causing "white middle class kids" to swap Myspace for Facebook. A large media buyer told Bloomberg that this was causing advertisers to quit Myspace. As he said, Advertisers, in general, have some difficulty with content and environments that they perceive to be edgy. Especially when the audiences that they value are available in environments that are less edgy."

Case Analysis

News Corp.'s failed effort to achieve growth from its acquisition of Myspace reveals four important principles of failure that will make it difficult for a company to grow through capabilities:

- **Assume past capabilities will apply to new businesses.** Success causes managers to repeat what they think worked in the past. Sadly, what managers think was the cause of their success may not be its true source. For example, Murdoch achieved tremendous success by hiring Roger Ailes to start and manage Fox News. Murdoch assumed that his success with Fox News implied a simple formula—hire the right person and set ambitious goals—would work again. Sadly for DeWolfe and Miller—both of whom Murdoch charged with meeting his ambitious goals—this formula was a failure when it came to building Myspace.

- **Set unrealistic expectations.** Typically a public company faces enormous pressure to boost quarterly revenues and profits. That pressure can make it easy for a CEO to push responsibility for those goals onto lower level managers. And if that pressure is too much for the business to bear, it will respond by taking actions that are good for meeting quarterly earnings targets—but bad for the long-term value of the business. This is exactly what happened when Murdoch announced that Myspace needed to achieve $1 billion in advertising revenue.

- **Ignore competitor strategies.** Rapid growth tends to attract rivals. And the fastest growing rivals pursue strategies that other industry participants ought to study. If that examination of competitor strategies reveals a company's weaknesses, the company should adapt. Facebook surpassed Myspace in part by applying growth strategies that News Corp. either ignored or noticed but did not perceive as worth studying. Rather than adapt by implementing competitively superior strategies, Myspace made its service worse than Facebook's from the perspective of demographically attractive consumers and the advertisers who hoped to reach them.

- **Weaken combined capabilities.** Each industry requires different combinations of capabilities to grow faster than rivals. When a large company makes an acquisition to obtain capabilities it lacks, the combined company ought to be able to perform those capabilities more effectively than either company could have previously done on their own. In retrospect, it is clear that News Corp. and Myspace were weak in several key capabilities—for example, neither could outdo Facebook when it came to product development. And while News Corp. was good at selling advertising for broadcast TV, it was not as skilled in doing so for social media content. Ultimately, Murdoch's overly ambitious financial expectations—and his impatience with the executives he charged with meeting them—doomed Myspace in its race with Facebook.

Principle Three   Small companies seeking growth from current capabilities should identify and attack untapped markets where their unique capabilities will enable them to gain significant market share.

Some of the most successful start-ups are run by CEOs who have extensive experience working with executives at well-established firms. That experience helps them to understand the strengths and weaknesses of those incumbents. And perhaps most important, helps them to imagine in detail how those incumbents might react to a carefully planned assault on their customers.

Such entrepreneurs can array their strengths against these incumbents' weaknesses to design, market, and service new products that customers find so compelling that they are willing to take the chance of giving some of their business to a start-up.

Such start-ups can achieve growth from current capabilities by applying three principles:

- **Focus on customers who are dissatisfied with currently available products.** Potential customers—whether businesses or consumers—are hesitant to try or pay for a start-up's product. The reason for that is simple—start-ups generally fail—thus stranding the customers with unsupported products. A start-up's best chance to overcome this reluctance is to offer potential customers a product that delivers a dramatically better solution to their problem than do products offered by current vendors. In so doing, entrepreneurs can boost the chances that customers will be willing to try—and ultimately pay for their products.

- **Stress capabilities that deliver superior value to customers.** New product development is the key capability at which most start-ups must excel. For example, if a start-up can listen with an open mind to customers, can envision how to use new technology to develop a product that will solve their problems better than the competition, and can build new products with a team approach that includes different functions—such as engineering, sales, finance, manufacturing, and early-adopter customers—it has a good chance of building products that customers are eager to buy. Such an approach to new product development could give a start-up an advantage over an incumbent that builds new products that are tied into all of its other products—with the goal of selling customers a complete bundle—regardless of whether that bundle solves the customers' problems.

- **Keep renewing capabilities.** It has become a cliché that some companies founded to become the opposite of an incumbent end up becoming so successful that they acquire all of the bad habits and characteristics which they were founded to overturn. To avoid this ironic fate, entrepreneurs must maintain intellectual humility and bear in mind that if unchecked, the pride that goes along with success can blind a leader to changes in customer needs, technology, and the competitive playing field that turn their capabilities from growth drivers to growth inhibitors.

Successful: SailPoint Grows to $100 Million in Revenues through Superior Product Development

Introduction

Founded in 2005, Austin, Texas-based identity management software provider, SailPoint's exceptional product management and customer service skills propelled it to over $100 million in revenue with bookings growing at 40% a year. By April 2016 it had 530 customers and 550 employees with hopes for filing for an IPO in 2017. (Identity management software protects companies against hackers—think about the 2014 hack of Sony Pictures—by among other things controlling how new employees get access to computing resources when they join a company and revoking those identities when they leave.)

Case Scenario

In April 2016, I interviewed its CEO Mark McClain, who explained how he built SailPoint after two successful ventures. McClain joined Tivoli Systems as it went public—and after IBM acquired it in 1996 for $743 million he ultimately ran its global marketing function. He also started and ran identity management software maker Waveset Technologies (Sun Microsystems bought it in 2003 for $150 million).

To explain SailPoint's success, McClain offered five management imperatives that spring from its advantages in product development, customer service, and human resource management:

- **Listen to customers with a "broader/forward" perspective.** *To grow, companies ought to listen to customers and give them what they need. McClain seems to agree—especially since changes in his customer's computing and business environments make it difficult for SailPoint to invent the future. So he meets with customers, asks them about their problems, and listens to their answers. He keeps an open mind—taking a broad approach and looking toward the future. Once he hears the same themes from many customers, he reaches the conclusion that it is time to act. So he gets different people involved, including engineers and product managers who synthesize this feedback and build a prototype of a product that he thinks will solve the customer problems. He puts the prototype in front of customers, gets their feedback, and "iterates." SailPoint's product development process contrasts starkly with that of big rivals who follow what McClain calls a "narrow/ backward" perspective. A case in point is IBM. As McClain said, "Big technology companies acquire companies that make point products. Their product managers fit acquired products* *with their existing ones. They don't listen enough to customers and product managers can't get engineers to respond to new customer needs." SailPoint's approach is winning it customers from the big players—half of its revenue is from customers of IBM, Oracle and CA Technologies, McClain says.*

- **Focus first on customers with the most pain.** *For a start-up, anyone could be a potential customer. Given its limited money and staff, the start-up should pitch its products to the group of customers that's most likely to buy. SailPoint targeted industries that would be most vulnerable to hackers— trying to create customers in "financial services, healthcare, federal government and later manufacturing and retail," said McClain. You can grow more quickly by selling to the potential customers who will buy the most quickly because they benefit most from your product.*

- **Turn customers into raving fans.** *Growth can come from making a customer much happier with your service than what competitors provide. Outstanding service pays two growth dividends—happy customers want to buy more from a company and sing its praises to potential customers. SailPoint turns customers into raving fans. As McClain said, "We have a 96% customer approval rating. This puts us in the position where the customers are saying, 'I wish you had more to sell to me, because you're different than other vendors I deal with'. This happens by overinvesting in our customer relationships and customer satisfaction because it creates this virtuous cycle where they want to buy more," said McClain.*

- **Use R&D and acquisitions to add new products.** *If a company has saturated its best customer groups around the world with its current products, where should it go next for growth? Get a bigger share of its current customers' budgets by inventing or acquiring new products that customers want to buy? SailPoint did both—in 2015 it acquired an Israeli company, Whitebox Security, to help its customers "secure and manage unstructured data" like social media postings even as it introduced a new version of its core product. Doing this well requires a vision of how a company will stay valuable to customers. "The ultimate strategy is how we touch other parts of not only the identity market, but also enterprise security and the broader IT ecosystem," said McClain.*

- **Attract great people and make them happy.** *Underlying excellent product development and effective customer service is the ability to attract and motivate talented people. SailPoint* has done this as evidenced by winning one of the highest Glassdoor ratings in the world—including 100% approval from its employees. SailPoint hires A-players who share its values and enjoy working with other smart people. Thanks to SailPoint's clearly articulated values, people who pass through its hiring process can take initiative to seize opportunities and adapt to change. SailPoint's values are dubbed the 4-Is and include the following:

- **Integrity** "means delivering on the commitments we make. We base our relationships with fellow employees, customers, partners, and investors on trust, every person who works in or with our company—our customers, our partners, and to each other—knows they can depend on us to do what we say we'll do," he explained.

- **Individuals** "refers to how much we value every person at SailPoint. We have learned that those who are confident in their abilities, yet humble enough to admit their shortcomings, make the best possible colleagues. As a result, we attract and retain the smartest, most engaging, most talented people in the industry," said McClain.

- **Impact** "means measuring and rewarding results, not activity. While we do our best to ensure that everyone on our team has the competence, skills and knowledge required to succeed, we expect people on our team to deliver those great results with a great attitude," explained McClain.

- **Innovation** "means developing creative solutions to real customer challenges that deliver significant, positive impact on the customer's bottom line. By combining an intimate knowledge of their businesses with our cutting-edge knowledge of technology, our customers view us as a critical, trusted partner," he said.

Case Analysis

SailPoint's success in achieving growth from its capabilities highlights three principles of small company grow through capabilities:

- **Empathize with customers.** The most successful small companies gain an advantage over rivals by viewing the world through the eyes of their customers. This is often because the company's founder started the company to solve her own problem and saw an opportunity to sell this solution to others. Large companies tend not to be able to empathize with customers—or if some of the large company's employees do empathize, their effort to respond to customer needs is muted by the company's senior executives. As a result, small companies can envision products that better meet the needs of potential customers. SailPoint's concept of listening with a broader/forward perspective is an excellent application of this principle—leading to its ability to design products that customers are eager to buy.

- **Cultivate capabilities that deliver competitively superior value to customers.** Capabilities are a means to deliver value to customers at scale. More specifically, companies perform processes such as product development, customer service, and marketing in order to design, make, deliver, and service products that are so valuable that large numbers of customers buy them repeatedly and recommend them to others. Capabilities enable companies to create and keep customers in a way that the company can repeat as it expands. SailPoint's skills in product development, service, and human resources management have contributed to its competitively superior customer value—which in turn has propelled its rapid growth.

- **Keep learning.** Capabilities lose their value over time because of changing customer needs, new technologies, and upstart rivals. Unless a company stays keenly attuned to these changes and adapts, its capabilities are likely to turn from core capabilities into core rigidities. Small company CEOs seeking to avoid this fate—which will ultimately lead to slower growth and loss of market share—must empathize with customers while maintaining intellectual humility. SailPoint demonstrated its ability to do this as it tailored its product to new industries and by acquiring a company that could deliver a new service that its customers were demanding. To sustain growth through capabilities, a CEO must be willing to keep learning—in spite of the company's success.

Unsuccessful: Despite 100,000 Users and $1.6 Million in Capital, GoCrossCampus (GXC) Fails

Introduction

In 2007, five Yale undergraduates started GXC—an online gaming company that raised $1.6 million in funding, had more than 100,000 users, and signed up over 100 institutions—mostly colleges and universities. By 2010, it had run out of money and shut down. Underlying this failure was the absence of many key capabilities needed to grow and operate a start-up.

Case Scenario

GXC was a "territorial-conquest game, like Risk," founded in September 2007 by four Yale undergraduate students and one Columbia undergrad. According to the **New York Times,** *"GXC more closely resembles an intramural or interscholastic sport than the typical online video game, where individuals or small groups are pitted against each other. GXC teams, made up of hundreds and sometimes thousands of players, play on behalf of real-world dorms or schools—even presidential candidates—by jostling for hegemony on maps of their campus or locale and conducting their campaigns as much in the real world as online."*

GXC was based in New Haven and was seeking revenues from companies—such as Google's Manhattan campus—seeking to build camaraderie among its employees. By March 2008, GXC had raised what was then an undisclosed amount of seed money—with the hope of raising more capital after they graduated and devoted themselves full time to building the game.

GXC sought to tap into intergroup competition at colleges and universities. As Brad Hargreaves, GXC's CEO explained, "We try to harness the feelings of various competitive groups in order to create really intense and enthusiastic groups of online gamers, essentially out of people who have often never played an online game before in their lives." And its chief marketing officer Matthew Brimer said that GXC's advantage over established gaming companies that might try to copy the game was its relationships with student governments who help in getting approval from university administrators.

By March 2008, 11,000 Ivy League students were playing its game and its total number of players ultimately grew to 100,000 before GXC burned through the $1.6 million it had raised. Its failure can be seen as the result of its weakness at performing three critical capabilities:

- ***Targeting the right market.** Small companies should target large markets whose customers have significant unmet needs that their start-up can address more effectively than rivals. GXC did not realize the importance of this capability* *until after it failed. GXC's product was intended for college students with campus pride who enjoyed playing strategy games, most of whom had little money to spend on anything other than alcohol. This market was too small to build a sustainable company.*

- **Raising capital for the long term.** *Investors, assuming that a company can win at most 10% market share, like to invest in start-ups targeting markets of at least $1 billion since they believe that in order to go public a company must generate at least $100 million in revenue. GXC's target market was smaller than that so it was only able to raise small amounts of capital at very short-term intervals. As Brimer said, "We raised $300K for our seed round from New York VCs. Four months later, we raised $300K more. And four months after that, we raised another $300K, and four months after that, another $300K."*

- **Developing products that meet user requirements.** *To develop winning products, small companies must work closely with customers—as well as cross-functional teams—to create products with features that customers want. GXC did not work with the right customers in developing its product, the game's interface was too difficult to use, and it failed to anticipate how rapidly growing customer demand would strain its ability to keep the game operating properly. For example, GXC launched its game in fall 2007 to capture the interest of students as they were arriving on campus—but technical problems forced it to shut down until Thanksgiving. Moreover, its developers lacked a product plan and they were only taking product feedback from friends and family to which they reacted immediately—so they did not make the right product improvements efficiently.*

Case Analysis

The GXC case highlights three principles that inhibit small companies' achievement of growth via current capabilities:

- **Put founders' interests ahead of customers' and investors'.** Some first-time entrepreneurs assume that applying the founders' skills to their interests will be sufficient for a successful launch. This can work if the founding team happens to include people who are capable of understanding and addressing the concerns of external stakeholders such as customers and investors. However, if a team lacks those skills then the company's direction will not be set effectively—or it will flow slowly from extensive internal debate among the founders based on the interaction between their shared interests and disagreements. GXC clearly suffered as a result of this problem and therefore it never recognized and closed its critical capability gaps.

- **Build team that lacks the capabilities needed to gain market share.** When start-ups seek to get off the ground, their founders ought to look objectively at the skills required to build a company that can grow. Failure can result if the team lacks critical capabilities because work that needs to be done to launch and grow the company does not happen. GXC's team had people with vision and coding ability but was lacking in sufficiently strong capabilities in product development, setting strategic direction, and raising capital.

- **Fail to acknowledge and adapt quickly to mistakes.** Mistakes are inevitable—and a crucial difference between start-ups that succeed and the ones that fail is their approach to acknowledging, analyzing, and fixing mistakes. Start-ups whose founders believe that they will create and define their industries can fall victim to confirmation bias—which leads them to ignore information that is inconsistent with their vision. As a result, they dismiss market signals that suggest the company may have made a mistake that it needs to fix. As we discussed earlier, GXC failed to identify, acknowledge, and fix several important mistakes—it picked the wrong target market and its team lacked critical skills in product development, strategic direction setting, and raising capital. It only recognized these mistakes after the company had failed. Successful start-ups do that while there is still hope for using the fixed mistakes to continue their expansion.

Principle Four   Small companies seeking growth from new capabilities should envision new market opportunities and build, partner, or acquire the skills need to gain share.

When seeking to achieve revenue growth, well-managed small companies ask themselves a difficult question—Do we have the capabilities needed to meet our growth goals? The honest answer to that question is often 'No"—but some entrepreneurs display false bravado and answer in the affirmative.

An effective CEO will recognize that the company may be missing critical capabilities and will evaluate how to add them to its capability portfolio. Such an evaluation will focus on questions such as:

- Which market opportunity is best for our company?
- Which companies are growing fastest in that market?
- Why do customers buy from these growth leaders and what are their critical capabilities?
- What are our company's strengths and weaknesses in each of these key capabilities?
- What are the best options—for example, hiring experienced management, partnering, or acquiring—to close our company's capability gap?

Small companies seeking growth from new capabilities answer these questions effectively by conducting in-depth analysis—driven by business instincts honed from their founders' prior business experience—into customer needs, growth leaders' capabilities, their strengths and weaknesses, and options for closing the resulting capability gaps. This analysis leads to decisions and actions that generate rapid growth.

Successful: Five Years after Founding, Commonwealth Dairy's New Capabilities Drive 100% Growth

Introduction

In 2009, Commonwealth Dairy's founders applied their skills at identifying growth opportunities to the Greek yogurt market—growing 100% a year to $140 million in revenues by 2015. Critical to this success was the financing it received from Ehrmann, a German yogurt maker, which helped the company's cofounders to add new capabilities including how to make, market, and distribute yogurt and how to manage the company as it grew.

Case Scenario

Commonwealth Dairy, with operations near Brattleboro, Vermont; and in Casa Grande, Arizona, made Greek yogurt that accounted for 70% of its $70 million in estimated 2013 revenues. Commonwealth made yogurt for private label retailers such as Wegmans, Costco, and others. They also sold the product under its own brand, Green Mountain Creamery. With help from YoYummy, introduced in late 2013 as children's yogurt in a pouch, Commonwealth expected to reach $140 million in revenues by the end of 2014.

Massachusetts entrepreneurs Thomas Moffitt, president and CEO; and Ben Johnson, vice president and CFO, cofounded Commonwealth in 2009. Both had left the same big-company employer, launching their start-up at the depth of the global financial crisis, which made it difficult for them to raise capital for their yogurt-making venture. Moffitt majored in biology and creative writing at Colby College and entered the biology PhD program at the University of Wisconsin, Madison. While there, he started a small company distributing milk, juice, and soda. After a few years of "mediocre success," he headed back east. From there, he went to a food broker where he observed who was buying what and which categories were growing. From there, he took a job at Ahold, an international retailer headquartered in Amsterdam, sourcing dairy commodities and helping to manage the risk associated with purchasing the hundreds of millions of dollars of dairy it bought every year.

Johnson was a Boston-area restaurant veteran who had left that industry and returned to finish his bachelor's degree in marketing at the University of Alabama. He stayed at Alabama to continue studying marketing for his master's degree, and then returned to Boston. He joined Ahold shortly after Moffitt had started there, working on dairy contracts. As Moffitt explained, "Ahold is where I met Ben. It had six retail banners and a food service business. Ahold had been an aggregator, found its strategy not working, and began to sell off products and downsize. Ben and I were sourcing dairy products and saw opportunity. Ahold was buying 30 million pounds of yogurt a year, demand was growing at 10%, and the product options were poor."

In 2008, the financial markets shuddered, which helped push Moffitt and Johnson to start a company to capture these opportunities. In so doing, they immediately recognized the importance of partnering to supplement their experience identifying emerging market opportunities with the capabilities they would need in order to turn their vision into a successful company. According to Moffitt, "A light bulb went off in our heads. We saw Ahold doing more downsizing and that there was an opportunity in yogurt. We started talking to people, including attorneys in Boston, who introduced us to entrepreneurs. One of the founders of Staples helped us identify missing links in our plan.

Moffitt and Johnson first recruited a board of advisors to help them meet people and raise capital. This board comprised that they felt were the major skillsets a venture capitalist would want to see. The board members included a former secretary of agriculture, because they believed that the dairy industry was very political and there was a significant amount of government money for dairy companies; a former president of TCBY yogurt, a yogurt expert from the University of Wisconsin; a successful entrepreneur who was between start-ups; and the owner of a company that built food plants. This latter individual's personal guidance and involvement was a game changer for them. As Moffitt said, "These people meant that Ben and I could walk into any meeting and gain the respect of any audience we were speaking to."

And they did not know how to make yogurt so they recruited someone who did. Said Moffitt, "We recruited a yogurt maker, an Austrian who was a vice president of Kozy Shack, a pudding-maker. He knew how to make yogurt and told us, 'I was in conversations four or five years ago about this with a German firm. I will give them a call.'"

In addition, Moffitt and Johnson raised capital for their venture in the midst of the financial market collapse from Ehrmann AG, a billion-dollar, family-run international yogurt company based in Germany. Soon, they were invited to Germany for a meeting with the Ehrmann AG board. "In September 2008, the worst part of the financial crisis, we made our pitch. For three months, we heard nothing. So we kept trying to find other partners, but Ehrmann had the capital and knowhow. In September 2009, we signed with Ehrmann and started constructing our dairy in Vermont," explained Moffitt.

Ehrman was attracted to the investment by the opportunity to get a foothold in the rapidly growing market for Greek yogurt in the United States, which took very little time to go from infancy, to rapid growth, to attracting many new competitors which presaged its maturation. The U.S. market for yogurt grew rapidly from $5 billion in 2010 to $7 billion in 2014. But Greek yogurt accounted for $2 billion of 2014 industry revenue was growing "at thousands of percent a year," according to Moffitt. While U.S. consumers were behind Europe in yogurt consumption, they were catching up fast, increasing their consumption from "one-seventh the amount of yogurt that Europe does—to one-fifth," he said.

But in 2013, the relative market share of industry leaders changed. Among the biggest rivals was New Berlin, New York-based Chobani, launched in 2007, which makes tart, Mediterranean-themed yogurt, and which claimed to have boosted revenue by 32% in 2013, and expected sales above $1.5 billion in 2014. The company, run by founder Hamdi Ulukaya, had a 19% share of the $6.5 billion U.S. market for refrigerated yogurt, according to Nielsen. And it controlled 38% of the U.S. Greek yogurt market.

This represented a growing revenue opportunity for Commonwealth. As Moffitt explained in 2014, "We will do $70 million in revenue this year and employ 150 people—and we think we will hit $140 million in revenue in 2015 with help from YoYummy—tapping into the $1 billion kids' yogurt market. And its expectations for the future were even more ambitious. The company had set a 2019 revenue target "in excess of $250 million." Explained Moffitt and Johnson, "We would like to be in a position where we continue to create innovative, market-changing products and grow our market share. We are actively looking at new markets in terms of geographic distribution and product categories."

To achieve these ambitious goals, Moffitt and Johnson added three new key capabilities that enabled Commonwealth to attract customers, fulfill demand reliably for a high quality product, and build its organization as it scaled. These capabilities included the following:

- **Yogurt Manufacturing.** When Moffitt and Johnson started Commonwealth, they did not even know how to make yogurt. But by hiring an experienced Austrian yogurt maker, they began to build the company's manufacturing capabilities. From there, they built a plant in Vermont that would make its premium, branded yogurt and a lower-cost facility in Arizona that could supply demand for lower-priced private label yogurt.

- **Raw Materials Purchasing.** *The economics of the yogurt industry were challenging and purchasing milk effectively was critical to their success. As Moffitt explained, "Milk accounts for most of our cost—it represents 15% to 17% of the price consumers pay for yogurt—fruit represents another 10%. In Vermont, we pay that milk price—80% of which is set at the federal level—to a co-op that represents about 1,000 farms which, on average, have 150 cows. Retailers get high margins on our product—they can mark it up 40%."*

- **Managing Growth.** *As the company grew, Moffitt and Johnson needed to let go of their day-to-day involvement in activities such as hiring and other decisions at all levels of the organization. With a strong push from Ehrmann, they also hired professional functional executives and introduced more formal systems for planning and control. For example, they boosted the professionalism of their raw materials purchasing. "We have set up a Strategic Sourcing team to manage all of our Vendor relationships and ensure we are well informed buyers with clear authority for purchasing and not a company with lots of poorly trained buyers who buy at will and without a formal review of alternatives," they said.*

Given the rapidly changing nature of its markets, Commonwealth needed to keep introducing new products. In April 2016, Commonwealth helped launch into the United States an Ehrmann pudding that was popular in Europe. Would Commonwealth continue to be able to add new products and new capabilities in order to achieve its ambitious goals?

Case Analysis

The Commonwealth Dairy case exemplifies four principles that small companies seeking growth from new capabilities should follow:

- **Know which capabilities are essential for winning in the target market.** When a company seeks to take market share, it must understand each of the key capabilities required to get and keep customers. When founding Commonwealth, Moffitt and Johnson realized that they needed a range of capabilities—most of which they lacked. Fortunately, their industry experience and the resulting network of relationships made them confident that they could build the company—despite lacking all the key capabilities.

- **Assess objectively your company's competitive position in each essential capability.** It is common for founders to express great confidence in their competitive superiority. However the most successful founders are able to gather data—comparing themselves objectively to rivals—so they can identify whether their company will truly enjoy a competitive advantage. Commonwealth's cofounders had sufficient confidence and objectivity to realize that they enjoyed one competitive advantage—the ability to see emerging new product opportunities before most rivals.

- **Hire, partner, or acquire to close the capability gap.** If a small company can identify objectively its capability gaps, then it ought to hire, partner, or acquire to gain access to the capability portfolio needed to grow. Commonwealth did an excellent job of closing the capability gap—its partnership with Ehrmann gave it capital and a management approach that helped it grow and it hired a yogurt industry veteran to lead its manufacturing capability.

- **Reassess your capability portfolio for each new market opportunity.** Companies ought to take a fresh look at their capability portfolios for each new growth opportunity that they target. Companies may find it more profitable to target new markets where a small number of capabilities must be modified and many of their current capabilities will help them compete as they are. Commonwealth was able to accomplish this when it targeted the private label yogurt market—in so doing it chose to add a lower-cost manufacturing facility where it could make yogurt at a lower cost than it did in its Vermont facility.

Unsuccessful: HealthSpot Immolates $44 Million Due to Weak Capabilities

Introduction

In January 2016, Dublin, Ohio-based telehealth kiosk maker, HealthSpot, shut down after burning through $46.7 million in equity and debt capital. Its top management tried to apply its experience in health care technology to a new market. Its kiosk and the inconvenience and cost of scheduling appointments did not generate sufficient demand for the new service. Ultimately, this failure can be traced to a mismatch between the strengths of HealthSpot's founding team and the requirements for competitive success in the telemedicine industry.

Case Scenario

HealthSpot, founded in 2011, made telemedicine kiosks intended to provide rapid access to doctors. By the time it filed for Chapter 7 bankruptcy four and a half years later, it had built 190 such kiosks that had been equipped with medical instruments and two-way video conferencing. Fifty-four of these kiosks were operating at customer sites including Rite Aid Corp.—its biggest customer with telemedicine kiosks in 25 stores that acquired HealthSpot for $1.15 million out of bankruptcy—and Marc's pharmacies in Ohio. Over three years, HealthSpot had generated "$1.1 million in revenue—$600,000 of which came in 2015 as it delivered its kiosks to hospitals, pharmacy chains and employers."

The most remarkable thing about HealthSpot was that it had convinced capital providers to part with $46.7 million. After all, the company's CEO Steve Cashman had no prior experience in the health care industry—before starting the company he had been an information technology consultant. Moreover, HealthSpot's top management team spent an inordinate amount of investor cash on their own salaries—$1.46 million was paid out to its seven senior officers (an amount equal to its total revenues). Ultimately, HealthSpot failed due to its weak performance of three critical capabilities:

- **Strategic Vision.** *Cashman's decision to connect patients with doctors via kiosks in pharmacies was a deeply flawed strategy. Among the most obvious flaws was the notion that a physician would be able to diagnose a patient via a remote camera, rather than a face-to-face conversation that would include physical examination; the notion that doctors would benefit economically from providing this service—rather than increasing their professional liability; and the idea that patient medical records could be safely checked and updated on a kiosk. What is most remarkable is that Cashman was able to persuade capital providers that this was a good investment opportunity.*

- **Product Development.** *HealthSpot was able to design and build kiosks—when it went bankrupt it had 137 kiosks valued at $3.5 million in its inventory. However, kiosks alone did not address the consumer need for on-demand medical treatment that the kiosks implicitly offered to satisfy. That's because HealthSpot required prearranged appointments— therefore the kiosk promised to deliver a scheduled appointment with a doctor in a location that resulted in far poorer* quality health care than would meeting at a doctor's office. HealthSpot's kiosks did not offer patients or doctors any advantages over the means of delivering care that they were designed to replace.

- **Marketing**. It is difficult to sell a product that doesn't give customers a compelling reason to buy. Despite his skills at raising capital, Cashman was clearly not as good at building a team that could generate sufficient revenue. With $1.1 million in total revenue generated by the HealthSpot during its existence—representing 5,000 patient consultations by May 2015, according to Cashman—the company's marketing skills were deeply flawed. It is possible that what Cashman counted as patient consultations did not generate much in the way of revenues. Moreover, the significant number of kiosks that it held in inventory suggest that its marketing team was not up to the task of persuading customers to buy them.

Case Analysis

HealthSpot's failure highlights three principles that small companies seeking growth from new capabilities should avoid:

- **Assemble a weak founding team.** HealthSpot's founder had no experience running a telemedicine company nor did members of his senior team. To be fair, Cashman was exceptionally effective at raising capital—yet in retrospect the enormous gap between HealthSpot's failure and its promise suggests that the company's capital providers lacked investment acumen. It is very unusual for a start-up with such a weak founding team to raise significant outside capital.

- **Ignore key capability gaps.** As we discussed earlier in the chapter to achieve growth, a founder must identify key capabilities required to gain market share and close the gap between the company's current capabilities and those needed to win. HealthSpot's CEO either did not see the need for product development and marketing or decided to staff those capabilities with the wrong people doing the wrong things. Without the ability to perform these activities in a way that delivered competitively superior value to customers, HealthSpot was unable to generate enough revenue to survive.

- **Spend capital on executive pay.** One key difference between large companies and small ones is top executives' pay. In big companies, those executives typically make millions in base salary, bonus, and stock options. In small companies, they typically earn modest six figure salaries and make up for the difference in the form of stock options that will only become valuable if the company is successful. HealthSpot violated this principle by paying millions in salary to its executives—thus accelerating the company's demise.

Applying the Principles of Growth through New Capabilities

Leaders seeking to assess whether they apply these principles to their organizations should be able to answer Yes to these six questions:

- What are the critical capabilities that support the fastest growing companies in your industry?

- How do these growth leaders use their capabilities to win new customers and keep them buying?

- How must your company modify its capabilities in order to accelerate its growth rate?

- Are there growth opportunities that your company could tap by applying its current capabilities?

- What capability gaps have you identified between your company's current capabilities and those needed to tap those opportunities?

- Should your company close the capability gap through targeted hiring, acquisition, or partnership?

Chapter 8: Growth Road Maps provides a detailed methodology for applying the principles of growth through new products.

Summary

A growing company's capabilities—such as product development, marketing and sales, manufacturing, distribution, and service—enable it to provide customers better value than do rivals.

If a company has developed the right capabilities, it should use them to enter new markets so that it will be able to offset declining revenues derived from maturing markets with rising revenues from rapidly growing new ones.

In general, capabilities must be modified to fit with each new growth opportunity. The profitability of these modifications will be highest if they both contribute to the company's rapid growth and do not cost too much to implement.

If a company chooses growth through new capabilities, it will benefit most if the new capabilities give it a significant share of a market that is growing quickly and likely to become large. Moreover, the investment in new capabilities will be particularly valuable to the company if they can be used to help gain share in a series of new market opportunities.

In Chapter 6, we'll explore the fifth dimension of growth—culture. While often dimly understood—culture is a set of values that underpin decisions such as whom to hire, promote, and manage out of the company and how people ought to act in their interactions with customers and partners. As we'll see, growth flows from a culture based on values in which the CEO believes, that talented people find compelling, and that motivate people to deliver superior customer value.

Growth via Culture

In Chapter 5, we saw how capabilities can help or hinder a company's growth. In Chapter 6, we explore how a company's culture—its shared values and the actions it takes to realize them—can contribute or constrain a company's growth.

Many years ago I worked for a consulting firm that was known as the world's expert in corporate culture. Given my analytical bent, I had difficulty at the time understanding what culture was and why it mattered so much. However, in the intervening decades, I've worked with many companies and witnessed firsthand the meaning and significance of culture—one CEO I interviewed spends 20% of his time on culture. Moreover, Daniel Kahneman's *Thinking Fast and Slow*—which I use in my Strategic Decision Making course—presents a conceptual framework—System 1 (causes people to make snap, intuitive decisions) and System 2 (makes a choice after carefully analyzing its pros and cons). This framework helps me to understand that culture engages workers emotionally (System 1) and helps leaders evaluate decisions such as whom to hire, promote, and manage out of the company (System 2).

© Peter S. Cohan 2017
P. S. Cohan, *Disciplined Growth Strategies*, DOI 10.1007/978-1-4842-2448-9_6

In teaching entrepreneurship students, I've seen that culture starts with values and that the right values occupy the center of a Venn diagram representing the intersection of three sets:

- **CEO's values.** Effective culture reflects the CEO's fundamental beliefs about what matters to other people including the founding team, customers, employees, and investors. If a CEO does not believe in the company's values, they will become empty words—and any effort to use those words to influence key decisions will result in confusion. Moreover, a company is in for a world of trouble when its stated values don't match the behavior of the CEO or employees.

- **Employee magnets.** The CEO's values should also help the organization to hire and motivate the best employees. Simply put, a company ought to develop values that flow from the CEO and will help the company to attract the best people because they find inspiration in the company's purpose and the way it operates.

- **Customer benefits.** Ultimately, values will only help a company grow if they attract people whose work is valuable to its customers. As we have explored throughout this book, growth flows from happy customers who keep buying from a company and tell others about their happiness. A company should develop values that flow from the CEO, attract and motivate the best employees, and encourage them to perform activities—such as building products and delivering service—that help a company to get customers and keep them happy.

Principles of Growth from Culture

How can culture accelerate a company's growth? A company is likely to grow faster than its industry if it develops values at the intersection of those three sets; uses them not only to hire and promote, but also to manage people who do not fit the values out of the company; and rewards employees who turn the values into actions that attract customers and keep them so happy that they strongly recommend the company to others. Culture can also slow a company's growth—especially if the CEO feels compelled to impose her values on the organization without regard to their appeal to employees or their ability to drive behavior that attracts and keeps customers. Culture can also impede a company's growth if the company's stated values slow employees' career success. Such cognitive dissonance can lower productivity and high turnover.

Large and small companies differ considerably in their approaches to achieving growth through culture. Most large companies are not run by their founders. Therefore, when a new CEO takes over, he may be faced with the significant challenge of reviving the company's growth. As we'll see later in this chapter, the key difference between a large company with a culture that encourages growth and one that impedes growth is the way it treats employees. How so? An effective large company growth culture respects its employees and eases their efforts to build new product prototypes so they can test out potential growth opportunities. Such a large company encourages experiments and even celebrates the learning that comes from failed ones. By contrast, a large company whose culture impedes growth views employees as costs to be minimized and encourages them to leave through layoffs, very limited salary increases, and ongoing pressure to outsource work to lower-cost countries, even as it cuts back on the quality of its customer service and builds new products with an eye toward locking in customers to all its products rather than delivering the industry's best solution to customer problems.

Small companies take a different approach to growth culture—much of which springs from the personality of the CEO. A small company CEO should create a culture that recognizes the importance of hiring people who are willing to take responsibility for achieving the company's growth goals and to express their opinions respectfully about the best strategy to achieve those goals. An effective small company growth culture urges employees to build products that deliver the industry's best performance at the most competitive price, and they deliver excellent customer service so that customers will recommend the company to others and keep buying as their needs change. By contrast, there are many kinds of ineffective small company growth cultures—one we will explore in this chapter is a company that believed that growth comes from hiring sales people and urging them to meet unrealistically high sales targets—trading off regulatory compliance and customer service in that pursuit.

Let's examine pairs of case studies of successful and unsuccessful applications of two principles of growth from culture:

- **Big companies seeking growth through culture** unleash growth potential by encouraging employees to spot opportunities, experiment frugally, and take initiative to create new businesses.

- **Small companies achieve growth through culture** by hiring and rewarding people who value rapid prototyping, excellent customer service, and disciplined execution.

Principle One Big companies unleash growth potential by encouraging employees to spot opportunities, experiment frugally, and take initiative to create new businesses.

Large companies often get that way thanks to exceptionally talented founders. Steve Jobs at Apple, Jeff Bezos at Amazon, and Mark Zuckerberg of Facebook come to mind. In many ways understanding how these icons of entrepreneurship achieved success provides useful insights for managers. However, more ordinary CEOs will never be gifted with the genius—whether it be in envisioning better products or challenging traditional ways that people interact or retailers operate—that enables such leaders to create and build fast-growing large companies.

In short, large company CEOs ought to create a culture that distributes responsibility for growth to all employees. Developing new products is risky. If any employee can build an inexpensive prototype of a new product idea and get feedback from potential customers, then the odds of success will rise. To create such a culture, a CEO ought to follow four principles:

- **Study successful corporate innovation.** A large company CEO ought to take personal responsibility for creating a culture that encourages its people to identify and develop new product ideas. Without the CEO's leadership, the company is likely to become too dependent on a small number of visionaries. To create a growth culture, the CEO ought to study how companies have encouraged innovation among their employees, the challenges companies have faced in achieving that outcome, how companies have overcome those challenges, and which ones remained unresolved.

- **Adopt applicable lessons.** The CEO must evaluate the results of this research and identify relevant lessons that the CEO can use to create a growth culture. From there the CEO should define the company's values and articulate a vision of how that culture will encourage employees to innovate.

- **Hire entrepreneurial leaders.** Such a culture will be more effective if the company has hired individuals who are entrepreneurial leaders—that is, people who have started companies or who have identified and captured business opportunities. To generate faster growth, a company must be able to attract these talented people.

- **Enable them to innovate.** Ultimately the company must create a process that will enable such employees to imagine and develop new products—giving them adequate resources with a minimum of interference from managers—and embracing the learning that comes from failed experiments during the process.

Case Studies

Successful: Intuit's Culture of Innovation Boosts Employee Innovation and Growth

Introduction

Intuit, a $4.7 billion (2016 revenues) Mountain View, California-based personal financial software provider, grew rapidly. Investors who purchased shares in March 1993 at $2.64 enjoyed a 17% annual gain—as of October 7, 2016, the shares traded at $107.45. That stock price increase seemed to result from Intuit's persistently rapid growth—for example, in the quarter ending January 2016, Intuit enjoyed 23% revenue growth abetted by a 49% increase to 1,257,000 of its QuickBooks Online subscriber count. Intuit's culture of innovation helps explain that high growth.

Case Scenario

Intuit's growth culture started with its founder and chairman of the executive committee, Scott Cook—a Harvard MBA and former Bain & Co. consultant. As he explained in a 2012 interview, he had a passion for assuring that Intuit was capable of both strengthening its core business and creating innovative new ones. His key finding was that big companies must create a culture of frugal experimentation.

By 2012, Cook—who did not see himself as a visionary innovator in the mold of Apple's Steve Jobs or Amazon's Jeff Bezos and therefore wanted to make sure Intuit would keep growing after he left—had been studying for at least four years. He believed that no market category could keep growing for so long that an incumbent company could avoid eventually perishing unless it hitched its wagon to a new market. As an example, Cook cited Microsoft, which "had been unable to invent successful new disruptive businesses—causing its growth to slow down." Cook found it strange that large successful companies could not invent new industries. After all, he reasoned, they have the best people, a high profit flow, the largest customer base, and the broadest channels of distribution.

And yet, Cook noted, if you look at enterprise and consumer technology companies, the game changing innovations almost never come from the big incumbents such as Oracle, SAP, and Microsoft. With the exception of Apple during Steve Jobs's second stint as CEO, all the big innovations came from start-ups. Cook decided to investigate whether there were any large companies that had been able to buck this trend. He studied companies such as Hewlett Packard, 3M, Procter & Gamble—where he had worked, and Toyota Motor. He found that the common thread during the periods of their most successful product and process innovations was the systems they put in place to encourage employees to conduct frugal experiments.

Intuit adopted this idea—inventing new businesses by creating an environment that encouraged employees to come up with new business hypotheses and test them by getting feedback from customers. Cook described an example—a debit card for people without bank accounts. An Intuit finance employee—not a "product person"—noticed that the people who needed tax refund checks the most were often ones who don't even have bank accounts. She envisioned the idea giving those people debit cards and having Intuit accept the tax refunds in its accounts and transfer the funds to the debit card. She came up with the idea in February and wanted to test it by April 1st before tax season ran out on April 15th. Cook criticized the kludgy website she developed but she argued that it was better to get something crude that would test her idea than to wait another 10 months. She expected 100 takers but got 1,000. And the surprise was that half the ones that wanted the debit card already had bank accounts. In this way, Intuit discovered that the need for this product was much greater than it expected. One interesting feature of this story is that Cook was not wild about the website that the employee had developed, but she was able to pursue her idea anyway. This echoes one of Cook's findings when he studied Hewlett Packard.

His conversation with the author of a 650-page book on its history revealed that seven of the eight big new businesses that HP invented came "from the bottom" and were opposed by CEO David Packard. The pattern Cook found was that in all these cases, three things were true:

- The company "liberated the inventive power of new people";

- It created a "culture of experimentation"; and

- It changed the role of the boss from a decider of whether to pursue or cancel innovation projects to an installer of systems that encourage endless cycles of hypothesis generation, testing with customers, and learning from the gap between quantitative expectations and measured market truth.

Cook believed that there was nothing more rewarding to employees than to see their idea being used by people. To that end, Intuit created an idea collaboration portal that let employees post ideas, get feedback, coaching, suggestions, and sign up other employees to help implement it. This idea encouragement happened without a manager getting involved. According to Cook, by 2012, this portal had turned 30 ideas into "shipping products and features" that boosted Intuit's revenues. Cook's culture of innovation recipe consisted of eight steps:

- **Leader's vision.** A culture of experimentation starts with the CEO's vision. In Cook's case, the vision was to change peoples' financial lives so profoundly that they could not imagine going back to the old way;

- **Strategy-by-experiment.** Rather than trying to curry favor with their bosses, Cook believed it was essential to enable Intuit employees to make data-based decisions. This meant encouraging them to conduct experiments—and importantly celebrating the learning that resulted from these experiments rather than harshly punishing failure—and collected data on customer behavior;

- **Leap of faith assumptions.** Cook encouraged people to identify the two or three key assumptions that had to be true for the idea to succeed—but might not be. Then he argued that people needed to test those assumptions with customers at a low cost in a very short time frame;

- **Numeric hypothesis.** Next Cook wanted people to come up with an estimate of, say, the number of customers that would order the new product;

- **Experimental run.** He expected the employee to run the experiment to test whether that numeric hypothesis was right or not;

- **Analysis of variance.** Then Cook wanted people to analyze the gap between the hypothesis and the actual results and dig deep to find the reason for that gap;

- **Surprise celebration.** Cook was adamant that people should not try to bury surprises to keep from being embarrassed but to savor them because they exposed a market signal that had not yet been detected; and

- **Decision.** Finally, Cook wanted Intuit people to make a decision about whether to pursue the idea or try a different one.

Intuit's culture of innovation was still going strong in 2016 as evidenced by the company's rapid growth in the number of users of its small business accounting software as a service, QuickBooks Online, which Intuit CEO Brad Smith initiated in response to a threat from Wellington, New Zealand-based Xero—a small business accounting mobile app—to QuickBooks, Intuit's PC-based accounting software for small businesses. Xero started in 2006 based on the idea that Intuit had focused its attention on small business accounting software for the United States and Canada and ignored the rest of the world. And as small business owners started using smartphones and the cloud, Xero saw a chance to seize an opportunity to offer a mobile accounting app that would win over those small businesses.

Xero—which went public in Australia in 2012 and raised $111 million in 2015 from U.S. venture capitalists—had 600,000 subscribers to its $9 a month app by 2016. Rather than operate a closed system as Intuit's PC-based QuickBooks did, Xero "opened up its platform so that banks and financial app makers could plug their services into it, offering users the ability to customize Xero and offering partner companies the ability to strengthen ties with their customers," according to the New York Times. After establishing a strong foothold in New Zealand and Australia, Xero took its software to Britain and the United States.

Intuit responded by turning a neglected product—QuickBooks Online—into a Xero rival—ultimately opening up the mobile accounting package to 2,000 apps like PayPal and Square and moving into Australia, a Xero stronghold. And in 2016, Intuit sold the PC-based Quicken and some other businesses to a private equity firm, raising $500 million. Smith developed QuickBooks Online as a rival to Xero through a previously established product line—focusing on building a product that would appeal to small businesses that were seeking to use an app for their accounting. Intuit was wise to keep its old PC-based business going—because many small businesses were still using it and it generated a substantial amount of cash to fund QuickBooks Online. As UBS analyst Brent Thill told the Times, "Whenever Intuit makes a wrong turn, they quickly get off the gravel and back onto the blacktop. That's why the company has done so well for such a long time."

Case Analysis

Intuit's continued growth brings into focus four principles that large companies seeking to create a culture of innovation ought to follow:

- **CEO must relinquish innovator-in-chief role.** Most large companies that are still run by their founders could be at risk when those founders depart. To be sure, those founders savor running their creations so much that they cannot imagine stepping down voluntarily. However this mindset endangers the company's long-term survival. Leaders who lack the innovative genius demonstrated by Jobs and Bezos ought to put a premium on their company's ability to grow after they leave. To achieve that, they ought to create a culture of innovation that lessens the company's dependence on a single individual to identify and capture growth opportunities.

- **Urge employees to innovate.** For a company to keep growing, its culture must attract and motivate individuals with a passion for identifying and capturing growth opportunities. If a company employs such individuals, it can only tap their full value by empowering them to innovate. Intuit's culture provided employees with psychic rewards in the form of recognition and empowerment to encourage them to innovate. Other companies such as Google and 3M carve out 20% of an employee's time to work on projects that interest them. Such intangible rewards encourage employees to innovate.

- **Remove innovation roadblocks.** Large companies tend to place primary responsibility for new products in the control of a research and development department—which imposes a highly structured process for approving and providing resources to competing product development proposals. These formal organizations and processes tend to slow down decision making and to approve a small number of proposals—many of which have limited potential for commercial success. For large companies to create a culture of innovation, they must eliminate such roadblocks. Cook recognized that Intuit not only erected typical innovation roadblocks—such as blocking access to resources for employees to test out new ideas; but it also had not given employees a systematic way to think about experimenting frugally.

- **Celebrate the learning that comes from failed experiments.** The environment outside large companies—such as customer needs, technology, and competitors—changes and in order for companies to adapt to that change, they must keep learning. Cook approached the challenge of creating a culture of innovation at Intuit with an intense focus on researching models of companies that have done so in the past. His scholarly approach reveals a critical principle for organizations committed to preserving such a culture—they must maintain intellectual humility despite the successful growth that ensues. History has proven repeatedly that overconfidence inevitably leads an organization to ignore external change—the survival of a culture of innovation hinges crucially on a commitment to continue learning. Moreover, too many companies destroy learning and growth by harshly punishing those whose growth experiments fail.

Unsuccessful: IBM Bureaucratic Culture Shrinks Revenues for 17 Consecutive Quarters

Introduction

In 2016, IBM, the 105-year-old computing giant, had fallen from grace—shrinking while its industry was growing. In the 17 quarters ending June 2016, its revenues declined every quarter on an annual basis even as IT spending rose at a 2% to 3% annual rate. Since taking over as CEO in January 2012, Virginia Rometty oversaw a 25% drop in revenues from $106.9 billion in 2011 to $80.3 billion; a 25% profit decline from $15.8 billion in 2011 to $11.9 billion; and by

October 10, 2016, its stock price had fallen 16% from $183.88 to $155 under her leadership.

At the core of its decline was a culture that hampered the effectiveness of IBM's investments in growth. And that inability to grow was quantified by Sanford C. Bernstein analyst Toni Sacconaghi who wrote in a February 2016 research note, "IBM's financials suggest that its strategic imperatives don't appear to be improving its wallet share at customers—rather, since overall revenues are contracting, it suggests that IBM is not even keeping up with its customers' shifting priorities". He highlighted a $16 billion gap between growth from what IBM dubbed "strategic imperatives"—new products and acquisitions targeted at growth businesses that generated $13.8 billion in revenue between 2011 and 2015 and the nearly $30 billion plunge in revenues from IBM's old businesses.

A closer look at these strategic imperatives revealed that IBM was hopelessly behind in one and the other represented an opportunity that was too small to make a difference in IBM's revenue growth. The first was the so-called cloud services market—estimated to account for $60 billion worth of revenue. IBM lagged far behind its rivals with little prospect for catching up due to its inability to grow much faster than its rivals. Synergy Research estimated that in the second quarter of 2015, Amazon's AWS business controlled 29% of the market while growing at 49%; Microsoft's 12% surging at 96%; and IBM a mere 7%—though increasing revenue at a respectable 54%. Meanwhile, IBM was proudly touting its Watson business—a provider of data analysis services—arguing that Watson was "large and growing" part of its $18 billion business analytics business. However, since IBM did not disclose those revenues, investors had no way of knowing how significant Watson was—though Sacconaghi estimated IBM's Watson revenues were below $200 million.

Case Scenario

A fundamental change in its culture contributed to IBM's inability to grow. Under its most famous leader, Thomas Watson, Sr., IBM's culture rested on three values: respect for the individual, the best customer service in the world, and excellence. By 2016, a description of what IBM truly valued, based on its conduct, was approximately the opposite of the values Watson articulated. Before getting into the details of this analysis, it is worth reinforcing the general proposition that we have explored in previous chapters—rapid growth flows to companies that deliver products that provide customers with competitively superior value. Such products are the byproduct of a culture of innovation—along the lines described in the Intuit case—which attracts and motivates the best people in the industry and enables them to bring their most viable ideas to market efficiently.

Respect for the individual?

In 2016, IBM's conduct toward employees did not appear consistent with the value of respecting the individual. For 70 years, IBM never laid off workers. If business changed, workers might be retrained and forced to adapt—possibly moving people across the country or overseas. According to D. Quinn Mills, an emeritus professor at Harvard Business School, Watson "believed people worked better when they were secure, not insecure. Watson "believed people would make a full commitment to the company if they knew they could count on the company to make a full commitment to them."

This began to change in the 1980s, thanks to IBM's ineffective effort to stop personal computers from taking market share from mainframes. By the time former McKinsey partner Lou Gerstner took over as CEO in 1993, IBM was running low on cash and he announced 60,000 layoffs. That marked the beginning of the end of IBM's respect for the individual, which by 2016 featured regular rounds of layoffs, slashing employee benefits, minimal raises, and ongoing efforts to shift work from the United States and Europe to locations such as India that pay lower salaries. As Robert Ochoa, an IBM employee who retired in May 2016, told Marketplace the company is not the same, "It's no longer respect for the individual. It's respect for the stockholders." As IBM's declining revenues, profits, and stock price suggest, it's not that either.

Indeed IBM's lack of respect for the individual was anathema to a growth culture. As a result, IBM was not the prime destination for the most talented young engineers and scientists—they tended to prefer companies like Google and Facebook or took their chances on the most promising start-ups. IBM's culture had repelled extremely talented engineers—a case in point was Shmuel Kliger. Kliger—who earned a PhD in computer science from Israel's Weizmann Institute, was employed at IBM's T.J. Watson Research Center when his IBM boss, Shaula Alexander-Yemini, senior manager for Distributed Systems Software Technology at T.J. Watson, "where she received an IBM Outstanding Innovation Award for Optimistic Recovery for Fault Tolerant Distributed Systems"—and her now ex-husband, Columbia University professor, Yechiam Yemini—persuaded Kliger to bolt with them to start a company.

IBM's culture repelled a pair of superstars. As Kriger explained to me in a July 2013 interview, "I did not have the patience to do all the maneuvering up and down all the layers of IBM's management needed to turn a patent into a new product that IBM would sell." Since Kriger and Yemini were frustrated that their IBM research would never find its way into a product that people would use, they started a company—event automation and real-time network systems management software provider, System Management Arts (SMARTS). In 2005, EMC bought SMARTS for $260 million. According to Kliger, "SMARTS generated $70 million in revenue in 2004, the year before EMC bought it." From there, Kliger became the Resource Management Software Group CTO at EMC—but it did not take. "I had as little power as EMC CTO as I did as a researcher at T.J. Watson," said Kliger.

He left EMC and in 2008, Kliger started VMTurbo—headquartered in Burlington, Massachusetts with R&D in Valhalla, New York (making it easier to recruit talent from IBM and Columbia)—based on Yemini's idea of applying economic theory to IT resources. As Kliger explained, "Yemini had the idea of putting a price on IT resources—those that were not being used much would have a lower price than the ones that were stretched to the limit. VMTurbo is a control system that uses this pricing system to keep IT resources in equilibrium." By 2012, VMTurbo was growing fast. As he said, "In 2012, our revenues and customer counts tripled. We expect both of those to double by the end of 2013. We are winning because we offer companies a rapid payback period on their investment. We charge them between $1,000 and $1,200 per socket and they recover that investment in three to four months."

The best customer service in the world?

Indeed with its loss of respect for individuals like Kriger and Yemini, IBM lost some of its ability to create new businesses that would grow because they created value for customers. But the loss of talent—particularly shifting resources to India—seriously degraded customer service at IBM. Oddly, the American Customer Satisfaction Index stopped measuring IBM's customer satisfaction rating in 2001—after it had declined from 78 in 1995 to 71 in 2001—Apple topped the list in 2016 with a score of 84. Shedding light on IBM's relatively weak score is a story of a customer service manager whose company had been acquired by IBM. This manager stayed at IBM after the acquisition and was working closely with customers to solve their knotty technical support problems. But after IBM shifted that customer service work to India, the customers became extremely frustrated by the resulting decline in service. Customers were so desperate that they contacted him to ask if he could help, but it was no longer his job and he was thinking of retiring from IBM. While it is difficult to draw a definitive conclusion about IBM's customer service from this example, it seems reasonable to me that there is a connection between IBM's shift of staff to lower-cost countries and a decline in the quality of its customer service.

Excellence?

Watson wanted IBM people to be the best in the industry by doing excellent work. One form of excellence that contributes directly to growth is whether a company makes products that outperform rivals in providing benefits to customers.

And on that front, IBM's product development process systematically impeded product development excellence. For example, IBM imposed numerous internal requirements on its product development teams—such as requiring that products were usable by vision-impaired individuals regardless of whether there was strong demand for the feature; that software could run on mainframes—regardless of whether there was a large market of mainframe users for the product; and that the product was available in at least nine languages (again without regard to the market requirement). These executive-imposed mandates could consume as much as half of product development teams' budgets and time. As a result, too many IBM products become available to customers after rival vendors had introduced their products—and those late products offered customers insufficient benefits to compel them to switch from rivals' products to IBM's.

A case in point was IBM's loss of market share in the $2 billion market for so-called identity management services, which keeps unauthorized employees out of different parts of a company's computer systems—in which SailPoint, a $100 million company founded by a former IBM executive, was cleaning Big Blue's clock. As SailPoint CEO Mark McClain, a veteran of IBM's Austin, Texas-based Tivoli, explained in a February 2016 interview, IBM had trouble listening to customers and responding quickly with product improvements that helped customers alleviate the real pain they were feeling. As McClain said, "Big technology companies [including IBM] acquire companies that make point products. [IBM] product managers focus on making the acquired products compatible with other [IBM] products such as database software and middleware. Their product managers don't spend enough time listening to customers and if a customer wants new features, they struggle to get the engineering resources to respond." While IBM did win business because it had strong relationships with top executives and it bundled identity management software with other IBM products at no charge, SailPoint was growing at 30% per year and won in competitive bids against IBM 80% to 90% of the time. "We have 530 customers and a 96% customer approval rating. Potential customers want to see a proof of concept and we welcome the opportunity to shine," said McClain.

These examples indicate that a culture of growth—along the lines of Watson's three values—no longer existed at IBM.

Case Analysis

The most essential element of IBM's values during the Watson, Sr. era was its respect for the individual. That respect was lost in the 1990s and its current absence highlights four principles that leaders should avoid if they want to create an effective growth culture:

- **Focus on quarterly earnings per share targets.** Companies that obsess over achieving quarterly earnings per share targets use cash to repurchase shares and to pay severance to fired employees. The short-term focus makes it difficult to justify investing in employees over the long term—and instead makes them fodder for each quarter's EPS target. Moreover, this quarterly focus creates a powerful incentive to keep pushing outmoded, overly pricy products onto customers in order to keep revenues from declining.

- **Raise compliance with executive mandates above building products that deliver superior value for customers.** Companies that focus too much on complying with the wishes of senior executives run the risk of behaving insensitively to customers. Such lack of market responsiveness is likely to cost the company market share—particularly if rivals exploit this weakness and deliver products that satisfy customer needs much more effectively.

- **Persistently cut staff, reduce benefits, and push jobs to lower-cost countries.** This focus demoralizes employees, repels the most talented people from wanting to join the company, and encourages people to focus their attention internally to keep their jobs. As a result, IBM has had difficulty attracting and motivating people who could develop new products that might contribute meaningfully to its revenue growth.

- **Make cost reduction a more important priority than customer satisfaction.** IBM formerly placed tremendous emphasis on customer satisfaction. However, as we saw in the case scenario, IBM has made a practice of trading off customer service in favor of lowering its salary costs. The resulting customer dissatisfaction hurts IBM's growth potential for two reasons: first, IBM customers will eagerly seek to buy from suppliers that offer better service than IBM; and second, IBM customers will hesitate to recommend IBM to other companies.

Principle Two   Small companies achieve faster growth by hiring and rewarding people who value rapid prototyping, excellent customer service, and disciplined execution.

Small companies are much closer to the edge of perishing than large ones. Often small companies have taken capital from investors who are so eager for revenue growth that they don't mind so much if the company loses money. Burning through cash puts a company on edge—if investors decide that they are no longer interested in investing when the small company is getting close to running out of cash, the company's survival could be at stake.

One of the most important ways to keep a small company growing is to ensure that its people are productive and working toward a common goal. A company's culture can increase the odds that this will happen—and just as significantly, can keep out people who do not fit—and thus distract the rest of the company from what needs to be accomplished.

An effective small company culture must be tailored to its CEO and the skills a company needs to attract and keep customers. To that end, a company ought to follow three principles:

- **Develop the right values.** At the beginning of this chapter, we saw that the right values for a company flow from the CEO's beliefs; will help attract talented people; and will motivate them to design, build, make, deliver, sell, and service products that attract and keep customers.

- **Attract and reward people who fit the culture.** Once a small company articulates its values, it must act on them. And one of the most common ways that small companies use those values is in deciding which people to hire. And once hired, the company should promote and celebrate the ones who act according to its values and manage out of the company those who do not.

- **Spend 20% of the CEO's time on culture.** To preserve a small company growth culture, the CEO ought to spend 20% of her time on culture. This means that as the company grows, the CEO should make sure that all the people in the company understand its values because the CEO tells stories about employees who took actions that embody those values. Moreover, the CEO ought to spend time each week communicating with the company about how it is doing in pursuit of its aims and seek input from employees on how they believe the company ought to improve.

Successful: SimpliVity Execution Culture Propels over 100% Annual Growth

Introduction

Doron Kempel, the CEO of Westborough, Massachusetts-based SimpliVity—a maker of so-called hyperconverged infrastructure (HCI)—created a culture of excellence in execution that enabled it to sustain over 100% annual growth between the time it launched its product in 2013 and the third quarter of 2016. HCI combined as many as a dozen data storage and retrieval functions into a single appliance that used a relatively inexpensive server to run customized software. The industry grew 137.5% to generate about $481 million in revenue in the second quarter of 2016. SimpliVity was founded in 2009 and by October 2016 had over 750 employees worldwide and was doubling its year-over-year revenue with 6,000 systems shipped globally since 2013. SimpliVity had a reseller network of 1,000 partners in 73 countries, enabling the company to generate 50% of its sales outside of the Americas.

Case Scenario

SimpliVity's ability to grow flowed from its culture of execution. As former Kleiner Perkins partner Matt Murphy, who led a September 2012 $25 million investment in SimpliVity, told me, Kempel is "an execution machine." In an October 2012 interview, Kempel told me that as a major in Israel's Defense Force, at 26, he was a decorated, second in command of an elite unit, and led "meticulously planned and scrupulously executed missions far away from Israel and way behind enemy lines." Following degrees from Tel-Aviv University and Harvard Business School, he started and grew a division of EMC "from zero to multi hundred million dollars in annual revenue." After that, he partnered with the "technologically brilliant" Moshe Yanai to start Diligent Technologies. In 2008, Kempel sold Diligent to IBM—which called Diligent "the best run small company IBM has ever acquired."

In setting up SimpliVity's culture, Kempel articulated six principles of effective execution:

- **Match the company's strengths to its mission.** *If a company's mission is to win in a highly competitive market, it must be able to build, sell, and support a technologically superior product and persuade customers and the market of that superiority. If the company's skills are not the ones needed to achieve the mission, the company should either get those skills or pick a mission that it can achieve.*

- **Hire people who buy into a company's norms.** *A company should hire people who are good at those skills and who eagerly follow the company's norms. SimpliVity sought people with self-discipline, who were process driven, results oriented, and imbued with an entrepreneurial spirit.*

- **Let the best ideas win.** *Managers must encourage debates about ideas and let the best, fact-supported thinking win. Kempel made roles and responsibilities clear, but minimized hierarchy, a value he reinforced by occupying a cube, rather than an office. When Kempel gave a presentation to his people, he expected them to share their skepticism and voice their opinions. If not, he encouraged them to do that afterward during a Post Activity Review (PAR). His goal was to reinforce risk taking and to depersonalize failure—using it as an opportunity to learn and improve.*

- **Motivate the right operating style.** *Kempel used a quarterly Alignment By Objective (ABO) process to reinforce behavioral norms that could account for 10 percent to 15 percent of a person's bonus. For example, a manager might have an ABO related to communication. Kempel gave the example of a* team member who wanted to learn how to disagree with her manager. He influenced her and her manager to assume ABO quarterly goals—for his part, "the manager would encourage her and she would express at least three unpopular views per quarter." The lesson here was that a company would get more out of its people if it respected their views.

- **Make action item tracking the company's life blood.** Kempel believed that SimpliVity should keep track of the tasks people had agreed to complete to achieve the company's mission—what he called "action item accountability." An action item was a team member's specific, measurable, time-stamped goal that she agreed on with her manager. SimpliVity trained managers how to define and track them. After all "if action items are not recorded, tracked and measured, our whole spirit of execution will be undermined," explained Kempel. He and his managers used an "action item log" to keep track of whether the goal was achieved, on time and as specified—and what the company "learned from deviations." A company without such an obsessive focus on tracking the achievement of goals was likely to slip behind those that did in Kempel's view.

- **Lead by example.** Despite all the processes, nothing was more compelling than the power of leaders to influence others through their actions. "In 35 years of leadership and management—in sports, military and business—I have seen no substitute for leadership by example. If the managers and leaders do not live, breathe and exemplify the norms, then the execution system will fail," Kempel said.

Two customers offer anecdotal evidence that SimpliVity's culture contributed to its growth.

As Kempel explained in an October 2016 interview, "We have a global 50 customer [a financial services firm] that consolidated six global data-centers down to just three; and displaced all legacy storage products with our HCI product. This company anticipates that our product will enable it to cut capital and operating expenditures by $100 million over five years and reduce its floor space by a factor of 10."

Another customer, The Container Store, sounded quite satisfied with SimpliVity. Its Platforms director Jay Whering said, "We evaluated a number of vendors—both hyperconverged and legacy. What we found with SimpliVity, and why we chose it over Nutanix, was that SimpliVity offered a far more complete solution—not just storage, but all data services, including built-in data protection, WAN optimization, and more. This was something no other company was offering, and is still unique to SimpliVity to this day. We are incredibly happy with our decision to go with SimpliVity and have felt the benefits of the solution throughout our entire business."

Indeed Kempel argued that this breadth of functionality is helping it win bids from rivals. "When we bid against competitors including Nutanix and EMC, we win 80% of the time because we offer customers more—not just storage, but enterprise-grade backup and native deduplication. Our faster growth springs from several factors: our value-added resellers (VARs) are engaged; we are doing more large deals; we have more repeat business in large enterprises and we are unique in just selling software—offering it on x86 servers from Cisco, Lenovo and Dell. In 2017, we expect that over 80% of our revenues will come from software. Though our per-customer revenues may be lower than they would be had we also sold low-margin hardware, we enjoy very high software gross margins," he said.

In January 2017, SimpliVity's culture of execution met with a mixed end when Hewlett Packard Enterprise announced plans to but the company for $650 million in cash. While this was more than the estimated $200 million IBM paid for his previous startup, it fell short of Kempel's goal of an IPO and the $3.9 billion that HPE was rumored to be planning to pay in November 2016.[1]

Case Analysis

SimpliVity offers insights into how a small company can create a growth culture. While it would be difficult for most CEOs to achieve SimpliVity's results, the success of its culture suggests four general principles for small-company CEOs seeking to growth through culture:

- **Develop the right values.** As we have already discussed, developing the right values is essential. In SimpliVity's case, it is clear that its CEO was quite accustomed to setting very ambitious goals and building and leading teams that could achieve them. When SimpliVity got started, the goal was to deliver a product that would save companies significant amounts of money and inefficiency in managing their data.

- **Hire people who fit with the values.** SimpliVity used its values to hire people that it believed would be eager to act according to its values. It is difficult to make sure that all employees will fit with the values before they are on-board. However, conducting early interviews that test whether potential hires will be able to act according to the company's values is a good place to start. If people who do not fit are told early in the process, a company can at least be more efficient in its pursuit of the right people.

---

[1]Chris Mellor, "What's SimpliVity CEO Doron Kempel and Arnie got in common? They'll both be back," The Register, January 20, 2017, http://www.theregister. co.uk/2017/01/20/doron_kempel_will_be_back/

- **Set goals that drive people to attract and retain customers.** Between hiring people and setting goals for them, there is much work that leaders must do. Specifically, CEOs ought to choose a business strategy, identify key skills the company needs, and decide who within each skill area should be responsible for which goals.

- **Monitor achievement of the goals.** An effective growth culture is good at using processes to keep track of what people promised to do in pursuit of those goals along with whether they actually delivered results. SimpliVity seems to have done this better than most companies—and they ought to learn from its approach.

Unsuccessful: Growth-at-Any-Cost Culture Collapses Zenefits

Introduction

In Chapter 1, we saw an example of a large pharmaceutical company Valeant that achieved very rapid growth boosting revenue, stock price, and executive compensation by acquiring well-established drugs with limited competition and raising prices dramatically. Along the way, it came to light that Valeant had a tainted relationship with a distributor that—when combined with accounting irregularities—threw into question its financial results and resulted in forcing out Michael Pearson, the CEO behind Valeant's undisciplined growth.

Small companies are equally capable of pursuing a culture of undisciplined growth. Zenefits is a San Francisco-based software company that provides small businesses with an app that replaces a company's benefits department. In exchange for software, Zenefits gets a commission on health insurance that its clients purchase via its software. Ben Horowitz, cofounder of Andreessen Horowitz, which, with another venture capital firm, Institutional Venture Partners, invested $66.5 million in Zenefits valuing the company at $500 million in the summer of 2014 said, "It's the ultimate entrepreneur tool. How do you deal with anything that is very complicated that you need to learn about to be in business? Are you really going to go learn about the Affordable Care Act? Probably not. Once you have Zenefits, that's it. You're compliant." One customer—Justin Winter, cofounder of Diamond Candles, an online store based in Durham, North Carolina—explained Zenefits's appeal. "The traditional brokers came here and we had a face-to-face meeting, and they were knowledgeable and very nice. But we're getting so many extra bonuses with Zenefits for the exact same price, we had to choose them," said Winter.

Case Scenario

In 2014, Zenefits was thought to be one of the fastest growing companies in Silicon Valley and it had raised $500 million in capital at a valuation of $4 billion. But by 2016, its CEO Parker Conrad had been fired after it was discovered that he had written software that enabled Zenefits employees to cheat on their health insurance brokerage licensing exam. Conrad—who was forced to take a leave of absence from Harvard College because he neglected his studies in favor of editing the Harvard Crimson—had subsequently been fired from SigFig, a portfolio management start-up he cofounded.

When he started Zenefits in 2013, he was terrified of failing again so he built the company around an obsession with meeting very aggressive growth goals—putting employee satisfaction and regulatory compliance far down on its list of values. Its revenue and employee counts grew dramatically. Between 2013 and 2016, Zenefits' headcount soared from 15 to 1,600. From $1 million by the end of 2013, the company's revenue hit $20 million by late 2014, and was projected to reach $100 million by late 2015—but it fell short by $30 million. Employees were jammed into office space with limited training and heavy drinking—beer kegs in its Scottsdale, Arizona, offices flowed during the workday—was coupled with an obsession with meeting sales goals.

Operational problems abounded. Zenefits was bringing in new customers far more quickly than it could enter them into its computer system, thus making customers frustrated As Conrad said, "It was a 5-pound-bag, 10-pounds-of-poop problem. Every day, we were able to load six to eight companies, but we were signing up 16 to 18. [There was a backlog of more than a month and a half.] It was a company-ending thing." Employees received low salaries coupled with promises of raises when funding came through—Zenefits raised $500 million at a $4 billion valuation in 2015—but people never received the promised raises.

Conrad was ultimately tossed out by Zenefits's board, replaced by chief operating officer David Sacks, in February 2016 when insurance regulators in California and Washington State discovered software that Conrad created to let Zenefits's employees cheat on the state's insurance broker license course. Sacks tried to change Zenefits's culture from "Ready, Fire, Aim" to "Operate with Integrity." Sacks tried to counter Zenefits's perception problem with a culture of "radical candor," he dubbed "Admit, fix, settle and repeat." He fired several executives who embodied Zenefits's fast-growth-at-any-cost culture and agreed with investors to slash the company's valuation in half to $2 billion. By October 2016, it was unclear whether Zenefits would survive or rivals with better growth cultures would usurp its customers.

Case Analysis

The Zenefits case highlights three principles that small companies seeking growth through culture should avoid:

- **Use company to heal CEO's psychological wounds.** As we explored earlier in this chapter, a small company's founder is an important source of its values. If a CEO has suffered psychological wounds from previous experience, there is a danger that he will use his latest start-up to heal them. And it appears as though Conrad's fear of failing—as he saw himself having done at Harvard and SigFig—instilled a deep fear of failure that motivated him to create a culture that valued rapid growth above all other considerations. As with many previous companies, such as Enron or Valeant, that culture yielded trouble.

- **Base culture on what CEO thinks investors want.** Investors are an important stakeholder of a small company—but a CEO who places their interest far above those of customers and employees is likely to endanger the company's long-term survival. CEOs must recognize their responsibility to push back against investor appetite for growth. Since Conrad was so eager to enrich his investors and himself—and perhaps to redeem himself in his own eyes—he decided to create a culture that would push the interests of only one stakeholder.

- **Ignore the needs of employees, regulators, and customers.** Such a culture led Conrad to hire people aggressively and urge them desperately to bring in new customers. Important management imperatives such as paying people competitive salaries, satisfying regulatory requirements, and upgrading operations to sustain high levels of customer satisfaction and boost customers' willingness to refer the company to others were all neglected. Conrad mistakenly assumed that rapid revenue growth would wash away all these problems. History shows that these problems eventually surface and severely threaten the company's survival.

Applying the Principles of Growth through Culture

Leaders seeking to grow through culture should ponder these five questions:

- Should I spend 20% of my time on our company's culture?

- Do our values reflect what I believe, what should be important to our people, and what will encourage them to deliver the industry's best products and customer service?

- Do we use our values to hire, promote, and manage people out of the company?

- As our company grows, do all our employees understand and act in ways consistent with our culture?

- If I am contributing to a culture that impedes growth, how can I find a leader who will overcome those impediments?

Chapter 8: Growth Road Maps provides a detailed methodology for applying the principles of growth through culture.

Summary

Growth through culture flows from an organization that has the right values and uses those values to hire the best people and motivate them to achieve ambitious goals in a sustainable manner. Since culture is largely a reflection of the CEO's personality, a company's board must assess carefully whether a new CEO will be more likely to create a culture based on values in which the CEO believes passionately that appeal to highly talented employees and that will encourage those employees to make decisions that result in industry-leading products and outstanding customer service. Such a culture can contribute to a company's rapid growth over the long term only if the CEO keeps evaluating its effectiveness and fixes its flaws as customer needs, technology, and the company's rivals change.

In the next chapter, we introduce the concept of growth trajectories—how companies chain together various combinations of the five dimensions of growth over time. In so doing, we examine growth insights drawn from a large database of public companies. We then examine growth trajectories of successful and unsuccessful companies—synthesizing general principles that leaders can use to guide their development of effective growth trajectories.

Constructing Growth Trajectories

Growth Trajectories

To sustain a company's growth over time, leaders must chain together growth trajectories from the five dimensions we examined in Chapters 2 through 6. The most growth trajectories tap revenue from a dimension in which the company currently participates and invests in new ones from which it will grow in the future. For example, consider the following five-vector growth trajectory:

- **Customer segment.** A company starts by selling its initial product to a specific group of customers—and seeks to gain as large a share of that customer group's growth as it can before its demand begins to become saturated.

- **New geography.** The next link in this company's growth trajectory may be to target the same customer group in new geographies by forging distribution partnerships in those locations or building local sales and marketing forces.

- **New products.** This company's third link might be to identify unmet needs among its current customers and develop or acquire new products that it can sell to those customers.

- **New capabilities.** Next the company might develop new capabilities or modify current ones in order to capture new growth opportunities created by changing technologies.

© Peter S. Cohan 2017
P. S. Cohan, *Disciplined Growth Strategies*, DOI 10.1007/978-1-4842-2448-9_7

- **New culture.** While a change in culture may be difficult to trace directly to changes in a company's growth rate, each time a company changes its CEO, its culture is likely to change. And if the new culture follows the principles outlined in Chapter 6, it is likely to accelerate growth.

Principles of Effective Growth Trajectories

While different growth trajectories have proven effective for large and small companies, the general approach of refining a company's business strategy within a focused customer group and subsequently expanding it to more geographies is quite common. In Chapter 7, we compare two large company case studies—Alexion Pharmaceuticals and Yahoo—to illustrate the difference between the fastest growing 5% of Forbes 2000 companies and the 5% most rapidly declining ones. We also compare a small company that grew quickly and ultimately went public in 2016 and contrast that with another small company that reached $100 million in revenue as a private company before imploding short of an IPO and ultimately being sold to a rival for an undisclosed price.

CEOs that choose effective growth trajectories— whether of large or small companies—are generally skilled at product development and excel at adding new capabilities—such as marketing and manufacturing—that the company requires in order to turn its initial product success into substantial revenue growth.

Large and small companies do differ importantly in their approach to building growth trajectories. The major difference is that small company CEOs are often intensely focused on achieving rapid growth as they reach for the $100 million revenue benchmark often considered the minimum revenue level required to go public. While some CEOs who preside over growth from founding to IPO stay with the company—Jeff Bezos at Amazon is a prominent example—a large number of such founders take their winnings and do other things. Therefore, the growth trajectories they choose generally involve focusing on a specific customer group—ideally one representing a market opportunity of at least $1 billion—with a product that those customers are eager to buy and then expanding globally to find more such customers in new geographies. As we will see in this chapter, data storage appliance maker Nutanix boosted customers' productivity and helped them adapt to changing business needs while app marketer Fiksu saved app developers money but was too easy for rivals to surpass and for a key partner to stifle.

Large companies must appoint CEOs who can identify new growth curves and invest in new products or acquisitions that can take a significant share of that new growth while creating a culture that encourages employees to identify and capture growth opportunities that they observe through their work with customers. While new products are generally the best avenue for new growth, large companies ought to consider acquisitions if they are analyzed using four tests for successful acquisitions. Moreover, even if these acquisitions succeed in adding sufficient profit to more than offset their purchase price, large companies must also foster a culture that stimulates employee creativity and initiative—leading to organic revenue growth. As we will see in this chapter, Alexion Pharmaceuticals did these things well whereas Yahoo made many acquisitions that failed and created a culture that stifled innovation.

Let's examine pairs of case studies of successful and unsuccessful applications of two principles of building effective growth trajectories:

- **Large companies building effective growth trajectories** expand from start-up to large growing public company by chaining together growth vectors in a way that sustains industry-leading growth.

- **Small companies building effective growth trajectories** expand initial product success within a customer group to new geographies.

Principle One   Large companies expand from start-up to large growing public company by chaining together growth vectors in a way that sustains industry-leading growth.

Case Studies

The case studies in this book reveal a basic truth—a company's ability to sustain industry-leading growth depends heavily on its CEO. If a CEO leads a company to superior growth over a period of decades, a new CEO is hardly guaranteed to sustain that growth. What's more, despite its best efforts, it is difficult for a company's board to be fully confident that its pick for a new CEO will be able to sustain the company's growth. Even if a board is fortunate enough to have overseen the performance of a successful CEO, the skills that this CEO exercised to sustain rapid growth in the past may be very different from the skills needed to keep that company growing rapidly in future decades by that CEO's successor.

Despite all these difficulties, a company's long-term success depends on making the right CEO choice—which means that a board needs guidance. To sustain the company's industry-leading growth, a board should seek a CEO who can do the following:

- **Match a value-creating product to a specific customer group's unmet need.** In order to get off the ground, a company must pick a group of customers whose needs are not being met by incumbent vendors and build a product that satisfies their needs so well that customers are eager to buy it. Often founders start a company with a specific technical expertise—however they are unsure of how to match that knowledge to a significant unmet need. Boards should focus on CEO candidates who demonstrate a willingness to experiment frugally with different possible product/market matches to discover one or two that work before the company runs out of money.

- **Sell that product to new geographies and/or to new customer groups.** Should a CEO satisfy that first test, the next challenge is to sustain that product's sales by seeking out new customers residing in new geographies and/or belonging to new customer groups that are similarly eager to buy the company's product. Boards should appoint a CEO with previous experience exploiting these twin growth vectors to achieve a rapid increase in revenue growth.

- **Adapt the company's capabilities to satisfy customers' current and future needs.** At the same time that the CEO is seeking new customers, she must make sure that the company can satisfy their needs. To that end, the CEO must build out the company's sales and marketing capabilities, expand its production and distribution resources, build its regulatory staff to make sure the company can operate in new geographies, and bolster its service organization to assure that new customers remain satisfied with the company and are willing to buy more in the future. Boards should seek CEOs who can manage this process effectively to keep the company's growth from stalling due to poor execution.

- **As older products mature, invent and/or acquire new products to sustain the company's growth.** As we pointed out in Chapter 1, new products start off growing slowly, accelerate steeply, mature, and ultimately decline. A company can only sustain industry-leading growth if it can sell new products—possibly obtained through a combination of internal development and acquisition—to take up the slack from the older ones that are declining. Of all the CEO skills needed to sustain a company's industry-leading growth, this is perhaps the most difficult. Excessive dependence on acquisitions often creates the perception of success at the beginning—followed by silent disappointment and a loss of industry-leading growth.

Success: Alexion Pharmaceuticals Grows at 44% Annual Rate from Molecule to $4 Billion along Four Growth Vectors

Introduction

Alexion Pharmaceuticals makes drugs that cure rare, life-threatening diseases—charging mind-bogglingly high prices for them. Yet despite the tiny number of people who buy its products and its high prices, Alexion has grown rapidly—at a 44% annual rate—between 1996 when it first started to generate revenues by providing contract research services and 2015. Over that 19-year stretch, Alexion's growth trajectory chained together four key dimensions of growth:

- **Customer group.** For its first decade, from 1996 to 2006, Alexion sold to drug researchers while it was advancing its first product through the process of regulatory review. Once it launched its first product, Alexion focused on two customer groups—the roughly 8,000 sufferers of atypical hemolytic uremic syndrome (aHUS) a fatal disease that destroys a person's hemoglobin every day and the estimated 10,000 to 20,000 people afflicted with paroxysmal nocturnal hemoglobinuria (PNH), a disease that leads to disabling anemia, does not go away, and kills a third of patients within five years.

- **Product.** Alexion changed its product focus significantly between 1996 and 2016. Between 1996 and 2006, it provided contract research services to provide the company with cash flow until it could sell its first product—Soliris. Beginning in 2008, Alexion began acquiring companies that it believed had the potential to add to its marketable product line; and by 2015 it had added two new products—Strensiq and Kanuma.

- **Capabilities**. Alexion matched its capabilities to the requirements of competing in its different markets. Once it launched its first product in 2007, Alexion added to its staff of drug researchers—building a drug manufacturing facility in Rhode Island and enhancing its sales and marketing departments to sell its products globally.

- **Geography**. Alexion provided contract research services in the United States and once it began selling Soliris in 2007, the company marketed globally—generating sales both in the United States and in Europe—which between 2008 and 2015 was Alexion's largest geographic market. In 2011, Alexion began selling in Asia/Pacific while it generated some additional revenue elsewhere—reaching 50 countries by 2015.

Case Scenario

Alexion was founded in 1992 by a Yale Medical School professor and a friend. The company nearly ran out of money before its CEO decided as a last ditch effort to try to focus Alexion on a disease with a tiny number of sufferers. The professor in question was Leonard Bell—an attending physician at Yale-New Haven Hospital and an Assistant Professor in the Department of Internal Medicine at the Yale University School of Medicine who became Assistant Professor of Medicine and Pathology and Co-Director of the program in Vascular Biology at Yale Medical School before leaving in February 1992 to found and run Alexion.

Alexion was founded at a supermarket ice cream freezer and nearly ran out of money before Bell decided to stop resisting his scientists' suggestion that he bet its remaining resources on curing a disease that affected fewer than 10,000 patients worldwide. Bell—who then had three children under the age of seven—was buying sweets at a supermarket when he bumped into a friend named Steve Squinto, a researcher at biotech Regeneron. Bell—whose father had built homes in New York— told Squinto he wanted to start a company. By the end of the shopping trip, he had recruited Squinto to join him as its head of R&D.

Bell knew the area of microbiology on which he wanted Alexion to focus but it took six years before the company turned that scientific interest into a revenue-generating product. The science that interested Bell was a series of enzymes that destroy foreign substances in the body—called complement—and their corresponding complement blockers that keep this destruction under control. Bell and Squinto thought complement blockers might be turned into drugs to fight inflammation from arthritis to kidney problems. By 1995, Alexion discovered that complement blockers would not make good drugs because they only worked when attached to cell surfaces. Alexion was saved from oblivion by U.S. Surgical, which gave the company $5 million to make pig organs that could be inserted into people without being destroyed by complement thanks to a fragment of a complement-blocking monoclonal antibody that Alexion would provide—aping the then-popular approach of Centocor, which had developed a successful treatment for post-heart-attack inflammation. On the strength of Centocor's success, Alexion was able to raise $21 million in a 1996 IPO.

Sadly for Alexion investors, that monoclonal antibody fragment did not work against the most widespread diseases—sending the company careening toward another cash crisis. After evaluating 10,000 possibilities, Squinto's R&D team found a monoclonal antibody that became Soliris. However, Soliris—which went into production in 1997—did not work as a cure for rheumatoid arthritis and kidney disease or post-heart-attack inflammation. Bell ultimately decided that Alexion should focus on PNH—a tiny market with no competition—designating Alexion scientist Russell Rother to work with Peter Hillmen—a UK-based global expert on PNH. Since complement kills the red blood cells of PNH patients within two days—those cells live for four months in healthy people—the two scientists thought Soliris would work on PNH. While Bell thought the PNH market was too small, Cambridge, Massachusetts-based Genzyme was able to generate $500 million in sales with its product to treat Gaucher, another rare disease. After a successful 2012 trial of Soliris on 11 patients, Bell worked with the FDA to design two trials of Soliris—the second one on 97 PNH patients helped everyone who got the drug. The drug was approved by the FDA in March 2007 and by 2016 sold for $440,000 a year per patient—a price usually paid for by insurance companies.

Once Alexion received approval to sell Soliris in the U.S. PNH market, its sales accelerated dramatically and its growth trajectory spanned three dimensions—geography, customer group, and capabilities. Between 1996 and 2006, its sales fluctuated from about $2 million to as high as $11 million in 2001 before drifting back under $2 million. But in 2007, its sales soared to $72 million and hit about $541 million by 2010 as it began to expand along two growth vectors—geography (in June 2007, the EC approved Soliris for PNH in Europe)—and customer group (in April 2009 the FDA approved Soliris for sale to U.S. aHUS patients and the EC granted the same approval for European aHUS patients in August 2009).

To satisfy the demand for its products, Alexion expanded its capabilities in manufacturing and marketing. In July 2006, it acquired a manufacturing plant in Smithfield, Rhode Island; and in December 2009, the EC approved that facility for production of Soliris. By 2013, Alexion had established an organization to support sales of Soliris in the United States, in the major markets in European Union, Japan, Asia Pacific countries, and other territories. In the United States, Alexion's customers were primarily specialty distributors and specialty pharmacies that supplied physician office clinics, hospital outpatient clinics, infusion clinics, or home health care providers. Alexion also sold Soliris to government agencies. Outside the United States, its customers were primarily hospitals, hospital buying groups, pharmacies, other health care providers, and distributors.

Alexion realized that its potential for growth in these products was limited so it began to make acquisitions focused on rare diseases. As Bell said, "We focus on patients with absolutely devastating disorders that are also either lethal or life-threatening. They're also very, very rare, so they get no attention from anybody. They're left with *no hope, and we only go forward not with treatments that will make it a little bit better but with treatments that will transform their lives. At the end of the day, everyone accepts that is high-level innovation."* To that end, Alexion acquired products focused on such rare disease markets between 2011 and 2015 as its sales grew from $783 million to over $2.6 billion, including the following:

- **Taligen.** In January 2011, Alexion acquired this privately held development stage biotechnology company based in Cambridge, Massachusetts, whose portfolio included novel antibody and protein regulators of the complement inflammatory pathways.

- **Orphatec.** In February 2011, Alexion acquired patents and assets from this company related to an investigational therapy for patients with an ultra-rare genetic disorder characterized by severe brain damage and rapid death in newborns—MoCD Type A.

- **Enobia.** In February 2012, Alexion acquired this privately held clinical-stage biotechnology company that was developing asfotase alfa, a human recombinant targeted alkaline phosphatase enzyme-replacement therapy for patients suffering with an ultra-rare, life-threatening, genetic metabolic disease—hypophosphatasia (HPP).

In 2015, Alexion also added to its product portfolio when the FDA approved two of its drugs:

- **Strensiq.** In 2015, the FDA approved Strensiq for patients with perinatal-, infantile-, and juvenile-onset HPP; the EC granted marketing authorization for Strensiq for the treatment of patients with pediatric-onset HPP; and Japan's Ministry of Health, Labor and Welfare approved Strensiq for the treatment of patients with HPP.

- **Kanuma.** In 2015, the FDA approved Kanuma for the treatment of patients of all ages with Lysosomal acid lipase deficiency (LALD)—a disease that causes children and adults to accumulate certain fats in the liver and spleen—and EC granted marketing authorization of Kanuma for long-term enzyme-replacement therapy in patients of all ages with LAL-D.

Bell retired as CEO in April 2015, leaving David Hallal in charge. Hallal had been Alexion's CEO from September 2014 to April 2015 and in senior commercial positions, including senior vice president, U.S. Commercial Operations from June 2006 until November 2008; senior vice president, Commercial Operations Americas from November 2008 to May 2010; senior vice president, Global Commercial Operations from May 2010 until October 2012; and then executive vice president and chief commercial officer from October 2012 to September 2014.

By the third quarter of 2016, Hallal seemed to have been doing well sustaining Alexion's growth after Bell's retirement. For the nine months ending September 2016, Alexion's sales had increased 21% to $2.3 billion while its net income for the period increased 294% to $307 million. Ninety-one percent of Alexion's revenues came from Soliris in the first nine months of 2016, about 6% came from Strensiq, and the remaining 3% from Kanuma. Sadly for Alexion, Hallal could not hold into his job as CEO. Due to accounting problems, in December 2016 Hallal was out as CEO as was CFO Vikas Sinha because "senior management pressured staff to get customers to order [Soliris] earlier than needed to meet financial targets." Would Alexion's board appoint a new CEO who could restore its rapid growth?[1]

Case Analysis

Bell followed the four principles for constructing an effective large company growth trajectory:

- **Match a value-creating product to specific customer group's unmet need.** Alexion's decision to focus its technology on orphan diseases was an excellent example of finding an unmet need and delivering a uniquely effective solution—thus yielding a very high willingness to pay, which spurred its initial growth spurt.

- **Sell that product to new geographies and/or to new customer groups.** Alexion sold Soliris globally and was able to provide it to patients with different diseases in order to sustain its initial growth.

- **Adapt the company's capabilities to satisfy customers' current and future needs.** Alexion expanded its manufacturing and marketing presence globally to support the growing global demand for its products.

- **As older products mature, invent and/or acquire new products to sustain the company's growth.** Alexion acquired technologies targeted at orphan diseases and developed its own new products. By the time Bell retired, his successor was beginning to generate revenues from the new products in an effort to keep Alexion growing.

---

[1]Jonathan Rockoff, "Alexion Says Senior Management Improperly Pressured Staff to Boost Sales," Wall Street Journal, January 4, 2017, http://www.wsj.com/articles/alexion-says-senior-management-improperly-pressured-staff-to-boost-sales-1483582564

Unsuccessful: Yahoo Grows Then Shrinks—Selling Out to Verizon for $4.8 Billion

Introduction

As the Alexion case demonstrates, to sustain rapid growth a large company's board must choose a CEO with the right mindset. And it stands to reason that a board that installs the wrong CEOs could find itself overseeing misguided investments that squander corporate resources without generating industry-leading growth. With the possible exception of Tim Koogle, the former Motorola executive who ran Yahoo from 1995 to 2001—leading its 1996 IPO at $13 a share followed by a huge stock price run-up before the dot-com crash, Yahoo's CEOs did not craft effective growth trajectories.

Yahoo's early CEOs built effective growth trajectories—but later ones fell short. Things started off well—during Koogle's tenure, Yahoo revenue soared from $2 million to $1.1 billion and its stock spiked over 1,300% until January 2000 when it began a 38% plunge from its IPO price in March 2001 when he left. Following Koogle, Terry Semel, a former Warner Brothers executive took over—overseeing a nice run-up in revenue from about $717 million to nearly $7 billion—acquired a big stake in Alibaba before it went public and declined a chance to invest in Google. From there, a string of executives presided over a steady revenue decline from $7.2 billion in 2008 to about $4.9 billion in 2015 after interference from activist investors. In 2016, Verizon agreed to pay about $4.8 billion for Yahoo's web assets—over $40 billion less than Microsoft offered in 2008.

Yahoo peaked out in the first Internet wave but hung on long after it had ceded leadership to Google and others. As the Web went mainstream in the 2000s, Yahoo could not keep up. Google used its algorithm-based web-query approach paired with keyword search advertising to take the lead. In 2005, Google's revenue surpassed Yahoo's. But Yahoo survived another decade. According to Paul Saffo, who teaches forecasting at Stanford, "It lasted a whole hell of a lot longer than I thought it would. It made some right moves, but it could never get ahead of the curve."

Case Scenario

Yahoo's less than stellar growth trajectory can be traced to the history of its leadership that was too often ineffective at foreseeing the evolution of its industry and crafting a vision that would enable Yahoo to capture the growth from these evolving trends. Instead, its CEOs made a string of acquisitions and investments—most of which did not pay off—even as it bungled what turned out to be the best investment opportunities. After its cofounders, Yahoo lacked top leadership with the ability to develop new services that consumers and advertisers found compelling—so its CEOs acquired other companies hoping that they would close the growth gap.

Yahoo was founded by graduate students at the Stanford School of Engineering. In 1994, Jerry Yang, a Taiwanese math genius; and David Filo, a programmer from Louisiana, created a directory of links called Jerry and David's Guide to the World Wide Web—web surfers embraced their map to what at the time was a difficult-to-navigate digital landscape. In 1995, Sequoia Capital invested in Yahoo and put Koogle—who presided over 16 acquisitions in the first five years of his tenure—in the CEO slot. Filo stayed on as technical leader—writing the first version of Yahoo's search engine while Yang was involved in strategic decision such as replacing Koogle with Semel.

Semel was a media executive who brought other media executives to Yahoo—thus creating the enduring identity struggle within Yahoo—was it a media or technology company? Semel lacked the strategic skill to see where market opportunity would reside and how to capture it. While Google was inventing a text advertising business that augmented web search results, Yahoo's persisted with its increasingly annoying banner ads. Semel passed on acquiring Google in 2002 and could have acquired Facebook in 2006 if he had not lowered his offer from $1 billion to $850 million after a disappointing earnings report.

Yang took over as CEO from Semel in 2007 and turned down what in retrospect was Yahoo's best exit offer—a $45 billion bid in 2008 from Microsoft that then-CEO Steve Ballmer believed would help it compete with Google. After Yang came a string of hapless CEOs—ex-Autodesk CEO, Carol Bartz and former president of PayPal; and Scott Thompson—who was fired after four months for faking a degree on his resume. Finally Marissa Mayer—hailed as someone who could reinvent Yahoo's services—took over in 2012—spending $2.8 billion on 53 acquisitions, including social-blogging platform Tumblr ($1.1 billion that was expected to contribute a mere $25 million in 2016 operating income on $80 million in revenue) and video-ad-tech company Brightroll ($650 million). Yahoo also invested in original-video programming like the Community series, which it wrote off in 2015. Once merged with Yahoo, these services did not become popular enough to stop Yahoo's revenue slide.

Mayer believed strongly that she should be the ultimate arbiter of Yahoo's product— thus stifling the creativity of her staff. A former Yahoo senior manager said, "Marissa is one of those people who's always certain she's right. She would undermine us, change her mind, or make everything go through her at the end of the day. It was a nightmare." Another employee said, "There's a uniform, recurring theme of bureaucracy in too many layers. Nobody was ever fully empowered." And in an interview with Charlie Rose, she refused to admit failure—a trait that inhibited Yahoo's ability to learn. As she told Rose when asked about Yahoo's mergers, "I actually think they did work. I think that it really was a matter of; we needed to rebuild some of the talent base. Obviously, we have fallen slightly behind where we hoped to be in terms of our plans, but I'm still very optimistic about Tumblr."

Ultimately she acceded to the demands of activist investors and sold off various pieces—leaving the rest for Verizon—although by January 2017 it was unclear whether a massive data breach at Yahoo might unwind the deal. In July 2016, Verizon Communications agreed to buy Yahoo! Inc.'s web assets—that attracted a billion monthly users to its mail, news and sports content and financial tools—for

$4.83 billion—leaving Yahoo with its stakes in Alibaba Group Holding Ltd. and Yahoo Japan Corp.—then worth about $40 billion in combined market value.

Case Analysis

The Yahoo case study illustrates three principles that large company boards should avoid when mapping a growth trajectory:

- **Install CEOs without product vision.** With the exception of Marissa Mayer, Yahoo's board consistently installed CEOs whose background was outside the Web search and advertising industry. As a result, each of the CEOs was unable to envision the direction of technology, competitor strategies, and evolving customer needs to create a new vision for Yahoo's service that would keep it ahead of rivals. While Yahoo's board hoped that her Google experience would ignite product innovation, she did not meet expectations.

- **Acquire companies that fail the four tests of a successful acquisition.** Yahoo made many acquisitions over its 21-year history. However, those deals did not add enough revenue or profit to offset their purchase price. To be sure, the stock market value of Yahoo's Alibaba and Yahoo! Japan stakes show that some of its deals were successful. This suggests that the strategic rationale for most of the deals was fairly flimsy—it appears that Yahoo's CEOs did not apply the four tests of a successful acquisition that we discussed in Chapter 4.

- **Create a culture that stifles employee creativity and initiative.** Yahoo suffered from cultural problems. For example, the 2006 Peanut Butter Manifesto highlighted the way Yahoo under Semel spread resources evenly across all its product lines without regard to their different levels of profit potential. As a result, employees concluded that management did not care about winning—rewarding unproductive employees for their long tenure and scrimping on pay for excellent performance. And when Mayer became CEO in 2012, her insistence on controlling all product decisions demoralized staff and repelled talent.

Principle Two Small companies grow from start-up to public company by expanding initial product success within a customer group to new geographies.

To achieve a successful exit for investors, a small company's growth trajectory depends heavily on finding a group of customers willing to buy its product—followed by an urgent effort to expand into new geographies in which the product will find significant demand. More specifically, a common benchmark for a small company seeking an initial public offering is to achieve $100 million in revenues and annual growth exceeding 30%. To build a growth trajectory to reach those targets a small company should follow four principles:

- **Appoint a CEO with product vision and execution skills.** A start-up's odds of achieving success grow significantly if its CEO has the right skills. As we have seen in many cases in this book, among the most important of these skills are the abilities to envision a product that customers will want to buy and to build a team that turns that vision efficiently into a tangible product.

- **Find a large market opportunity with significant customer pain.** To turn such a product into a business, the CEO must codevelop it with customers who have a significant unmet need that other vendors are not satisfying. As we saw in the Alexion case, in rare cases a small number of potential customers can turn into a large market if the price for the product is sufficiently high. However, Alexion is the exception that proves a more common rule—CEOs should seek to develop products that will solve a large unmet need shared by a large numbers of potential customers. Often CEOs become aware of these opportunities because they formerly worked for large companies that are creating them by providing customers with over-priced, inflexible products that contribute heavily to the large company's growth and profitability.

- **Build a product that delivers an irresistible jump in value to customers.** Start-ups generally do not survive very long because most of them run out of cash before they start to generate enough revenue to be acquired or go public. Sometimes, start-ups get large quickly but competitors witness that success and introduce a better product that takes away the start-up's customers. This makes potential customers reluctant to buy a start-up's product because the company may go out of business and not be able to support the product. To overcome such hesitancy, a start-up must offer customers an irresistible jump in value (what I call a Quantum Value Leap (QVL))—the ratio between the product's benefits and its price—relative to competing products.

- **Expand quickly into new geographies with strong demand for that product.** If a company enjoys rapid growth selling its product to a specific customer group in its home geography, it should expand into new geographies with similar customer groups that are similarly eager to buy that product. Although the start-up should understand the CAGE differences between its home country and the new geography, this geographic expansion strategy may enable the company to grow quickly without making significant changes to its product or marketing strategy.

Successful: Nutanix Grows at 140% Annual Rate to Go Public Seven Years after Launch

Introduction

Nutanix, a San Jose, California-based HCI supplier, was founded in September 2009 and started selling its first product in October 2011—five years later it went public. HCI offered companies a QVL, because this product category—in which Nutanix led the industry—combined up to 12 different corporate data processing functions such as server, virtualization, and storage—into a single device running on an inexpensive piece of computer hardware run by sophisticated software. By July 2016, this strategy won Nutanix 3,768 end customers supported by 1,980 employees generating $445 million in revenues (with a net loss of $168 million)—up at a four-year annual growth rate of 187%.

Case Scenario

Nutanix grew rapidly because compared to rivals such as EMC, NetApp, and VMWare, Nutanix's product saved customers money and helped them adapt to change. Not only did Nutanix's products reduce companies purchase costs by 20% cost and operating cost by another 50% it, but it also boosted the customer's ability to adapt to change in its business. As a result, Nutanix said it was taking customers from EMC. In November 2014, Nutanix senior vice president of Product and Marketing, Howard Ting, told me "Nutanix beats EMC in many large enterprise accounts. We recently won the business of a major biotechnology company that previously bought from EMC. The company wanted to reduce its IT headcount 15% and get more agile while lowering costs. We saved the company 15% to 20% over EMC in capital expenditures and 40% to 50% on operating expenditures." Ting also believed that Nutanix helped customers in more qualitative ways. "We make them more nimble—it takes 15 minutes to install our product to 14 days for VBlock and enable them to add storage capacity in smaller increments—rather than the three year increments that EMC requires them to buy. We are in the second inning of this game," said Ting.

Nutanix believed that it was targeting a huge market that was growing rapidly. As Ting said, "IDC estimates that the market for converged infrastructure is $15 billion and it grew 60% in the last quarter. We save big companies tens of millions of dollars in total cost of ownership (a national mortgage bank lowered its capital expenditures 43% and its total cost of ownership 62% over five years compared to VBlock—a converged product sold through VCE, an EMC/Cisco joint venture.)"

One of Nutanix's cofounders was a serial entrepreneur who appeared to love starting new businesses but not sticking around until they either got acquired or went public. Mohit Aron—founder and long-departed chief technology officer of Nutanix—owned 10.7 million shares of its common stock, which represented 8.7% of its Class B shares. That meant he had many reasons for hoping that Nutanix went public and did well thereafter. But Aron was not concerned about money. As he explained in a September 14, 2016, interview, "The IPO is a funding event. Money is not why I do things. For me it's about passion."

And perhaps that explains why he left Nutanix in January 2013 to start Cohesity. As he said, "We started Nutanix because when I got my PhD from Rice University I talked with the founder of NetApp who told me that storage was most efficient if it was managed as a network. But that never made sense to me; I thought storage would work better if it was local. And that's what Nutanix does for primary storage."

In September 2016, Aron told me that Nutanix had the potential to make money because it and its competitors were adapting to a change in the venture capital climate. As he said, "A few years ago, venture capital firms were investing in hyper-convergence companies and were willing to subsidize their price cuts so they could gain market share and accelerate revenue growth." The appetite for fast growth and cash immolation has cooled." Public market investors punished companies like Pure Storage that were losing money and venture capitalists changed their perspective—urging their portfolio companies to cut costs to become profitable. They are not cutting prices the way they used to," said Aron.

Meanwhile CEO Dheeraj Pandey had created a culture at Nutanix that blended humility in the face of its customers with bravado toward rivals. As Pandey explained in a December 2014 interview, caring about employees, customers, and partners was the key to the company's success. Said Pandey, "Empathy for individuals can lead to great things. First is employees. They are fully in the company, they signed on. Second is customers—they signed on as well. Third is partners who can benefit from network effects. Pandey believes it is more important to do what brings you joy than to pursue riches. As he said, "We look at them not as portfolios to try to make us rich—but as individuals. This drives us to feel compassion and to listen to what they are actually saying to us. Even when we become a public company, Wall Street will be a side effect."

Pandey took a different view of the competition. As he said, giving before taking is critical to competitive success. "In the 1990s, companies were scrambling to build an infrastructure to take advantage of the Internet. Companies that could supply it were in a strong bargaining position to squeeze customers. But now there are 50 competitors and we believe we must be humble, have empathy for customers, and give to them before we can expect to get," argued Pandey. There was a kind of schizophrenia at Nutanix. "We are humble in the presence of our customers and aggressive with the competition," Pandey explained.

Nutanix also wanted to create a sense of camaraderie among its employees. According to Pandey, "We use Yammer as a way to keep our organization flat. We operate in 28 or 29 countries and our people can communicate with others at almost any time of day. Even though they don't see each other in person, they feel close." Nutanix also offers great employee benefits. It pays 100% of an employee's health costs; 100% of any dependents; and $10,000 per family reimbursement of unexpected medical costs.

With customers, Nutanix wanted long-term, repeat business rather than a focus on massive multimillion dollar deals. And the company also had empathy for how the partners did business and make money so it did not squeeze them too much on margin. Nutanix believed that the most iconic brands offered experiences rather than products. "The biggest brands sell an experience (right brain) rather than a thing (left brain). Brands like Williams Sonoma, Amazon, and Apple manage the customer's experience. We try to do that by, for example, making sure that customers do not have to go very long before they get the right answer to their questions," Pandey said, "Ultimately, the necessary and sufficient condition to build a large business is to use empathy to fully realize an excellent customer experience."

Nine months after filing for its initial public offering, Nutanix finally went public—in a very successful first day of trading that sent its shares above the offering price. A few days later, Nutanix stock peaked at about $47 a share but by November 15, they had lost 31% of their value. Would Nutanix be able to keep growing and ultimately achieve profitability?

Case Analysis

Nutanix illustrates five principles that can help small companies build effective growth trajectories:

- **Appoint a leadership team with product vision and sales and other key capabilities.** Nutanix's former CTO and its current CEO combined in two people the capabilities needed to start and sustain its rapid growth. While Aron was a product visionary and talented engineer, he lost patience with building an organization to support Nutanix's sustained growth. Here Pandey excelled at attracting and motivating talent, building up a global customer base, and raising capital.

- **Find a large market opportunity with significant customer pain.** HCI targets a huge market—Nutanix estimated it as a $15 billion opportunity. While that figure may exaggerate the sales potential for HCI, growth over the last several years has been very rapid—which suggests that many early-adopters of this technology experienced significant pain from incumbent products due to their very high cost to purchase and operate as well as their inflexibility to customers' evolving business requirements.

- **Build a product that delivers an irresistible jump in value to customers.** Nutanix's growth is largely a result of the QVL it provides customers. As Nutanix said, one customer cut its capital expenditures 15% to 20% when swapping out technology from EMC, cut operating expenditures 40% to 50%, and accelerated installation times from 14 days to 15 minutes while being able to add much smaller capacity increments to support growth.

- **Create a culture of growth**. Thanks to Pandey, Nutanix's culture motivated people to act in ways that helped it to attract and motivate talented people, to provide great service to customers, to collaborate well with partners, and to compete fiercely with rivals. These values helped Nutanix to sustain its industry-leading growth rate.

- **Expand quickly into new geographies with strong demand for that product**. Nutanix expanded its initial product from the United States to the rest of the world—and in the years from 2012 to 2016, about 60% of its revenues came from the United States while a bit under 40% were from the rest of the world. This global expansion helped Nutanix to scale to the point at which it could go public.

Unsuccessful: Fiksu Revenues Spike to $100 Million in 3.5 Years, and Then Implode

Introduction

An MIT math major earned a PhD in theoretical computer science at the University of California, Berkeley, and got tenure as a professor at the University of Massachusetts. He went on sabbatical—and started three companies. In 2010, he started app marketer Fiksu—it means smart in Finnish—which raised $17.6 million in venture capital and grew to $100 million in revenue in 3.5 years targeting a $19 billion revenue opportunity that was growing at over 60% a year. Then its revenues fell, and by 2015 it had scrapped plans for an IPO and dismissed 10% of its workforce. In June 2016, Fiksu sold itself for an undisclosed price to an obscure marketing agency.

Case Scenario

Between 1986 and 2005, Micah Adler, Fiksu's founder and CEO, proved his excellence as a student and professor—and by 2012 he had demonstrated what appeared to be exceptional courage by chucking his academic career to start five companies. In May 2005, Adler was a tenured associate professor in the Computer Science department at UMass Amherst. He had a sabbatical coming up and originally had planned to "travel around the world, visiting various computer science departments, working with world class collaborators who lived in interesting places. Then, [he] unexpectedly came up with an idea for a business and decided to cancel the travel plans and use [his] sabbatical to start CourseAdvisor—[a Wakefield, Massachusetts-based online lead generator serving the education industry he cofounded in 2004 that the Washington Post bought in October 2007]. Five companies later, he [saw that being an entrepreneur was] an incredibly fun and rewarding way of life, where every single day brings interesting challenges," Adler explained.

Fiksu was founded to solve a business problem that Adler faced when he developed apps. Given the relative ease of building apps and making them available for sale on platforms such as Apple's iTunes store, app developers needed a way to stand out from the pack and encourage people to download their apps so they could get paid for their efforts. Fiksu was originally named Fluent Mobile—launching a news reader in July 2009. But Adler struggled to market Fluent Mobile's apps. As he said, "We were building our own news reader and we had a very positive launch. It was app of the week. It was written about in the New York Times. We were seeing 50,000 down-loads a day, but things dried out very quickly." Adler tinkered with ways of getting users to download its apps—ultimately slashing its cost per download from $3 to about 26 cents. By July 2011 Fiksu was operating a platform—used by Groupon, Gilt Groupe, and numerous game developers—that helped app developers find the least expensive way—from among 20 mobile advertising networks and incentivized install companies such as FreeMyApps that gives users free gift cards for playing games—to achieve client-defined outcomes such as getting users to buy or open their app three times.

Adler saw in Fiksu a way to tap a huge market that he could serve with his passion for and skill at building algorithms. As Adler told me, "I did some analysis and reached a conclusion that many people saw as shocking—there would be $100 billion worth of acquisitions of mobile companies. One thing that helped me reach this conclusion is that Google estimated that mobile ads would reach 30% of its traffic. I decided that I needed to get in and build something and we would learn as we go. We started to develop algorithms to make digital marketing efficient. We reached out to AdMob (acquired by Google), Quattro (bought by Apple), and Millennial Media—which went public. I brought in some PhDs to figure out how to get more efficient. [After lowering the cost per download to 26 cents], we realized that we had invented something that was powerful, unique, and with broad commercial appeal. We surged to the number one position in the news category on the app store because our algorithm has better *targeting—get the right ad to the right person at the right time; reach—[in August 2013 Fiksu aggregated] across over 200 mobile ad networks, and efficiency—making decisions that must be made 50,000 times per second in under 100 milliseconds each."*

Fiksu grew quickly. In April 2011, it had 23 employees and by August 2013, it employed "between 190 and 200. 150 in Boston and the others in London, Helsinki, Tokyo, Seoul, Singapore and San Francisco" serving 500 customers such as Coke, Disney, eBay, and Groupon. By August 2014, Fiksu was up to $100 million in revenue, expecting to end 2014 with 300 employees, more than 800 customers, "promoting more than 2,300 mobile apps with profiles of nearly 60% of the world's smartphones and tablets, three billion app downloads, and 3.5 trillion marketing events."

It looked like Fiksu was poised for a 2015 IPO, but hopes for that were definitively crushed by June 2016. In 2015, it hired a chief financial officer who had helped take another company public but fired him in March 2015—dismissing 10% of its workforce or 26 people. Around September 2015, Fiksu dismissed another 25 employees and closed some international offices—leaving it with 115 employees by June 2016. That's when Fiksu was gobbled up for undisclosed terms by ClickDealer, a Menlo Park, California-based marketing agency part of an international asset management firm called Noosphere. Adler said of the deal, "As experts in transforming high-potential companies into definitive market leaders—with a diverse set of advertising technology businesses in their portfolio—Noosphere not only saw an incredible opportunity in Fiksu but also noted the remarkable synergy of our teams."

Fiksu's collapse can be attributed to two changes in the industry. In 2014, Apple began to crack down on incentivized installs—in fact, game developers were paying Fiksu but were working hard not to disclose the fact. Christian Calderon, chief revenue officer of game studio Ketchapp said, "It was totally common for user acquisition (UA) managers to straight-up lie about using it. I even heard of one UA manager that got a note from Fiksu's accounting team asking them to confirm that they were a client and the manager ignored the message because they didn't want a paper trail. It was always tricky for Fiksu because … the quality of that kind of traffic is not good. It was a critical part of Fiksu's growth, but it ended up being a bad business to be in because Apple looks down on it."

While incentivized installs have not disappeared, there is fierce rivalry over the remaining spoils. As Adler said, "Like many startups, Fiksu has not been immune to competitive pressures—this is a highly competitive market"—noting that 85 cents of every new dollar spent in online advertising went to either Facebook or Google in Q1 2016, according to Morgan Stanley. In 2013, Fiksu took a $5 million line of credit from Bridge Bank and in 2014 it added $10 million in debt financing from Silicon Valley Bank. As business slowed, Fiksu may have lacked sufficient cash to both operate the company and pay off its loans. Indeed, that may have triggered a loan contract term that enabled Bridge Bank to take ownership of Fiksu—which then sold it to Noosphere.

Case Analysis

Fiksu was exceptionally successful before it imploded. Its disappointing outcome suggests that Adler failed to follow three principles that small companies should use to construct effective growth trajectories:

- **Target a customer group that uniquely values your product.** Fiksu's rapid growth demonstrates that its customers found its product valuable. However, Fiksu's product was too easy for rivals to copy and too dependent on the bargaining power of a large partner, Apple. Fiksu targeted a customer group that valued its product—but that value was not unique enough to keep customers from switching to rivals' products. Fiksu might have done better had it found a customer group that uniquely valued its product.

- **Develop new products to stay ahead of competing products targeting that customer group.** It is unclear whether Adler was aware of how quickly its product was transitioning from rapid growth to decline. However, Fiksu was clearly unable to introduce a new product that could surf a new growth curve when revenue from its previous products began to decline. To sustain its growth, Fiksu should have introduced new products to take up the slack from the decline in its original products.

- **Create a growth culture that supports sustainable customer value.** Fiksu was too dependent on a product that its customers were embarrassed to admit they bought. This does not mean necessarily that Fiksu tolerated unethical conduct—however, it does suggest that it did not place enough value of building products that customers would be proud to recommend to other people. As a result, when Apple began to frown on incentivized installs, Fiksu's customers fled. Fiksu should have held itself to a higher standard of creating products that delivered sustainable customer value.

Applying the Principles of Effective Growth Trajectories

Leaders seeking to construct sustainable growth trajectories should consider five questions:

- Does my product offer so much value to a group of customers that they will choose it over competing products and recommend it enthusiastically to others?

- Is the market opportunity among this customer group large enough that the company can grow rapidly by expanding into new geographies with minimal CAGE distance from our home geography?

- Do we have the right capabilities to sustain rapid growth as we introduce new products or do we need to acquire a company to obtain them?

- Does our company have a deep bench of leaders with the blend of product vision and execution skills needed to sustain rapid growth?

- Does our company have a culture that listens with an open mind to customers, respects and motivates our employees, and aggressively competes with rivals?

Chapter 8: Growth Road Maps provides a detailed methodology for applying the principles of growth through new products.

Summary

To sustain growth over time, companies must construct effective growth trajectories. Whether large company or small, such trajectories match a new product with a customer group that is eager to buy because it satisfies an unmet need better than rival products. Once established, continued growth comes from selling the same product to similar customers in new geographies. Next, a company should seek growth from targeting the original product to new customer groups—or if that is not fruitful—to consider new products—whether developed internally or acquired—that a company's current customers will eagerly purchase. And as the company expands in these ways, it may also need to add new capabilities to sustain its rapid growth. Underlying this ever-adapting growth trajectory, a company seeking to sustain rapid growth must foster a growth culture that listens with an open mind to customers, respects and motivates employees, and spurs bold competitive moves to counter rivals.

Growth Road Maps

Chapter 2. Road Map for Growing Faster via Customers

A company aspiring to grow faster from current or new customer groups ought to assess its CEO before embarking on a new growth strategy. A company's independent board members ought to assess the CEO's fitness to boost the company's growth. To be sure, the CEO characteristics needed to lead a company to faster growth are likely to vary depending on the specific company, its industry, its performance, and its prospects. In general, there are six traits that may indicate to boards that the current CEO will be able to achieve faster growth:

- Prior experience conceiving and executing successful growth strategies

- Skill at leading diverse teams in a collaborative, rather than dictatorial, fashion

- Ability to attract and motivate strong functional executives—for example, vice presidents of engineering, manufacturing, sales, and service

© Peter S. Cohan 2017
P. S. Cohan, *Disciplined Growth Strategies*, DOI 10.1007/978-1-4842-2448-9_8

- Intellectual humility and willingness to engage in fact-based intellectual debate

- Resistance to assuming that past sources of success will lead to future success

- Recognition of the importance of winning by creating superior value for potential customers

Conversely, if the current CEO demonstrates the opposite of these traits, it that may indicate that a new person should take over:

- No prior experience conceiving and executing successful growth strategies

- Command and control style of management that shuts down team contributions

- Inability to attract and retain strong functional executives

- Tendency to listen only to information that confirms what the CEO already believes

- Desire to prove that strategies that worked in the past will work for different situations

- Belief that the CEO knows more than customers or competitors about where to find growth

The case studies we examined in this chapter suggest that a board would have judged the CEOs of McDonalds, Criteo, SoFi, and Actifio as possessing desirable traits for conceiving and executing an effective growth strategy. Easterbrook clearly had a helpful combination of experience inside and outside McDonalds. His inside experience helped him to understand how to persuade key stakeholders such as franchisees and employees to accept a change in strategy and his outside experience made him more open to listening to customers and observing competitor strategies. Rudelle clearly had the intellectual humility needed to listen to customers, observe their unmet needs, and lead his organization to develop and sell a new product that met the needs of its customers. And Ashutosh's broad technology industry experience and prior success at building Actifio's market position among large organizations made it more likely that he would be able to build a new service for a new customer segment. Similarly, Cagney's success getting SoFi into a leading position in student loan refinancing would suggest to the board that he might be able to sell more to customers in its installed base. By contrast, a board would be in a difficult position trying to decide whether DeLuca, Perez, or Nguyen would be good candidates to lead a growth strategy. DeLuca created Subway but by the time of the case had lost his creative edge. Perez was brought in from HP with the idea that he would build a profitable position in ink cartridges for Kodak as he had done with inkjet printers. And Nguyen picked investors who would be easily overpowered by his persuasive skills—despite his lack of success building sustainable companies.

If a company's current CEO is well-suited to the challenges of creating and executing an effective growth strategy, he or she should lead a three phased process:

- Diagnose current growth strategy
- Envision future growth strategy
- Execute growth strategy

I. Diagnose Growth Strategy

The CEO ought to begin creating a growth strategy via current or new customers by using the Five Dimensions of Growth framework described in Chapter I to diagnose the company's current strategy. This is an important place to start because it will help the company to assess its current resources and to evaluate the resources it needs to add before it can achieve its growth goals. To the end, the CEO ought to do the following:

- Assemble a team of people—leaders of business units or key functional divisions—within the company who will ultimately be in charge of achieving faster growth.

- Consider seeking outside assistance from an expert who can help collect and analyze data in an objective manner.

- Develop a detailed description of the company's current growth strategy with respect to customers. To that end, the strategy team should gather data to answer the following questions:

  - Which 20% of the company's customers account for 80% of its revenue?

  - Are these key customers organizations or individuals?

    - If the key customers are organizations, do they share common characteristics—such as industries, size (e.g., number of employees), or attitude toward new technologies (e.g., early- or late-adopters)?

    - If the key customers are individuals, do they share common characteristics such as age range, education level, income, or attitude toward new technologies?

- Based on these common characteristics, what customer groups are contributing most to the company's current revenues?

- Who are the company's competitors and what are their shares of the segment?

- In which segments does the company lead?

- How fast are these segments growing and what factors are driving that growth

- Why is the company leading in those segments and how sustainable is that lead?

- In which segments is the company lagging?

- How fast are these segments growing and what factors are driving that growth?

- Why is the company lagging in those segments and how difficult would it be for the company to improve its competitive position?

Actifio addressed many of these questions when it decided to focus on a new group of customers—SMEs. Ashutosh decided that his company's dependence on well-known large companies as customers had considerable marketing value. But he was concerned that the unpredictability of their cash flows put too much stress on the organization at the end of the quarter when he faced considerable pressure to meet sales targets and customers did not feel the same sense of urgency about signing contracts with Actifio. The cumulative effect of the uncertainty of how long it would take to close sales with large organizations led Ashutosh to the conclusion that he should start to seek revenues from the $580 billion market for IT spending by SMEs.

II. Envision Growth Strategy

Once the strategy team has answered these questions, the CEO should lead a process for envisioning a growth strategy from current or new customers. To that end, the team should brainstorm, evaluate, and choose a growth strategy from among many creative options through the following steps.

- Brainstorm many possible growth vectors among current or new customers. The team should base these ideas on four principles:

  - Listen to customers in segments where the company is winning and losing—discussing customer pain points and unmet needs

- Study fast-growing rivals and identify which customer groups are contributing most to their rapid growth

- Seek deeper understanding of the trends underlying customer pain and rivals' rapid growth

- Encourage participants not to self-censor and to generate both blend blue sky and more-grounded ideas

- Rank the growth vectors based on criteria such as these:

  - The size, growth, and profitability of the market segments

  - The company's current or potential competitive advantage

  - The net present value of the investment required to implement the strategy

- Scrutinize the best ideas by conducting more in-depth analysis such as customer interviews, cost analysis, and competitor analysis.

- Articulate the two best ideas emerging from this process in clear and specific terms. The growth strategies should answer questions such as the following:

  - In which customers' segments will the company compete?

  - What are the company's market share targets by year in those segments?

  - What products or services will the company offer those customers?

  - Why does the company believe that customers will prefer its products over competitors'?

  - Will the company sell the product via direct sales, distributors, or other means?

  - How much capital will be required to implement the strategy?

  - What does the company estimate will be the net present value of that investment?

Actifio's SME strategy suggests that it followed some of these steps—but not others. For example, Actifio seems to have developed a product for the SME market that would save customers money and enable their IT systems to be more responsive to customer needs. However, Actifio did not think enough ahead of time about the capabilities required to succeed in the SME market. It became clear within several months that Actifio would either need to invest in many new capabilities or change its strategy to one that better aligned with its strengths.

III. Execute Growth Strategy

Having assessed the company's current growth strategy and envisioning a future strategy, the final step is to execute that strategy so that the company can achieve the desired results. To do this, the CEO will need to transform both the strategy and organization to achieve faster growth premised on the idea that people who excelled in the old organization may find themselves out of a job and new people will come into the company. To that end, the CEO should do this:

- Persuade the board to dedicate the resources—such as capital and people—to making the growth strategy successful

- Communicate the growth vision clearly to the entire organization

- Identify employees who embrace the vision and those who seek to resist it

- Make any job cuts completely at once and with a minimum of delay

- Bring in new hires quickly and give them clear goals and the resources needed to achieve those goals

- Listen carefully to concerns and over-communicate progress in implementing the strategy

- Measure progress toward growth goals and adjust the strategy to overcome obstacles

In executing its SME strategy, Actifio did measure progress toward its goal and realized that it needed a significant change in its approach. Sadly for Actifio's investors, the new strategy did not appear to offer the cash-flow smoothing benefit that Ashutosh had hoped for when he launched Actifio One in February 2015.

Chapter 3. Road Map for Growing Faster via Geography

A company aspiring to grow faster from current or new geography ought to start by assessing how well the current CEO's skills fit with the demands of a geographic expansion strategy as we explored in Chapter 2.

I. Diagnose Growth Strategy

The CEO should start by assessing the company's current geographic growth strategy—assembling a team along the lines presented in Chapter 2 but focusing on a different set of questions. To that end, the CEO ought to do the following:

- Develop a detailed description of the company's current growth strategy with respect to geography. To that end, the strategy team should gather data to answer the following questions:

    - What proportion of the company's revenue comes from each geography in which it currently sells?

    - Are the key customers in these geographies organizations or individuals?

        - If the key customers are organizations, do they share common characteristics—such as industries, size (e.g., number of employees), or attitude toward new technologies (e.g., early- or late-adopters)?

        - If the key customers are individuals, do they share common characteristics such as age range, education level, income, or attitude toward new technologies?

    - Based on these common characteristics, what customer groups within these geographies are contributing most to the company's current revenues?

    - Who are the company's competitors in these geographies and what are their shares of the segment?

    - In which geographies does the company lead?

- How fast are the markets for the company's products in these geographies growing, and what factors are driving that growth?

- Why is the company leading in those geography, and how sustainable is that lead?

- In which segments is the company lagging?

- How fast are these segments growing and what factors are driving that growth

- Why is the company lagging in those segments, and how difficult would it be for the company to improve its competitive position?

II. Envision Growth Strategy

Once the strategy team has answered these questions, the CEO should lead a process for envisioning a growth strategy from current or new geographies. The team should break into two smaller groups—one to analyze potential growth from current geographies and another to assess opportunities from new geographies—that work in parallel.

Current Geographies

To that end, the team should brainstorm, evaluate, and choose a growth strategy from among many creative options through the following steps.

- Brainstorm many possible growth vectors among current geographies. The team should base these ideas on four principles:

  - Listen to customers in locations where the company is winning and losing—discussing customer pain points and unmet needs.

  - Study fast-growing rivals and identify which strategies are contributing most to their rapid growth in those locations.

  - Seek deeper understanding of the trends underlying customer pain and rivals' rapid growth.

  - Encourage participants not to self-censor and to generate both blue sky and more-grounded ideas.

- Rank the growth vectors based on criteria such as these:
  - The size, growth, and profitability of the market segments
  - The company's current or potential competitive advantage
  - The net present value of the investment required to implement the strategy
- Scrutinize the best ideas by conducting more in-depth analysis such as customer interviews, cost analysis, and competitor analysis.
- Articulate the two best ideas emerging from this process in clear and specific terms. The growth strategies should answer questions such as the following:
  - In which current geographies should the company seek to expand?
  - What are the company's market share targets by year in those geographies?
  - What products or services will the company offer customers in those geographies?
  - Why does the company believe that customers in these geographies will prefer its products over competitors'?
  - Will the company sell the product via direct sales, distributors, or other means?
  - How much capital will be required to implement the strategy?
  - What does the company estimate will be the net present value of that investment?

New Geographies

To develop options for growth from new geographies, teams should do the following:

- Develop a list of 50 or more possible countries from which to consider future growth

- Pick the 10 most compelling of these by ranking each countries' potential revenue for the company, revenue growth rate, and factors boosting and inhibiting the country's revenue growth potential

- For these 10 countries, evaluate the CAGE distance between each and the company's core geography. Teams should seek detailed data on each of the four CAGE factors from sources including:

  - Interviewing professors with country-specific cultural, political, and economic expertise

  - Meeting with government officials in the countries to understand their role in granting licenses and influencing the purchase and use of the company's product

  - Speaking with taxation and financial services experts within the country

  - Listening to potential customers in these countries to assess the likelihood that they would purchase the company's product

- Rank the 10 countries based on this:

  - The size, growth, and profitability of the local market for your company's products

  - Its CAGE distance between your company's home geography

  - The company's current or potential competitive advantage in the country

  - The net present value of the investment required to implement the strategy

- Scrutinize the most attractive countries by conducting more in-depth analysis such as customer interviews, cost analysis, and competitor analysis.

- For the two most compelling countries emerging from this process, articulate the growth strategy by answering questions such as the following:

  - In which customers segments will the company compete within the country?

  - What are the company's market share targets by year in the country?

- What products or services will the company offer those customers?

- Why does the company believe that customers will prefer its products over competitors'?

- Will the company sell the product via direct sales, distributors, or other means?

- How much capital will be required to implement the strategy?

- What does the company estimate will be the net present value of that investment?

Once the two teams have completed their analysis, the CEO should decide whether to seek resources to implement geographic expansion from current or new geographies—and if so, how to sequence them. To that end, the CEO might consider ranking the proposed geographic growth strategies based on the following criteria:

- Contribution to near-term revenue growth

- Capital and human resource requirements

- Expected time to generate results

- Potential for unexpected negative surprises

Netflix applied this approach in conceiving of its strategy to expand into 150 more countries between 2015 and 2017. Most interestingly, Netflix's emphasis in plotting its global strategy was on the similarities across countries of customer groups. Netflix used detailed information about how its customers use its service—measuring factors such as what shows they watch, how much time they watch them, on which devices—to identify 2,000 clusters based on viewers' tastes for specific types of programming.[1] Netflix customers in these clusters live in different countries. Todd Yellin, Netflix's head of product innovation told the *Telegraph* that 90% of Japanese anime shows on Netflix are watched by people outside Japan. Moreover, Yellin found that there were 15 people around the world in his cluster who were spread out from "Dalston in East London to Bangalore, India."[2] Nevertheless, Netflix did not believe that simply distributing the same content to such clusters around the world would achieve its ends. The company also planned to create international content in many languages—adding Arabic, Korean, Simplified and Traditional Chinese to the 17 languages it already supported.[3] Moreover, Netflix added the Spanish language shows described earlier in the chapter. In 2016, Hastings hoped to produce more international content. "We have a show in Germany, in France, in Spain, in Italy, several in Brazil, two in Mexico, several in Japan, but that needs to be 5x or 10x. We have to localize product, expand content and all that content needs to be available globally," Hastings told the *Telegraph*.[4]

In developing its global growth strategy, Netflix followed two of the important principles underlying the steps for envisioning growth strategy. First, it should be based on ambitious goals founded on detailed analysis of relevant data. Second, effective geographic growth strategies flow from original ideas about how to deliver compellingly better value to customers.

III. Execute Growth Strategy

Having assessed the company's current growth strategy and envisioning a future strategy, the final step is to execute that strategy so that the company can achieve the desired results. Successful implementation of a geographic growth strategy will depend on the same general principles outlined in Chapter 2.

For growth strategies that involve expanding to new geographies, the CEO must take additional steps:

- Meet with leaders in the new country to explain the company's goals and intended benefits to the country.

- Develop relationships with relevant regulators and obtain required licenses and permits.

- Establish partnerships where appropriate with local legal and accounting firms.

- Forge distribution and marketing partnerships.

- Establish mechanisms for collecting and disbursing cash and paying taxes.

Chapter 4. Road Map for Growing Faster via New Products

A company aspiring to grow faster from new products ought to start by assessing how well the current CEO's skills fit with the demands of a product expansion strategy as we explored in Chapter 2.

I. Diagnose Growth Strategy

The CEO should start by assessing the company's current product growth strategy—assembling a team along the lines presented in Chapter 2 but focusing on a different set of questions. To that end, the CEO ought to do the following:

- Develop a detailed description of the company's current growth strategy with respect to products. To that end, the strategy team should gather data to answer the following questions:

    - What proportion of the company's revenue comes from each product that it currently sells?

    - Are the key customers of these products organizations or individuals?

        - If the key customers are organizations, do they share common characteristics—such as industries, size (e.g., number of employees), or attitude toward new technologies (e.g., early- or late-adopters)?

        - If the key customers are individuals, do they share common characteristics such as age range, education level, income, or attitude toward new technologies?

    - Based on these common characteristics, what customer groups that buy these products are contributing most to the company's current revenues?

    - Who are the company's competitors in these product areas and what are their shares of the segment?

    - In which products does the company lead?

    - How fast are the markets for the company's products growing and what factors are driving that growth?

    - Why is the company leading in those product categories and how sustainable is that lead?

    - In which product categories is the company lagging?

    - How fast are these product categories growing and what factors are driving that growth?

    - Why is the company lagging in those product categories, and how difficult would it be for the company to improve its competitive position?

II. Envision Growth Strategy

Once the strategy team has answered these questions, the CEO should lead a process for envisioning a growth strategy from building or acquiring new products. The team should break into two smaller groups—one to analyze potential growth from building new products and another to assess opportunities from acquiring new products—that work in parallel.

Building New Products

To that end, the team should brainstorm, evaluate, and choose a growth strategy from among many creative options through the following steps.

- Brainstorm many possible growth vectors based on four principles:

    - Listen to customers in locations where the company is winning and losing—discussing customer pain points and unmet needs,

    - Study fast-growing rivals and identify which strategies are contributing most to their rapid growth in those locations,

    - Seek deeper understanding of the trends underlying customer pain and rivals' rapid growth,

    - Encourage participants not to self-censor and to generate both blue sky and more-grounded ideas,

- Rank the growth vectors based on criteria such as these:

    - The size, growth, and profitability of the market segments

    - The company's current or potential competitive advantage

    - The net present value of the investment required to implement the strategy

- Scrutinize the best ideas by conducting more in-depth analysis such as customer interviews, cost analysis, and competitor analysis.

- Articulate the two best ideas emerging from this process in clear and specific terms. The growth strategies should answer questions such as the following:

    - In which current products should the company seek to expand?

    - What are the company's market share targets by year in those product categories?

    - What products or services will the company offer customers?

    - Why does the company believe that customers will prefer its products over competitors'?

    - Will the company sell the product via direct sales, distributors, or other means?

    - How much capital will be required to implement the strategy?

    - What does the company estimate will be the net present value of that investment?

Amazon and New Relic followed many of these steps in developing their AWS and Insight products, respectively. Bezos clearly recognized that there would be a large market opportunity to sell large organizations access to AWS once it worked well for Amazon's e-commerce operations and had been made easier to use for companies outside Amazon. It is not clear whether Amazon set specific market share targets for AWS—however, given what has been written about his focus on measuring specific factors that determine customer satisfaction, growth, and productivity, market share goals would fit within Amazon's culture. The case presented in this chapter also makes it clear that AWS continues to receive investment from Amazon to keep the breadth and quality of its services ahead of rivals—thus securing its market leadership and contributing to scale economies that contribute to its relatively high profitability and significant contribution to Amazon's profits. New Relic took a different approach to developing Insight and its other new products. Specifically, Cirne spent a significant amount of time listening to its enterprise customers and gaining deep insights into what new products could relieve the pressure on IT operations managers. Moreover, Cirne showed inventiveness in developing a marketing strategy for New Relic that would turn influential users of its technology—Ruby on Rails developers—into passionate and effective advocates of its products. In this way, New Relic was able to invest more in product development and less in sales and marketing.

Acquiring New Products

To develop options for growth from new products, teams should do the following:

- In the same way as the team seeking to build new products, the team should brainstorm many possible growth vectors based on four principles:
  - Listen to customers in locations where the company is winning and losing—discussing customer pain points and unmet needs.
  - Study fast-growing rivals and identify which strategies are contributing most to their rapid growth in those locations.
  - Seek deeper understanding of the trends underlying customer pain and rivals' rapid growth.
  - Encourage participants not to self-censor and to generate both blue sky and more-grounded ideas.
- Develop a list of at least five possible new product categories from which to consider future growth.
- Rank each product categories' potential revenue for the company, revenue growth rate, and factors boosting and inhibiting the product's revenue growth potential.
- For the most attractive new product categories, evaluate the company's potential peak market share. Teams should seek detailed data on factors likely to determine the company's success in the most attractive product categories by doing this:
  - Interviewing potential customers to identify and rank the criteria they use to compare competing suppliers, how they rate those suppliers on the criteria, and what they see as their biggest unmet needs.
  - Meet with technology experts and professors to envision different scenarios about how relevant technology is likely to evolve to help satisfy those unmet needs better than do rivals.
  - Evaluate the capabilities required to outperform rivals in the new product categories.
  - Assess the strength of the company's capabilities relative to those of its competitors.

- Consider options for how to close this capability gap—including hiring key people or acquiring a company that can provide the needed capabilities.

- For the two most compelling product categories emerging from this process, articulate the growth strategy by answer questions such as the following:

  - To which customer segments will the company sell the new product?

  - What are the company's market share targets for the new product?

  - Why does the company believe that customers will prefer its products over competitors'?

  - Which company making that product will be acquired?

  - How will the company integrate the acquired company?

  - Will the company sell the product via direct sales, distributors, or other means?

  - How much capital will be required to complete the acquisition?

  - What does the company estimate will be the net present value of that investment?

Localytics used many of these principles in its acquisition of Splitforce. Aggarwal realized that its customers would appreciate its A/B testing capability and that he could only apply Splitforce's technology to help Localytics customers if he could persuade its key people to join Localytics and to work diligently to realize the merger's potential. To that end, Aggarwal met with key people at Splitforce, assured himself that they fit culturally with Localytics, worked out the details of how to merge their combined products and capabilities, and created a schedule of handing out equity to how well Splitforce's key people met jointly agreed-on objectives. Once the two teams have completed their analysis, the CEO should decide whether to seek resources to implement product growth strategies—from building or acquiring new products—and if so, how to sequence them. To that end, the CEO might consider ranking the proposed product growth strategies based on the following criteria:

- Contribution to near-term revenue growth

- Capital and human resource requirements

- Expected time to generate results

- Potential for unexpected negative surprises

III. Execute Growth Strategy

Having assessed the company's current growth strategy and envisioning a future strategy, the final step is to execute that strategy so that the company can achieve the desired results. For growth strategies that involve *building* new products, the CEO must:

- Win Board and shareholder support for building the new products

- Dedicate product development teams to the high-priority, new product categories

- Encourage those teams to be interdisciplinary—including sales, marketing, engineers, finance—and to work with early-adopter customers

- Urge the teams to build prototypes of the new product, give it to those customers, and get their feedback

- Evaluate whether new manufacturing, supply, distribution, and marketing and sales strategies will be needed for the new products

- Provide the resources required to bolster the company's skills

- Actively support the new product launches

For growth strategies that involve *acquiring a company* that supplies the new products, the CEO must:

- Form an interdisciplinary team to consider potential acquisition candidates within the new product industry

- Set specific acquisition candidate evaluation criteria as detailed earlier in the chapter:

  - Industry attractiveness

  - Better off

  - NPV > 0

  - Ease of integration

- Rank candidates based on these criteria:

- Meet with key people in the target company to assess their fit

- Discuss methods of combining products and capabilities

- Agree on compensation terms for key people

- Negotiate deal terms and finalize contracts
- Manage integration so that combined companies appear seamless to customers when deal closes

Chapter 5. Road Map for Growing Faster via Capabilities

Before building a road map for growing faster via capabilities, a company's board ought to assess whether the current CEO will be capable of creating and implementing such a strategy. To make that assessment the board should follow a process along the lines we discussed in the road map for growth via customer groups in Chapter 2. The outcome of this process should either make the decision to keep the current CEO or find a new one.

I. Diagnose Growth Strategy

The CEO should start by assessing the company's current capabilities-based growth strategy—assembling a team along the lines presented in Chapter 2 but through the following process:

- By interviewing customers, analyzing competitors, and assessing the company's current capabilities develop a detailed description of the company's current growth strategy with respect to capabilities. To that end, the strategy team should gather data to answer the following questions:

  - What specific, ranked criteria—for example, price, selection, quality—do your current customers use to decide among suppliers of the products your company provides?

  - What are the critical capabilities that companies in the industry must possess to satisfy each of these customer purchase criteria?

  - Compared to the industry's fastest-growing rivals, how well do customers perceive that the company is satisfying each of the purchase criteria?

  - How do the industry's fastest-growing rivals and the company perform these capabilities?

- In which capabilities does the company currently outperform these rivals? In what ways might rivals undermine the company's advantage in these capabilities over the next five years?

- In which capabilities does the company currently lag these rivals? In what ways might the company change the way it performs these capabilities to outperform rivals over the next five years?

Answering these questions thoroughly will provide the company with an objective assessment of its capabilities.

II. Envision Growth Strategy

Next the CEO should lead a process for envisioning a growth strategy from current or new capabilities.

In order to create independent perspectives, the team should break into two smaller groups—one to analyze potential growth from current capabilities and another to assess opportunities that would require a changed capability portfolio—that work in parallel.

Current Capabilities

The team should brainstorm, evaluate, and choose a growth strategy from among many creative options through the following steps:

- Brainstorm many possible growth opportunities. The team should base these ideas on four principles:

  - Listen to customers where the company is winning and losing—discussing customer pain points and unmet needs.

  - Study fast-growing rivals and identify which strategies are contributing most to their rapid growth in those locations.

  - Seek deeper understanding of the trends underlying customer pain and rivals' rapid growth.

  - Encourage participants not to self-censor and to generate both blue sky and more-grounded ideas.

- Rank the growth opportunities based on criteria such as these:

    - The size, growth, and profitability of the market segments

    - The fit between the company's capabilities and the requirements for competitive success in each segment

    - The net present value of the investment required to implement the strategy

- Scrutinize the best ideas by conducting more in-depth analysis such as customer interviews, capabilities and cost analysis, and competitor analysis.

- Articulate the two best ideas emerging from this process in clear and specific terms. The growth strategies should answer questions such as the following:

    - In which new markets should the company seek to expand?

    - What are the company's market share targets by year in those geographies?

    - What products or services will the company offer customers in those geographies?

    - Why does the company believe that customers in these geographies will prefer its products over competitors'?

    - What capabilities will the company be able to use to share in the selected markets?

    - Will the company sell the product via direct sales, distributors, or other means?

    - How much capital will be required to implement the strategy?

    - What does the company estimate will be the net present value of that investment?

New Capabilities

To evaluate whether growth opportunities will require new capabilities, the team should brainstorm, evaluate, and choose a growth strategy from among many creative options through steps similar to the ones described for current capabilities. The most significant difference between the two is that the team should focus with particular objectivity on four questions:

- Can the company build new capabilities required to gain a significant share of the growth opportunities identified by the team?

- If so, does the team have concrete recommendations regarding how to build these new capabilities?

- Will the new capabilities enable the company to grow faster than rivals contending for the growth opportunities?

- Will the profit from capturing the growth opportunities more than offset the investment required to build these new capabilities?

Once the two teams have completed their analysis, the CEO should choose from among the proposed capabilities-based strategies—and if so, how to sequence them.

The CEO might rank the proposed capabilities-based growth strategies based on the following criteria:

- Contribution to near-term revenue growth

- Capital and human resource requirements

- Expected time to generate results

- Potential for unexpected negative surprises

Following these steps can boost a company's growth. As we saw in Chapter 5, Apple's success in the smartphone industry flowed from applying—with modifications—the capabilities it had developed by competing with the iPod in the MP3 player market. Specifically, Apple's used its excellent skills in hardware design, supply chain, marketing, and customer service to the iPod and iPhone. Moreover, Apple applied its skills at partnering with others differently with the iPod and iPhone. Whereas Apple's iPod benefited from its partnering skills in building iTunes; Apple formed different partnerships—with AT&T and other wireless service providers and with app developers (creating the App Store)—to spur the iPhone's success.

III. Execute Growth Strategy

Having assessed the company's current growth strategy and envisioning a future strategy, the final step is to execute that strategy so that the company can achieve the desired results.

Successful implementation of a capabilities-based growth strategy will depend on the same general principles outlined in Chapter 2.

For growth strategies that involve creating new capabilities, the CEO must take additional steps:

- Identify the capabilities required to gain share in the new market.

- Evaluate the fit between the company's capabilities and the ones required for competitive success in the new market.

- Brainstorm ways to close the capability gap including these:

  - Acquiring a company with the needed capabilities

  - Partnering with firms that excel in the needed capabilities

  - Hire experts in the needed capabilities

  - Modify existing capabilities to better fit them to the competitive requirements of the new market

- Choose and implement the best option(s) for closing the capability gap.

Chapter 6. Road Map for Creating a Growth Culture

A company aspiring to create a growth culture ought to start by assessing how well the current CEO's skills fit with the demands of a creating a growth culture. Since a company's culture so strongly reflects the values and conduct of its CEO, if the CEO is not able to create a growth culture, the company's board may need to find a new one.

To that end, the board should hire an independent consultant to investigate and reach conclusions about the current CEO regarding questions such as the following:

- Has the company sustained industry-leading revenue growth?

- If not, does the board believe that the company has in place a practical strategy to boost its revenue growth?

- Does the company encourage and provide resources to employees so they can test and develop new products?

- If so, have these employee innovation resources led to measurable revenue growth improvement?

- If not, does the CEO encourage departments to fight for limited resources and insist on making all key decisions?

- If not, is the CEO open to and capable of changing the company's culture to encourage growth?

Based on the answers to these questions, the board will be able to make a more informed decision about whether or not to keep the current CEO. If not, the board ought to find a CEO who can create a growth culture and manage the CEO out of an executive role at the company.

I. Diagnose Culture

The board-chosen CEO should start by assessing the company's current culture—assembling a team along the lines presented in Chapter 2 but focusing on the following questions:

- Does the company have a well-defined culture?

- If so,

    - What are the company's values?

    - What stories does the CEO tell to explain each of the values to employees and others?

    - Does the CEO believe passionately that these values are important? If so, why?

    - Do the company's values inspire current employees and help attract new ones? If so, which employees were inspired and/or attracted to the company by which values and why?

    - Does the company use its values to hire, promote, and manage people out of the company?

- Do the company's values motivate employees to take actions that help the company attract and retain customers? If so, which employees helped attract and retain which customers and why did their actions motivate these customers?

- If not—possibly assuming a new CEO has been brought in to create a growth culture,

  - To assess why the company is lagging rivals, is the company's revenue growing faster than the industry? If not, why not?

  - To evaluate whether its culture is attracting and motivating top talent, is the company's employee turnover and productivity better than its industry? If not, why not? Compared to rivals, does the company attract more so-called A Players? If not, why not?

  - To determine whether its culture is encouraging employees to win and keep customers, does the company have a high net promoter score—the likelihood that a current customer will recommend the company enthusiastically to others? If not, why not?

II. Envision Growth Culture

A CEO should use the answers to these questions to reach a conclusion about whether the company has a strong growth culture or needs to create one. If the company's growth culture is helping spur industry-beating revenue growth, the CEO must focus on keeping the culture from becoming so rigid that it impedes growth. And if the company needs to create a growth culture, it should do so as described below.

Create Growth Culture

The company should create a growth culture through the following steps:

- Identify key stakeholders and ask them what they want:

  - Listen to current and potential customers to identify specific actions by the company's employees that will encourage them to buy and recommend the company's products.

- Study fast-growing rivals to identify the attributes of their cultures that help them to attract talented employees and motivate them to act in ways that create and sustain customer loyalty.

- Listen to current and potential employees to identify specific values and conduct that would encourage them to join and contribute to the company.

- Develop a list of values at the intersection of three sets:

  - What the CEO believes are the values essential to achieving the company's mission

  - The values that will attract and motivate the most talented employees

  - What employees should do in product development and service to attract and retain customers

- Develop compelling stories that the CEO and other executives can use to make the values meaningful to employees.

- Incorporate the values into employee interviews and performance evaluations.

- If employees act in ways consistent with the company's values, encourage their career development and reward them accordingly.

Keep Growth Culture from Calcifying

If a company is already growing faster than the industry, the CEO should investigate—possibly with help from independent consultants—whether the company is becoming complacent by taking the following steps:

- Ask employees who quit the company why they left, where they went and, and why the new employer was a better option for them.

- Ask the former managers of those employees why they think the employee left.

- If the manager and the employee have a different perception, investigate what might be causing the difference.

- Ask former customers why they stopped buying from the company, which supplier they buy from now, and why that supplier is better for them.

- Ask the former sales person for those customers to explain why they think the customer switched to a rival.

- If the sales person and the customer have a different perception, investigate what might be causing the difference.

- Interview industry experts and potential customers to seek information about trends in technology, new rivals, and evolving unmet needs that might threaten the company's business strategy.

- Based on this analysis, consider which aspects of the company's' culture ought to change in order to encourage the company to continue its rapid growth.

As we see in Chapter 7, growth comes from leaders who pick the right values and reinforce them through their own behavior; their choices of whom to hire, promote, and fire; how they set goals and encourage people to achieve them; and what they learn from success and failure.

A case in point is Nutanix that had grown at an average rate of 186% in the four years ending July 2016 and went public in October 2016—valuing its $445 million in 2016 sales at $4.5 billion on November 23, 2016.

Nutanix CEO Dheeraj Pandey created a culture that blended humility in the face of its customers with bravado toward rivals. As Pandey explained, empathy for employees, customers, and partners is the key to the company's phenomenal success. Said Pandey, "Empathy for individuals can lead to great things. First is employees. They are fully in the company, they signed on. Second is customers—they signed on as well. Third is partners who can benefit from network effects."

Nutanix encourages its employees to work together. According to Pandey, "We use Yammer as a way to keep our organization flat. We operate in 28 or 29 countries and our people can communicate with others at almost any time of day. Even though they don't see each other in person, they feel close."

It was not all sweetness and light—Pandey sought to give customers more value than competitors did. As he said, unlike in the past, customers have 50 competitors from which to choose so Nutanix must "have empathy for customers, and give to them before it can expect to get." There is a dichotomy at Nutanix. "We are humble in the presence of our customers and aggressive with the competition," Pandey explained.

III. Execute Growth Culture

Having assessed the company's culture and envisioning a growth culture, the final step is to change the culture so that the company can achieve the desired results.

To implement the envisioned growth culture, the CEO should:

- Meet with employees to ask them what they think the company should value and work with them to embrace the values of the new culture.

- Clearly articulate the company's values and tell stories that illustrate how the new values helped people in practical situations—making life better for employees and customers and helping the company generate industry-leading revenues.

- Take clear actions that indicate the CEO is following the new values and expects employees to do so as well.

- Change the interview process to screen out potential employees who do not fit with the new culture.

- Link reward systems to employee conduct that reinforces the value of the new culture.

- By getting objective feedback from employees, customers, investors, industry experts, and others, fight forces that make new culture overly rigid so the company can adapt well to change.

Chapter 7. Road Map for Building Growth Trajectories

In Chapter 7, we identified a common growth trajectory that chains together some or all of these five dimensions to sustain a company's long-term growth:

- Create a **growth culture** to help build an effective team to launch and grow the company.

- Develop a **new product** that uniquely satisfies the unmet needs of a specific **customer group.**

- Build **capabilities**—for example, product development, manufacturing, distribution, sales, and service—to provide and service the product.

- Add new capabilities—such as manufacturing, sales, and service—to support the sale of the product to a similar customer group in **new geographies.**

- Consider whether the product can be sold as is—or modified—to generate revenue growth by selling to a **different customer group.**

- Before the current product matures, **develop or acquire a new product** that will enable the company to tap the growth potential of a new, fast-growing market opportunity. Revisit the previous steps in the growth trajectory as needed to sustain revenue growth from the new product.

As a company considers which dimensions of growth to investigate as possible sources of industry-leading revenue growth, the CEO should follow the specific approaches for the most relevant growth dimension as detailed in Chapters 2 through 6 and earlier in this appendix.

Notes

Chapter 1: Introduction

[i] Daniel Sparks, "Ouch! A Close Look at LinkedIn Corporation Stock's 44% 1-Day Decline," *Motley Fool*, February 6, 2016, http://www.fool.com/investing/general/2016/02/06/ouch-a-close-look-at-linkedin-corporation-stocks-4.aspx

[ii] Peter Cohan, "4 Reasons Microsoft Wasted $26.2 Billion to Buy LinkedIn, *Forbes*, June 13, 2016, http://www.forbes.com/sites/petercohan/2016/06/13/4-reasons-microsoft-wasted-26-2-billion-to-buy-linkedin/

[iii] Derek Xiao, "Elizabeth Holmes Isn't the Only Billionaire to Blow a Fortune," *Forbes*, June 2, 2016, http://www.forbes.com/sites/derekxiao/2016/06/02/elizabeth-holmes-billionaires-gone-bust-eike-batista-allen-stanford-fortunes-lost-rebounds/

[iv] Charlie Gasparino, "Exclusive: Nelson Peltz Secretly Meets with DuPont Board," *FoxBusiness*, October 28, 2015, http://www.foxbusiness.com/features/2015/10/28/exclusive-nelson-peltz-secretly-meets-with-dupont-board.html

[v] Jacob Bunge, David Benoit, and Chelsey Dulaney, "DuPont, Dow Chemical Agree to Merge, Then Break Up Into Three Companies," *Wall Street Journal*, December 11, 2015, http://www.wsj.com/articles/dupont-dow-chemical-agree-to-merge-1449834739

[vi] Peter S. Cohan, "Westboro's SimpliVity Keeps on Hiring," *Worcester Telegram & Gazette*, December 13, 2015, http://www.telegram.com/article/20151213/news/151219819

[vii] Peter S. Cohan, "Will Westboro's SimpliVity Be Bought for $3.9 Billion?," *Worcester Telegram & Gazette*, November 20, 2016, http://www.telegram.com/news/20161120/peter-s-cohan-will-westboros-simplivity-be-bought-for-39-billion

© Peter S. Cohan 2017
P. S. Cohan, *Disciplined Growth Strategies*, DOI 10.1007/978-1-4842-2448-9_9

viii Peter Cohan, "3 Secrets for Growing from $1 Million to $100 Million in 3.5 Years," *Inc.*, August 11, 2014, http://www.inc.com/peter-cohan/3-secrets-to-grow-from-1-million-to-100-million-in-3-5-years.html

ix Lara O'Reilly, "At the Start of the Year, Ad-Tech Company Fiksu Was on a Hiring Spree and Preparing to Go Public—Now It Has Scrapped Its IPO Plans and Is Cutting 10% of Its Workforce," *Business Insider*, April 1, 2015, http://www.businessinsider.com/fiksu-scraps-ipo-plans-and-announces-layoffs-2015-4

x Curt Woodward, "Mobile Ad-Tech Company Fiksu Cuts Staff to Focus on New Product," *BetaBoston*, September 24, 2015, http://www.betaboston.com/news/2015/09/24/mobile-ad-tech-company-fiksu-cuts-staff-to-focus-on-new-product/

xi Mark Jones, "Fiksu Acquired by ClickDealer Having Lost Ground to AdTech Heavyweights," *Performance In*, March 6, 2016, http://performancein.com/news/2016/06/03/fiksu-acquired-clickdealer-having-lost-ground-ad-tech-heavyweights/

xii Peter Cohan. "3 Reasons Amazon Stock Will Soar in 2016," *Forbes*, December 31, 2015, http://www.forbes.com/sites/petercohan/2015/12/31/3-reasons-amazon-stock-will-soar-in-2016/

xiii Peter Cohan. "After Beating Estimates and Apple, Is Google Really an Alpha Bet?," *Forbes*, February 1, 2016, http://www.forbes.com/sites/petercohan/2016/02/01/after-beating-estimates-and-apple-is-google-really-an-alpha-bet/

xiv Richard N. Foster, *Innovation: The Attacker's Advantage*: Summit Books, 1986).

xv Peter Cohan, *Hungry Startup Strategy* (Oakland, CA: Berrett-Koehler, 2012).

xvi February 23, 2016, author interview with business development consultant Chris Lamb.

xvii Margi Murphy, "SAP Offers S/4HANA for Free," *ComputerWorldUK*, July 29, 2015, http://www.computerworlduk.com/it-management/s4-hana-what-does-saps-next-generation-erp-mean-for-customers-3596790/

xviii Murphy, Ibid.

xix Bert Hochfeld, "SAP: Taking Market Share at an Accelerating Pace from to Oracle," *Seeking Alpha*, January 19, 2016, http://seekingalpha.com/article/3818256-sap-taking-market-share-accelerating-pace-oracle

xx Peter Cohan, "Invest In Companies Like Netflix That Do the Opposite of What Clay Christensen Says," *Forbes*, July 14, 2014, http://www.forbes.com/sites/petercohan/2014/07/14/by-disrupting-disruption-netflix-reveals-new-investing-strategy/

xxi Dwight Gertz and Joao Baptista, *Grow to Be Great: Breaking the Downsizing Cycle* (New York: Free Press, 1995), ch. 2.

xxii Peter Cohan, "When the Blind Lead," *Business Strategy Review*, September 7, 2007, http://onlinelibrary.wiley.com/doi/10.1111/j.1467-8616.2007.00488.x/abstract

xxiii Peter Cohan, *Net Profit* (San Francisco: Jossey-Bass, 1999).

xxiv Noah Buhayar, "This Lender Lures Millennials with Free Cocktail Parties," *Bloomberg*, December 3, 2015, http://www.bloomberg.com/news/articles/2015-12-03/this-lender-lures-millennials-with-free-cocktail-parties

[xxv] Ari Levy, "Tech-Fueled Online Loans Face Stiff Test in 2016," *CNBC*, February 25, 2016, http://www.cnbc.com/2016/02/25/tech-fueled-online-loans-face-stiff-test-in.html

[xxvi] Board of Governors of the Federal Reserve System, "Consumer Credit—G.19," December 2015, http://www.federalreserve.gov/releases/g19/current/

[xxvii] It may make sense to consider using Michael Porter's five forces framework to conduct a thorough analysis of the forces that will influence the future attractiveness of these market segments.

[xxviii] Analysts should ask customers to list and rank their buyer purchase criteria and to assess how well their company satisfies those criteria compared to competitors' products.

[xxix] Analysts should consider using Porter's value chain as a way to identify the critical activities needed to outperform rivals on the customer purchase criteria. For each critical activity, analysts should compare how well they perform the activity to its rivals.

[xxx] Sophia Yan, "Starbucks Adding 1,400 New Shops in China," *CNN*, January 12, 2016, http://money.cnn.com/2016/01/12/investing/starbucks-china-expansion/

[xxxi] Helen H. Wang, "Five Things Starbucks Did to Get China Right," *Forbes*, November 10, 2012, http://www.forbes.com/sites/helenwang/2012/08/10/five-things-starbucks-did-to-get-china-right/

[xxxii] Ibid.

[xxxiii] Analysts may consider using the CAGE (cultural, administrative, geographic, and economic) distance framework to assess the fit between a company's home country and that of the new country as described by Pankaj Ghemawat, *Redefining Global Strategy* (Boston: Harvard Business Review Press, 2007).

[xxxiv] Peter Cohan, "Growth Guru Likes Facebook, Microsoft," *Forbes*, May 23, 2016, http://www.forbes.com/sites/petercohan/2016/05/23/growth-guru-likes-facebook-microsoft/

[xxxv] Benj Edwards, "The Birth of the iPod," *Macworld*, October 23, 2011, http://www.macworld.com/article/1163181/ipods/the-birth-of-the-ipod.html

[xxxvi] Peter Cohan, "Will Apple Stock Soar 50% in 2016?," *Forbes*, January 25, 2016, http://www.forbes.com/sites/petercohan/2016/01/25/will-apple-stock-soar-50-in-2016/

[xxxvii] Peter Cohan, "Netflix's Reed Hastings Is the Master of Adaptation," *Forbes*, October 22, 2013, http://www.forbes.com/sites/petercohan/2013/10/22/netflixs-reed-hastings-is-the-master-of-adaptation/#4934f4267b10

[xxxviii] Roberto Baldwin, "Netflix Gambles on Big Data to Become the HBO of Streaming," *Wired*, November 12, 2012, http://www.wired.com/2012/11/netflix-data-gamble/

[xxxix] Vijay Govindarajan and Srikanth Srinivas, "The Innovation Mindset in Action: 3M Corporation," *Harvard Business Review*, August 6, 2013, https://hbr.org/2013/08/the-innovation-mindset-in-acti-3/

[xl] Peter Cohan, "Can Scott Cook Revive Corporate America?" *Forbes*, February 29, 2012, http://www.forbes.com/sites/petercohan/2012/02/29/can-scott-cook-revive-corporate-america/

Chapter 2: Growth via New or Current Customers

[i] Amy Gutman, "What Startups Can Learn From McDonald's Turnaround," *Forbes*, January 29, 2016, http://www.forbes.com/sites/amyguttman/2016/01/29/what-startups-can-learn-from-the-egg-mcmuffin/

[ii] Jessica Wohl, "Behind 'The People's Launch' of All Day Breakfast at McDonald's," *Advertising Age*, September 4, 2015, http://adage.com/article/cmo-strategy/people-s-launch-day-breakfast-mcdonald-s/300214/

[iii] "McDonald's Beats Earnings on Surging US Sales, China Demand," *CNBC*, January 25, 2016, http://www.cnbc.com/2016/01/25/

[iv] Leslie Patton, "McDonald's to Expand All-Day Breakfast to Keep Sales Boost Going," *Bloomberg*, July 6, 2016, http://www.bloomberg.com/news/articles/2016-07-06/mcdonald-s-to-expand-all-day-breakfast-to-keep-sales-boost-going

[v] "Why McDonald's Sales Are Falling," *The Economist*, January 14, 2015, http://www.economist.com/blogs/economist-explains/2015/01/economist-explains-7

[vi] Peter Cohan, "The Inside Story Of McDonald's 35% Profit Growth," *Inc.*, May 31, 2016, http://www.inc.com/peter-cohan/growth-gurus-inside-scoop-on-mcdonalds-turnaround.html

[vii] Drew Harwell, "The Rise and Fall of Subway, the World's Biggest Food Chain," *The Washington Post*, May 30, 2015, https://www.washingtonpost.com/business/economy/the-rise-and-fall-of-subway-the-worlds-biggest-food-chain/2015/05/29/0ca0a84a-fa7a-11e4-a13c-193b1241d51a_story.html

[viii] Harwell, Ibid.

[ix] Danielle DeCourcey, "Subway Is Taking Another Big Blow as Sales Drop Again," *Attn.com*, April 2, 2016, http://www.attn.com/stories/7037/subway-sales-declining-2015

[x] Robert McFadden, "Fred DeLuca, Hands-on Co-Founder of Subway Sandwich Chain, Dies at 67," *New York Times*, September 15, 2015, http://www.nytimes.com/2015/09/16/business/fred-deluca-co-founder-of-subway-sandwich-chain-dies-at-67.html

[xi] Kelly Liyakasa, "Criteo Continues Growth Streak, Adding 730 Customers and Hefty Revenue Gains," *AdExchanger*, August 4, 2015, http://adexchanger.com/investment/criteo-continues-growth-streak-adding-730-customers-and-hefty-revenue-gains/

[xii] Criteo, "Schedule 14A," *sec.gov*, May 11, 2016, http://www.sec.gov/Archives/edgar/data/1576427/000157642716000232/defa14amay.htm

[xiii] Criteo, "Schedule 14A," Ibid.

[xiv] Liyakasa, Ibid.

[xv] Liyakasa, Ibid.

[xvi] Criteo, "First Quarter 2016 10Q," *sec.gov*, May 4, 2016, http://www.sec.gov/Archives/edgar/data/1576427/000157642716000218/criteo10qq12016.htm

xvii Peter Cohan, "How Success Killed Eastman Kodak," *Forbes*, October 10, 2011, http://www.forbes.com/sites/petercohan/2011/10/01/how-success-killed-eastman-kodak/print/

xviii Times Staff and Wire Reports, "Polaroid Wins $909 Million from Kodak: Photography: The Firms Have Been Involved in a Patent-Infringement Suit for Years. Analysts Had Expected the Award to Be Much Larger," *Los Angeles Times*, October 13, 1990, http://articles.latimes.com/1990-10-13/business/fi-1997_1_instant-photography

xix Sandra M. Chung, "Polaroid Goes Bankrupt; Plans to Sell Existing Assets," *The Tech*, October 23, 2001, http://tech.mit.edu/V121/N53/53pol.53n.html

xx Thomas Finnerty, "Kodak vs. Fuji: Battle for Global Market Share," *Pace University*, 2000, http://www.pace.edu/emplibrary/tfinnerty.pdf

xxi Kamal Munir, "The Demise of Kodak: Five Reasons," *Wall Street Journal*, February 26, 2012 http://blogs.wsj.com/source/2012/02/26/the-demise-of-kodak-five-reasons/

xxii Munir, Ibid.

xxiii Michael L. Millenson, "Kodak to Buy Sterling Drug," *Chicago Tribune*, January 23, 1988, http://articles.chicagotribune.com/1988-01-23/business/8803240788_1_kodak-pharmaceutical-industry-sterling-drug

xxiv "Kodak to Sell Remaining Sterling Winthrop Unit: Drugs: SmithKline Beecham Will Buy the Consumer Health Products Business for $2.925 Billion," *Associated Press*, August 30, 1994, http://articles.latimes.com/1994-08-30/business/fi-32940_1_health-products-business

xxv "Eastman Kodak Company 10 Q," June 30, 2011, *sec.gov*, https://www.sec.gov/Archives/edgar/data/31235/000003123511000117/ekq22011_10q.htm

xxvi Mike Spector and Dana Mattioli, "Kodak Seeks Help as Fears Mount," *Wall Street Journal*, October 1, 2011, http://www.wsj.com/articles/SB100014240529702041382045766030 53167627950

xxvii Dawn McCarty and Beth Jinks, "Kodak Files for Bankruptcy as Digital Era Spells End to Film," *Bloomberg*, January 19, 2012, http://www.bloomberg.com/news/articles/2012-01-19/kodak-photography-pioneer-files-for-bankruptcy-protection-1-

xxviii Ben McLannahan, "Upstart Lender SoFi Maintains Its Bravado as Gintech Fever Cools," *Financial Times*, May 2, 2016, http://www.ft.com/cms/s/0/5db33398-05d6-11e6-96e5-f85cb08b0730.html#ixzz4ChtVaUX7

xxix Peter Rudegeair and Telis Demos, "Slump Might Turn Anti-Bank SoFi Into a Bank," *Wall Street Journal*, July 12, 2016, http://www.wsj.com/articles/slump-might-turn-anti-bank-sofi-into-a-bank-1468339004

xxx Ainsley O'Connell, "Inside SoFi's Exclusive Club for 'Great' People," *Fast Company*, July/August 2016, http://www.fastcompany.com/3060461/most-innovative-companies/inside-sofis-exclusive-club-for-great-people

xxxi O'Connell, Ibid.

xxxii "SoFi CEO: Funding Boosts Pursuit of 'Aggressive' Ambitions," *CNBC*, October 1, 2015, http://www.cnbc.com/2015/10/01/nding-boosts-pursuit-of-aggressive-ambitions.html

xxxiii Peter Cohan, "5 Ways That SoFi Threatens Bank of America, *Forbes*, October 2, 2015, http://www.forbes.com/sites/petercohan/2015/10/02/5-ways-that-sofi-threatens-bank-of-america/

xxxiv Bill Swindell, "SoFi Seeks to Upend the Banking Business, *The Press Democrat*, July 12, 2015, http://www.pressdemocrat.com/business/4186680-181/sofi-seeks-to-upend-the?page=0&artslide=0

xxxv Hugh Son, "Bank of America Least Loved in Places Where It's Best Known,"*Bloomberg*, April 30, 2015, http://www.bloomberg.com/news/articles/2015-04-30/bank-of-america-is-least-loved-in-places-where-it-s-best-known

xxxvi Swindell, Ibid.

xxxvii Dan Primack, "SoFi Raises Whopping $1 Billion to Refinance Student Loans, *Fortune*, September 30, 2015, http://fortune.com/2015/09/30/sofi-raises-whopping-1-billion-to-refinance-student-loans

xxxviii " SoFi CEO: Funding Boosts Pursuit of 'Aggressive' Ambitions," Ibid.

xxxix Ainsley O'Connell, "Inside SoFi's Exclusive Club for 'Great' People,"*Fast Company*, July/August 2016, http://www.fastcompany.com/3060461/most-innovative-companies/inside-sofis-exclusive-club-for-great-people

xl O'Connell, Ibid.

xli O'Connell, Ibid.

xlii O'Connell, Ibid.

xliii Rudegeair and Demos, Ibid.

xliv Rudegeair and Demos, Ibid.

xlv Rudegeair and Demos, Ibid.

xlvi Biz Carson, "In Memoriam: 7 Once-Hot Startups That Shut Their Doors in 2015," *Business Insider*, December 14, 2015, http://www.businessinsider.com/startups-that-failed-in-2015-2015-12

xlvii Carson, Ibid.

xlviii Carmel DeAmicis, "Homejoy Shuts Down After Battling Worker Classification Lawsuits," *Re/code*, July 17, 2015, http://www.recode.net/2015/7/17/11614814/cleaning-services-startup-homejoy-shuts-down-after-battling-worker

xlix DeAmicis, Ibid.

l Many so-called gig economy companies such as Uber classified their workers as contractors instead of employees so they would not have to pay payroll taxes, social security benefits, vacation time, or other fees. Workers filed lawsuits and presidential candidates debated the topic.

li Christina Farr, "Homejoy at the Unicorn Glue Factory," *Backchannel*, October 26, 2015, https://backchannel.com/why-homejoy-failed-bb0ab39d901a#.j51tb1uxe.

lii Farr, Ibid.

liii Farr, Ibid.

liv Farr, Ibid.

[lv] Farr, Ibid.

[lvi] Peter Cohan "As EMC Struggles, Actifio One Targets $580 Billion Market," *Forbes*, February 9, 2015, http://www.forbes.com/sites/petercohan/2015/02/09/as-emc-struggles-actifio-one-targets-580-billion-market/

[lvii] "2016 IPO Prospects: Actifio Looks Ready," *sramanamitra.com*, January 5, 2016, http://www.sramanamitra.com/2016/01/05/2016-ipo-prospects-actifio-looks-ready/

[lviii] Kyle Alspach, "Actifio Raises $100 million, Valuing Company at $1 Billion," *BetaBoston*, March 24, 2014, http://www.betaboston.com/news/2014/03/24/actifio-funding-ipo-valuation-billion-dollar-boston-tech/

[lix] Cohan, Ibid.

[lx] Cohan, Ibid.

[lxi] Cohan, Ibid.

[lxii] "2016 IPO Prospects: Actifio Looks Ready," Ibid.

[lxiii] Peter Cohan, "$1.1 Billion Startup Recovers from Bad Advice on Managing 'Disruption,'" *Inc.*, July 13, 2016, http://www.inc.com/peter-cohan/11-billion-startup-recovers-from-bad-advice-on-managing-disruption.html

[lxiv] Fred Andrews, "MANAGEMENT: IDEAS INTO ACTION; A Primer on Weathering Technology's Storms," *The New York Times*, November 3, 1999, http://www.nytimes.com/1999/11/03/business/management-ideas-into-action-a-primer-on-weathering-technology-s-storms.html

[lxv] Cohan, Ibid.

[lxvi] Cohan, Ibid.

[lxvii] Cohan, Ibid.

[lxviii] "2016 IPO Prospects: Actifio Looks Ready," Ibid.

[lxvix] Tom Wright, "Actifio Makes IPO U-turn," *CRN UK*, June 28, 2016, http://www.channelweb.co.uk/crn-uk/news/2463079/actifio-makes-ipo-u-turn

[lxx] Wright, Ibid.

[lxxi] Wright, Ibid.

[lxxii] Adario Strange, "Color App Shutting Down Next Month," *PC Mag*, November 20, 2012, http://www.pcmag.com/article2/0,2817,2412335,00.asp

[lxxiii] Danielle Sacks, "Bill Nguyen: The Boy in the Bubble," *Fast Company*, October 19, 2011, http://www.fastcompany.com/1784823/bill-nguyen-the-boy-in-the-bubble

[lxxiv] Colleen Taylor, "Sources: Apple Paid $7 Million for Color Labs," *TechCrunch*, November 19, 2012, https://techcrunch.com/2012/11/19/sources-apple-paid-7-million-for-color-labs/

[lxxv] Sacks, Ibid.

[lxxvi] Jeffrey L. Wilson, "Color Brings Social, Multi-Lens Shooting to iPhone, Android Phones," *PC Mag*, March 23, 2011, http://www.pcmag.com/article2/0,2817,2382194,00.asp

[lxxvii] Strange, Ibid.

[lxxviii] Jeffrey L. Wilson, "Color Brings Social, Multi-Lens Shooting to iPhone, Android Phones," *PC Mag*, March 23, 2011, http://www.pcmag.com/article2/0,2817,2382194,00.asp

[lxxix] Strange, Ibid.

[lxxx] Claire Cain Miller, "Investors Provide Millions to Risky Start-Ups," *The New York Times*, June 19, 2011, http://www.nytimes.com/2011/06/20/technology/20color.html?pagewanted=1&_r=1

[lxxxi] Cain Miller, Ibid.

[lxxxii] Shayndi Raice and Spencer E. Ante, "Insta-Rich: $1 Billion for Instagram," *Wall Street Journal*, April 10, 2012, http://www.wsj.com/articles/SB10001424052702303815404577333840377381670

[lxxxiii] Maya Kosoff, "Here's How Two Analysts Think Instagram Could Be Worth Up to $37 Million," *Business Insider,* March 17, 2015, http://www.businessinsider.com.au/instagram-valuation-2015-3

[lxxxiv] Cain Miller, Ibid.

[lxxxv] Cain Miller, Ibid.

[lxxxvi] Sacks, Ibid.

[lxxxvii] Sacks, Ibid.

[lxxxviii] Strange, Ibid.

[lxxxix] Strange, Ibid.

[xc] Sacks, Ibid.

[xci] Sacks, Ibid.

Chapter 3: Growth via New or Current Geographies

[i] Pankaj Ghemawat, "Distance Still Matters," *Harvard Business Review*, September 2001, https://www.business.illinois.edu/aguilera/Teaching/Distance%20still%20matters%20HBR%202001%20Ghemawat.pdf

[ii] "Market Share of Wireless Subscriptions Held by Carriers in the U.S. from 1st Quarter 2011 to 1st Quarter 2016," *The Statistics Portal*, accessed July 8, 2016, http://www.statista.com/statistics/199359/market-share-of-wireless-carriers-in-the-us-by-subscriptions/

[iii] "Un-carrier at Three Years: Assessing T-Mobile's Disruptive Impact," *451 Research*, March 28, 2016, https://newsroom.t-mobile.com/news-and-blogs/3-years-Un-carrier-report.htm

[iv] Roger Cheng, "T-Mobile Cements Its Standing by Adding 1.8M Customers," *CNET*, April 28, 2015, http://www.cnet.com/news/t-mobile-cements-its-standing-by-adding-1-8m-customers/

[v] "A Look Back at T-Mobile's Eight 'Un-carrier' Moves," *The Latin Post*, January 3, 2015, http://www.latinpost.com/articles/28183/20150103/look-back-t-mobiles-eight-un-carrier-moves.htm

[vi] "A Look Back at T-Mobile's Eight 'Un-carrier' Moves," Ibid.

[vii] "Un-carrier at Three Years: Assessing T-Mobile's Disruptive Impact," Ibid.

[viii] "T-Mobile Income Statement," *Morningstar*, accessed July 9, 2016, http://financials.morningstar.com/income-statement/is.html?t=TMUS&region=USA&culture=en_US

[ix] "T-Mobile US, Inc Schedule 14A," sec.gov, April 26, 2016, https://www.sec.gov/Archives/edgar/data/1283699/000119312516564011/d75474ddef14a.htm

[x] Danielle Sacks, "Who The @!#$&% Is This Guy? John Legere's Strategy for Taking New Customers by Storm," *Fast Company*, June 2, 2015, http://www.fastcompany.com/3046877/who-the-is-this-guy-john-legeres-strategy-for-taking-new-customers-by-storm

[xi] Sacks, Ibid.

[xii] Sacks, Ibid.

[xiii] Sacks, Ibid.

[xiv] Sacks, Ibid.

[xv] Brian Fung, "T-Mobile Is Giving Pokémon Go Players Free Data, Because of Course," *The Washington Post*, July 14, 2016, https://www.washingtonpost.com/news/the-switch/wp/2016/07/14/t-mobile-is-giving-pokemon-go-players-free-data-because-of-course/

[xvi] Patricia Sellers, "How Avon Chose Its New CEO," *Fortune*, April 9, 2012, http://fortune.com/2012/04/09/how-avon-chose-its-new-ceo/

[xvii] "Avon Products Income Statement," *Morningstar*, Accessed July 9, 2016, http://financials.morningstar.com/income-statement/is.html?t=AVP&region=USA&culture=en_US

[xviii] Beth Kowitt, "Avon: The Rise and Fall of a Beauty Icon," *Fortune*, April 11, 2012, http://fortune.com/2012/04/11/avon-the-rise-and-fall-of-a-beauty-icon/

[xix] Glazer, Ibid.

[xx] Glazer, Ibid.

[xxi] Glazer, Ibid.

[xxii] Kowitt, Ibid.

[xxiii] Joann S. Lublin And Ellen Byron, "Avon Explores Strategic Alternatives," *Wall Street Journal*, April 14, 2015, http://www.wsj.com/articles/avon-explores-strategic-alternatives-1429030371

[xxiv] Lublin and Byron, Ibid.

[xxv] Kowitt, Ibid.

xxvi Yashaswini Swmaynathan, "Ding-Dong: Cerberus Comes Calling at Avon with $605 Million Investment," *Reuters*, Dec 17, 2015, http://www.reuters.com/article/us-avon-prdcts-divestiture-cerberus-capi-idUSKBNOU00KX20151217

xxvii Lublin and Byron, Ibid.

xxviii Gabriel Kane, "Moody's Downgraded Avon Products with a 'Negative' Outlook," *Market Realist*, June 28, 2016, http://marketrealist.com/2016/06/moodys-downgrades-avon-products-negative-outlook/

xxix "Best Buy Acquires Jiangsu Five Star," *Shenzhen Daily*, May 15, 2006, http://www.chinadaily.com.cn/bizchina/2006-05/15/content_589901.htm

xxx "Best Buy Plans Retreat From China. Good News or Bad?," *The Motley Fool*, June 26, 2014, http://www.fool.com/investing/general/2014/06/26/best-buy-plans-retreat-from-china-good-news-or-bad.aspx

xxxi "Best Buy to Sell China Business, Focus on North America," *Reuters*, December 4, 2014, http://www.reuters.com/article/us-best-buy-china-idUSKCN0JI0NV20141204

xxxii Todd Spangler, "Netflix Wants the World: Can It Really Expand to 200 Countries in 2 Years?," *Variety*, January 22, 2015, http://variety.com/2015/digital/news/netflix-wants-the-world-can-it-really-expand-to-200-countries-in-2-years-1201411740/

xxxiii Spangler, Ibid.

xxxiv Spangler, Ibid.

xxxv Spangler, Ibid.

xxxvi Spangler, Ibid.

xxxvii Spangler, Ibid.

xxxviii Spangler, Ibid.

xxxix Daniel Sparks, "A Close Look at Netflix, Inc.'s International Expansion," *The Motley Fool*, August 5, 2015, http://www.fool.com/investing/general/2015/08/05/a-close-look-at-netflix-incs-international-expansi.aspx

xl Sparks, Ibid.

xli Sparks, Ibid.

xlii Sparks, Ibid.

xliii Joshua Brustein, "Netflix's Utopian Plan to Conquer the World," *Bloomberg*, January 7, 2016, http://www.bloomberg.com/news/articles/2016-01-07/netflix-s-utopian-plan-to-conquer-the-world

xliv Brustein, Ibid.

xlv Peter Cohan, "Is Netflix's Big Miss a Buying Opportunity?" *Forbes*, July 19, 2016, http://www.forbes.com/sites/petercohan/2016/07/19/is-netflixs-big-miss-a-buying-opportunity/print/

xlvi Cohan, Ibid.

xlvii Cohan, Ibid.

xlviii Peter Cohan, "Is Netflix's Big Miss a Buying Opportunity?" *Forbes*, July 19, 2016, http://www.forbes.com/sites/petercohan/2016/07/19/is-netflixs-big-miss-a-buying-opportunity/print/

xlix Cohan, Ibid.

l Cohan, Ibid.

li Saritha Rai, "Apple's Push to Flood India with Used iPhonesIgnites Backlash," *Bloomberg*, April 3, 2016, http://www.bloomberg.com/news/articles/2016-04-03/apple-s-push-to-flood-india-with-used-iphones-ignites-backlash

lii Rai, Ibid.

liii Rai, Ibid.

liv Rai, Ibid.

lv Rai, Ibid.

lvi Rai, Ibid.

lvii Rai, Ibid.

lviii Rai, Ibid.

lvix Rai, Ibid.

lx Rai, Ibid.

lxi Rai, Ibid.

lxii Writankar Mukherjee, "Apple Wants More Clarity on Sourcing Rules before Opening Retail Stores in India," *Economic Times*, July 8, 2016, http://economictimes.indiatimes.com/tech/hardware/apple-wants-more-clarity-on-sourcing-rules-before-opening-retail-stores-in-india/articleshow/53106417.cms

lxiii Mukherjee, Ibid.

lxiv Mukherjee, Ibid.

lxv Arpinder Singh, "Bribery and Corruption: Ground Reality in India,"*EY*, accessed July 17, 2016, http://www.ey.com/IN/en/Services/Assurance/Fraud-Investigation—Dispute-Services/Bribery-and-corruption-ground-reality-in-India

lxvi "SEC Enforcement Actions: FCPA Cases," *sec.gov*, https://www.sec.gov/spotlight/fcpa/fcpa-cases.shtml, accessed July 17, 2016.

lxvii Sarah Maxjan,"Rethinking the Nail Salon by Glancing at the Starbucks Model," *New York Times*, January. 14, 2015, http://www.nytimes.com/2015/01/15/business/smallbusiness/rethinking-the-nail-salon-by-glancing-at-the-starbucks-model.html

lxviii Maxjan, Ibid.

lxix Elizabeth Segran, "The Nail Salon Where Manicurists Get 401Ks and Paid Vacation," *Fast Company*, July 15, 2016, http://www.fastcompany.com/3061006/the-nail-salon-where-manicurists-get-401ks-and-paid-vacation

[lxx] Maxjan, Ibid.

[lxxi] Maxjan, Ibid.

[lxxii] Maxjan, Ibid.

[lxxiii] Anthony K.Tjan,"Strategy on One Page," *Harvard Business Review,* June 1, 2011, https://hbr.org/2011/06/strategy-on-one-page/Strategy on One Page

[lxxiv] Maxjan, Ibid.

[lxxv] Maxjan, Ibid.

[lxxvi] Maxjan, Ibid.

[lxxvii] Tjan, Ibid.

[lxxviii] Maxjan, Ibid.

[lxxix] Brentney Hamilton, "The Pedicure Index: How Dallas' Freewheelin' Feet Brought a Boston Mani-Pedi Spot Here," *GuideLive*, February 19, 2015, http://www.guidelive.com/dallas/2015/02/19/pedicure-index-brings-miniluxe-to-dallas

[lxxx] Olivia Vanni, "MiniLuxe Secures $7.5M in Funding, Plans Expansion to Cali.," *BostInno*, July 6, 2016, http://bostinno.streetwise.co/2016/07/06/miniluxe-funding-from-cue-ball-horowitz-for-california/

[lxxxi] Kim Bhasin, "The Long, Agonizing Fall of PacSun," *Bloomberg*, April 8, 2016, http://www.bloomberg.com/news/articles/2016-04-08/the-long-agonizing-fall-of-pacsun

[lxxxii] Bhasin, Ibid.

[lxxxiii] Samantha Masunaga, "PacSun Files for Chapter 11 Bankruptcy Protection, Plans to Go Private," *Los Angeles Times*, April 7, 2016, http://www.latimes.com/business/la-fi-pacsun-bankruptcy-20160407-story.html

[lxxxiv] Hang Nguyen, "PacSun Seeks New Foot Traffic," *The Orange County Register*, February 28, 2006, http://www.ocregister.com/articles/stores-74607-business-johnson.html

[lxxxv] Nguyen, Ibid.

[lxxxvi] Nguyen, Ibid.

[lxxxvii] Bhasin, Ibid.

[lxxxviii] "PacSun CEO Seth Johnson Resigns to 'Pursue Other Interests,'" *Business Transworld*, October 26, 2006, http://business.transworld.net/products/pacsun-ceo-seth-johnson-resigns-to-pursue-other-interests/#l7u7HhkvJ5oMgoP8.99

[lxxxix] Bhasin, Ibid.

[xc] Bhasin, Ibid.

[xci] Bhasin, Ibid.

[xcii] Bhasin, Ibid.

[xciii] Bhasin, Ibid.

xciv Peter Cohan, "Critical Software Shows Portugal Can Grow," *Forbes*, June 3, 2011, http://www.forbes.com/sites/petercohan/2011/06/03/critical-software-shows-portugal-can-grow/

xcv Cohan, Ibid.

xcvi Cohan, Ibid.

xcvii Cohan, Ibid.

xcviii Cohan, Ibid.

xcix Cohan, Ibid.

c "Mozambique Profile—Timeline," *BBC*, January 15, 2015, http://www.bbc.com/news/world-africa-13890720

ci "Portugal: Critical Software Signs New Contracts in Mozambique," *Macauhub*, October 21, 2008, http://www.macauhub.com.mo/en/2008/10/21/5940/

cii "International Focus: Mozambique," *Criticalsoftware.com*. July 13, 2015, http://www.criticalsoftware.com/en/media-centre/short-news/posts/news-in-brief/international-focus-mozambique#.V5JS3mdTG1s

ciii "International Focus: Mozambique," Ibid.

civ "Marco Costa Is the New CEO of CRITICAL Software," *criticalsoftware.com*, January 3, 2012, http://www.criticalsoftware.com/en/media-centre/short-news/posts/news/marco-costa-is-the-new-ceo-of-critical-software#.V5IrSmdTG1s

cv "Marco Costa Is the New CEO of CRITICAL Software," Ibid.

cvi "CRITICAL Software Announces the Return of Gonçalo Quadros as CEO," *criticalsoftware.com*, July 24, 2014, http://www.criticalsoftware.com/en/media-centre/press-releases/posts/press-releases/critical-software-announces-the-return-of-goncalo-quadros-as-ceo#.V5Jbw2dTG1s

cvii "CRITICAL Software Announces the Return of Gonçalo Quadros as CEO," Ibid.

cviii "CRITICAL Software Has Today Announced Its 2015 Financial Results, Reporting Its Strongest Annual Performance to Date," *criticalsoftware.com* , April 12, 2016, http://www.criticalsoftware.com/en/media-centre/press-releases/posts/press-releases/critical-software-reports-record-annual-financial-results#.V5Jd02dTG1s

cix "CRITICAL Software Has Today Announced Its 2015 Financial Results, Reporting Its Strongest Annual Performance to Date," Ibid.

cx "rdio," *crunchbase*, accessed July 22, 2016, https://www.crunchbase.com/organization/rdio#/entity

cxi Janko Roettgers, "Pandora Is Acquiring Music Streaming Service Rdio For $75 Million (Exclusive)," *Variety*, November 16, 2015, http://variety.com/2015/digital/news/pandora-rdio-acquisition-1201641583/

cxii Casey Newton, "Why Rdio Died," *The Verge*, November 17, 2015, http://www.theverge.com/2015/11/17/9750890/rdio-shutdown-pandora

cxiii Newton, Ibid.

cxiv Newton, Ibid.

cxv Newton, Ibid.

cxvi Newton, Ibid.

cxvii Newton, Ibid.

cxviii Newton, Ibid.

cxix Newton, Ibid.

cxx Newton, Ibid.

cxxi Newton, Ibid.

cxxii Newton, Ibid.

cxxiii Newton, Ibid.

cxxiv Author interview with Chris Lamb, September 14, 2016.

Chapter 4: Growth via Building or Acquiring New Products

i "Amazon.com," *Morningstar*, accessed July 27, 2016, http://financials.morningstar.com/ratios/r.html?t=AMZN&region=USA&culture=en_US

ii AWS Remains Dominant Despite Microsoft and Google Growth Surges, Synergy Research Group, February 3, 2016, https://www.srgresearch.com/articles/aws-remains-dominant-despite-microsoft-and-google-growth-surges

iii TNW DEALS, "Why AWS Dominates the Cloud Services Market," *NextWeb*, March 11, 2016, http://thenextweb.com/offers/2016/03/11/amazon-web-services-dominates-cloud-services-market/

iv TNW DEALS, Ibid.

v TNW DEALS, Ibid.

vi Ritika Trikha, "How Amazon Web Services Surged Out of Nowhere, *HackerRank*, August 26, 2015, http://blog.hackerrank.com/how-amazon-web-services-surged-out-of-nowhere/

vii Trikha, Ibid.

viii Jack Clark, "How Amazon Exposed Its Guts: The History of AWS's EC2," *ZDNet*, June 7, 2012, http://www.zdnet.com/article/how-amazon-exposed-its-guts-the-history-of-awss-ec2/

ix Dan Frommer, "Amazon Web Services Is Approaching a $10 Billion-a-Year Business," *recode*, Apr 28, 2016, http://www.recode.net/2016/4/28/11586526/aws-cloud-revenue-growth

x Morningstar, Ibid.

[xi] Mathew Ingram, "When Will ESPN's Subscriber Numbers Finally Hit Bottom?," *Fortune*, November 24, 2015, http://fortune.com/2015/11/24/espn-subscriber-numbers/

[xii] Mike Farrell, "Cord Cutting Grew Four-Fold in 2015," *Multichannel News*, April 4, 2016, http://www.multichannel.com/news/content/cord-cutting-grew-four-fold-2015/403811

[xiii] Farrell, Ibid.

[xiv] "Cutting the Cord," *The Economist*, July 16, 2016, http://www.economist.com/news/business/21702177-television-last-having-its-digital-revolution-moment-cutting-cord

[xv] Ingram, Ibid.

[xvi] Ingram, Ibid.

[xvii] Ingram, Ibid.

[xviii] Ingram, Ibid.

[xix] Ingram, Ibid.

[xx] Clay Travis, "ESPN Loses Another 1.5 Million Subscribers As Cord Cutting Accelerates," *Outkick The Coverage*, May 28, 2016, http://www.outkickthecoverage.com/espn-loses-1-5-million-subscribers-as-cord-cutting-accelerates-052816

[xxi] "ESPN to Cut the Cord, But Will it Help Disney (DIS) Shareholders?," *Zacks*, July 8, 2016, http://finance.yahoo.com/news/espn-cut-cord-help-disney-203308269.html

[xxii] Peter S. Cohan, "Four Tests for Successful Acquisitions," *Babson Insight*, accessed July 28, 2016, http://www.babson.edu/executive-education/thought-leadership/strategy/Pages/successful-acquisitions.aspx

[xxiii] Josh Constine and Kim-Mai Cutler, "Facebook Buys Instagram for $1 Billion, Turns Budding Rival Into Its Standalone Photo App," *TechCrunch*, April 9, 2012, https://techcrunch.com/2012/04/09/facebook-to-acquire-instagram-for-1-billion/

[xxiv] David Gelles, "Citigroup Says Instagram Is Worth $35 Billion," *New York Times*, December 19, 2014, http://dealbook.nytimes.com/2014/12/19/citigroup-says-instagram-is-worth-35-billion/

[xxv] Shayndi Raice and Spencer E. Ante, "Facebook Inks Its Biggest Deal Ever; Neutralizes Threat from a Hot Photo Start-Up," *Wall Street Journal*, April 10, 2012, http://www.wsj.com/articles/SB10001424052702303815404577333840377381670

[xxvi] Josh Constine and Kim-Mai Cutler, Ibid.

[xxvii] Josh Constine and Kim-Mai Cutler, Ibid.

[xxviii] Shayndi Raice and Spencer E. Ante, Ibid.

[xxix] Josh Constine and Kim-Mai Cutler, Ibid.

[xxx] Jemima Kiss, "Instagram CEO Kevin Systrom: 'We're Working on Time Travel'," *The Guardian*, October 2, 2015, https://www.theguardian.com/technology/2015/oct/02/instagram-kevin-systrom-interview-working-on-time-travel

[xxxi] Kiss, Ibid.

xxxii Gelles.

xxxiii Kiss, Ibid.

xxxiv Andrew Griswold, "Instagram Explodes Past 500 Million Monthly Users and Why It Matters," *Fstoppers*, July 19, 2016, https://fstoppers.com/apps/instagram-explodes-past-500-million-monthly-users-and-why-it-matters-138786

xxxv "Digital Ad Spending to Surpass TV Next Year By 2020, TV's share of Ad Spending Will Drop Below One-Third," *eMarketer*, March 8, 2016, http://www.emarketer.com/Article/Digital-Ad-Spending-Surpass-TV-Next-Year/1013671

xxxvi Tom Johnson, "That's AOL folks," *CNNfn*, January 10, 2000, http://money.cnn.com/2000/01/10/deals/aol_warner/

xxxvii Johnson, Ibid.

xxxviii Johnson, Ibid.

xxxix Johnson, Ibid.

xl Johnson, Ibid.

xli David Gardner, "AOL Completes Spin-Off from Time Warner," *Information Week*, December 10, 2009, http://www.informationweek.com/e-commerce/aol-completes-spin-off-from-time-warner/d/d-id/1085495?

xlii Tom DiChristopher, "Verizon Closes AOL Acquisition," *CNBC*, June 23, 2015, http://www.cnbc.com/2015/06/23/

xliii Yinka Adegoke, "Time Warner to Complete Cable Spin-Off Next Month," *Reuters*, February 26, 2009, http://www.reuters.com/article/us-timewarner-idUSTRE51P82W20090227

xliv Anne Steele and John D. McKinnon, "Charter Communications Completes Acquisition of Time Warner Cable," *Wall Street Journal*, May 18, 2016, http://www.wsj.com/articles/charter-communications-completes-55-billion-acquisition-of-time-warner-cable-1463581387

xlv Peter Cohan, "4 Reasons AT&T Should Not Acquire Time Warner," *Forbes*, October 21, 2016, http://www.forbes.com/sites/petercohan/2016/10/21/4-reasons-att-should-not-acquire-time-warner/#6b0260a5598c

xlvi "AOL and Time Warner Unite." *BBC News*, January 12, 2001, http://news.bbc.co.uk/2/hi/business/1112358.stm

xlvii Munk, Nina. *Fools Rush In: Steve Case, Jerry Levin, and the Unmaking of AOL Time Warner.* (New York: HarperCollins Publishers, 2004), p. 133.

xlviii Munk, Ibid.

xlix Munk, Ibid.

l Munk, Ibid.

li A Material Adverse Change (MAC) clause is typically included in merger and other financial contracts. MAC clauses enable parties to a deal to pull out of the transaction before closing if there is a significant change in the business that materially alters the value of the deal.

lii Munk, Ibid.

[liii] David Shook, "AOL's Close Call on Debt; Had It Not Recently Renegotiated Its Loans, the Massive Writedowns It Has Made Would Have Put It in an Even tTougher Spot," *BusinessWeek Online,* January 31 2003, http://www.bloomberg.com/news/articles/2003-01-30/aols-close-call-on-debt One of the terms of AOL's borrowing contract was to maintain a net worth greater than $50 billion. The goodwill write-down was based on assumptions that were not disclosed to investors—leaving open the possibility that the write-down amount was set to avoid violating that debt contract term.

[liv] Paul Abrahams, "Yahoo! Warns of Slower Advertising Spending in 2001," *FT.com.*, January 10, 2001.

[lv] Rayner, Abigail. "Merger Hit Trouble from Day One—AOL Time Warner's Growing Turmoil," *The Times*, July 20, 2002, p. 47.

[lvi] Tim Arango, "How the AOL-Time Warner Merger Went So Wrong," *New York Times,* January 10, 2010, http://www.nytimes.com/2010/01/11/business/media/11merger.html

[lvii] Peter Cohan, "New Relic Up-Ends Tradition," *Forbes*, December 14, 2011, http://www.forbes.com/sites/petercohan/2011/12/14/new-relic-up-ends-tradition/

[lviii] Cohan, Ibid.

[lix] Cohan, Ibid.

[lx] Cohan, Ibid.

[lxi] Cohan, Ibid.

[lxii] Cohan, Ibid.

[lxiii] Cohan, Ibid.

[lxiv] Morgan Brown, "New Relic's Growth Playbook from Startup to IPO," *GrowthHackers.com*, accessed August 2, 2016, https://growthhackers.com/growth-studies/new-relics-growth-playbook-from-startup-to-ipo

[lxv] Cohan, Ibid.

[lxvi] Brown, Ibid.

[lxvii] Brown, Ibid.

[lxviii] Cohan, Ibid.

[lxix] Cohan, Ibid.

[lxx] "Edited Transcript of NEWR Earnings Conference Call or Presentation 10-May-16 9:00pm GMT," *Thomson Reuters StreetEvents*, May 11, 2016, https://finance.yahoo.com/news/edited-transcript-newr-earnings-conference-043252149.html

[lxxi] "Edited Transcript of NEWR Earnings Conference Call or Presentation 10-May-16 9:00pm GMT," Ibid.

[lxxii] "Edited Transcript of NEWR Earnings Conference Call or Presentation 10-May-16 9:00pm GMT," Ibid.

[lxxiii] "Edited Transcript of NEWR Earnings Conference Call or Presentation 10-May-16 9:00pm GMT," Ibid.

lxxiv "Edited Transcript of NEWR Earnings Conference Call or Presentation 10-May-16 9:00pm GMT," Ibid.

lxxv Derrick Harris, "New Relic CEO on How to Build a Cloud Company and Help Customers Play Offense with Software," *Medium*, December 18, 2015, https://medium.com/s-c-a-l-e/new-relic-ceo-on-how-to-build-a-cloud-company-and-help-customers-play-offense-with-software-d6150778770d#.p8sx9ab6t

lxxvi Harris, Ibid.

lxxvii Harris, Ibid.

lxviii "New Relic Recognized as a Leader in Gartner's Magic Quadrant for Application Performance Monitoring Suites for Fourth Consecutive Year," *New Relic*, December 18, 2015, https://newrelic.com/press-release/20151218

lxxix Keith B. Nowak, *LinkedIn*, accessed August 3, 2016, https://www.linkedin.com/in/keithbnowak

lxxx Keith B. Nowak, Ibid.

lxxxi Keith Nowak, "Postmortem of My First Company (A Reposting)," *Medium*, accessed August 3, 2016, http://keithbnowak.com/post/55830173333/postmortem-of-my-first-company-a-reposting

lxxxii Keith Nowak, "Postmortem of My First Company (A Reposting)," Ibid.

lxxxiii Keith Nowak, "Postmortem of My First Company (A Reposting)," Ibid.

lxxxiv Keith Nowak, "Postmortem of My First Company (A Reposting)," Ibid.

lxxxv Keith Nowak, "Postmortem of My First Company (A Reposting)," Ibid.

lxxxvi Keith Nowak, "Postmortem of My First Company (A Reposting)," Ibid.

lxxxvii The typical venture capital partner meets with 1,000 entrepreneurs a year and invests in two of them. Of those two, only one in 10,000 ends up being worth at least $1 billion.

lxxxviii Michael Yoshino and Srini Rangan, *Strategic Alliances: An Entrepreneurial Approach to Globalization.* (Boston: Harvard Business School Press, 1995), pp. 83–84.

lxxxix Robert Cringley, "Triumph of The Nerds: Part II," *pbs.org*, accessed August 4, 2016, http://www.pbs.org/nerds/part2.html

xc "Bill Gates Real Time Net Worth," *Forbes*, accessed August 4, 2016, http://www.forbes.com/profile/bill-gates/

xci "Microsoft Acquires 86-DOS," *Complex.com*, January 8, 2013, http://www.complex.com/pop-culture/2013/01/the-15-most-important-tech-acquisitions-of-all-time/Microsoft Acquires 86-DOS

xcii Peter Cohan, *The Technology Leaders: How America's Most Profitable High Tech Companies Innovate Their Way to Success.* (San Francisco, CA: Jossey-Bass Publishers, 1997), pp. 49-50.

xciii Jan Rivkin and Michael Porter, *Matching Dell.* (Boston: Harvard Business School Publishing, 1999), p. 2.

xciv Peter Cohan, "Six Winning Ways to Boost Growth by Acquisition," *Inc.*, April 17, 2015, http://www.inc.com/peter-cohan/six-winning-ways-to-boost-growth-by-acquisition.html

[xcv] Cohan, Ibid.

[xcvi] Cohan, Ibid.

[xcvii] Cohan, Ibid.

[xcviii] Cohan, Ibid.

[xcix] Cohan, Ibid.

[c] Cohan, Ibid.

Chapter 5: Growth from Current or New Capabilities

[i] Sam Costello, "How Many iPhones Have Been Sold Worldwide?" *ipod about.com*, August 22, 2016, http://ipod.about.com/od/glossary/f/how-many-iphones-sold.htm

[ii] "Why Apple's Investors Are Questioning Its Future," *Fortune*, January 6, 2016, http://fortune.com/2016/01/06/apple-wall-street/

[iii] Shira Ovide and Daisuke Wakabayashi, "Apple's Share of Smartphone Industry's Profits Soars to 92%," *Wall Street Journal*, July 12, 2015, http://www.wsj.com/articles/apples-share-of-smartphone-industrys-profits-soars-to-92-1436727458

[iv] Peter Cohan, "Apple's Profit Doom Loop," *Forbes*, September 1, 2016, http://www.forbes.com/sites/petercohan/2016/09/01/apples-profit-doom-loop/

[v] Ovide and Wakabayashi, Ibid.

[vi] David Yoffie and Eric Baldwin, "Apple in 2015," *Harvard Business School*, October 28, 2015, https://cb.hbsp.harvard.edu/cbmp/product/715456-PDF-ENG

[vii] Fred Vogelstein, "And Then Steve Said, 'Let There Be an iPhone'," *New York Times*, October 6, 2013, http://www.nytimes.com/2013/10/06/magazine/and-then-steve-said-let-there-be-an-iphone.html

[viii] Vogelstein, *New York Times*, Ibid.

[ix] Fred Vogelstein, "The Untold Story: How the iPhone Blew Up the Wireless Industry," *Wired*, January 2008, http://www.wired.com/2008/01/ff-iphone/

[x] Vogelstein, *Wired*, Ibid.

[xi] Vogelstein, *New York Times*, Ibid.

[xii] Vogelstein, *Wired*, Ibid.

[xiii] Vogelstein, *Wired*, Ibid.

[xiv] Christopher Minasians, "Ever Wondered Where iPhones and iPads Are Made and Assembled? We Researched Apple's Supply Chain and Distribution. Updated 18 April 2016 with iPhone SE Build Cost," *Macworld*, April 6, 2016, http://www.macworld.co.uk/feature/apple/are-apple-products-truly-designed-in-california-made-in-china-iphonese-3633832/

[xv] Peter Cohan, "After 101 Years, Why GM Failed," *DailyFinance*, May 31, 2009, http://www.aol.com/article/2009/05/31/after-101-years-why-gm-failed/19052641/

[xvi] Cohan, Ibid.

[xvii] Cohan, Ibid.

[xviii] Nancy Koehn et al., "GM: What Went Wrong and What's Next," *Harvard Business School Working Knowledge*, June 9, 2009, http://hbswk.hbs.edu/item/gm-what-went-wrong-and-whats-next

[xix] "A Giant Falls," *The Economist*, June 4, 2009, http://www.economist.com/node/13782942

[xx] Koehn, Ibid.

[xxi] "A Giant Falls," Ibid.

[xxii] Anita McGahan, "Saturn: A Different Kind of Car Company," *Harvard Business School*, November 21, 1994, https://cb.hbsp.harvard.edu/cbmp/content/sample/795010-PDF-ENG

[xxiii] McGahan, Ibid.

[xxiv] McGahan, Ibid.

[xxv] McGahan, Ibid.

[xxvi] McGahan, Ibid.

[xvii] Dave Hanna, "How GM Destroyed Its Saturn Success," *Forbes*, March 8, 2010, http://www.forbes.com/2010/03/08/saturn-gm-innovation-leadership-managing-failure.html

[xxviii] "IBM's Tough Transition Continues As Sales Shrink—Again," *Fortune*, July 18, 2016, http://fortune.com/2016/07/18/ibm-earnings-revenue-second-quarter/

[xxix] Peter Cohan, "5 Reasons IBM Is Buffett's Biggest Blunder," *Forbes*, February 29, 2016, http://www.forbes.com/sites/petercohan/2016/02/29/5-reasons-ibm-is-buffetts-biggest-blunder/

[xxxx] "Netflix 2006 10K," February 28, 2007, *sec.gov*, https://www.sec.gov/Archives/edgar/data/1065280/000119312507042689/d10k.htm

[xxxi] Peter Cohan, "How Netflix Reinvented Itself," *Forbes*, April 23, 2013, http://www.forbes.com/sites/petercohan/2013/04/23/how-netflix-reinvented-itself/#b4a104d74ea3

[xxii] Cohan, Ibid.

[xxiii] Cohan, Ibid.

[xxxiv] Cohan, Ibid.

[xxxv] Cohan, Ibid.

[xxxvi] Joe Nocera, "Can Netflix Survive in the New World It Created?" *New York Times*, June 15, 2016, http://www.nytimes.com/2016/06/19/magazine/can-netflix-survive-in-the-new-world-it-created.html

[xxxvii] Nocera, Ibid.

[xxxviii] Nocera, Ibid.

[xxxix] Peter Cohan, "5 Ways That Adobe Systems Disrupted Itself," *Forbes*, February 2, 2015, http://www.forbes.com/sites/petercohan/2015/02/02/5-ways-that-adobe-systems-disrupted-itself/#507b82064837

[xl] Felix Gillette, "The Rise and Inglorious Fall of Myspace," *Bloomberg*, June 22, 2011, http://www.bloomberg.com/news/articles/2011-06-22/the-rise-and-inglorious-fall-of-Myspace

[xli] Gillette, Ibid.

[xlii] Yinka Adegoke, "Special report: How News Corp Got Lost in Myspace," *Reuters*, April 7, 2011, http://www.reuters.com/article/us-Myspace-idUSTRE7364G420110407

[xliii] Stuart Dredge, "Myspace—What Went Wrong: 'The Site Was a Massive Spaghetti-Ball Mess'," *The Guardian*, March 6, 2015, https://www.theguardian.com/technology/2015/mar/06/Myspace-what-went-wrong-sean-percival-spotify

[xliv] Matthew Garrahan, "*The Rise and Fall of Myspace*," *Financial Times*, December 4, 2009, http://www.ft.com/cms/s/0/fd9ffd9c-dee5-11de-adff-00144feab49a.html

[xlv] Adegoke, Ibid.

[xlvi] Garrahan, Ibid.

[xlvii] Dredge, Ibid.

[xlviii] Adegoke, Ibid.

[xlix] Gillette, Ibid.

[l] Peter Cohan, "5 Growth Secrets of a $900 million Serial Entrepreneur," *Inc.*, April 17, 2016, http://www.inc.com/peter-cohan/5-growth-secrets-of-a-900-million-serial-entrepreneur.html5 Growth Secrets of a $900 Million Serial Entrepreneur

[li] Cohan, Ibid.

[lii] Cohan, Ibid.

[liii] Peter Cohan, "This $900 Million Startup CEO Drives Growth Through Culture," *Inc.*, July 22, 2016, http://www.inc.com/peter-cohan/this-900-million-startup-ceo-drives-growth-through-culture.htm

[liv] Alyson Shontell, "How One Startup Had Millions In Funding And 100,000 Users—And Still FAILED," *Business Insider*, August 19, 2010, http://www.businessinsider.com/how-gocrosscampus-startup-failed-2010-8?op=1/#u-dont-have-a-company-you-have-a-job-1

[lv] Brad Stone, "Storming the Campuses," *New York Times*, March 21, 2008, http://www.nytimes.com/2008/03/21/technology/21ivygame.html?_r=1

[lvi] Stone, Ibid.

[lvii] Stone, Ibid.

lviii Brad Hargreaves, "Capturing the Union or the Intersection," *bhargreaves.com*, http://bhargreaves.com/2010/03/capturing-the-union-or-the-intersection/ March 1, 2010

lvix Shontell, Ibid.

lx Shontell, Ibid.

lxi Peter Cohan and Sam Hariharan, "Growing Pains at Commonwealth Dairy," Babson College, August 1, 2016, Product #: 39-PDF-ENG

lxii The remainder of this case scenario is from Cohan and Hariharan, Ibid.

lxiii Neil Versel, "Why did HealthSpot fail? The telemedicine industry weighs in," *Medcity News*, January 6, 2016, http://medcitynews.com/2016/01/healthspot-fail-telemedicine/

lxiv Neil Versel, "Rite Aid picks Up Bankrupt HealthSpot's Assets for Just $1.15M," *MedCity News*, June 13, 2016, http://medcitynews.com/2016/06/rite-aid-healthspot/

lxv Carrie Ghose, "HealthSpot Files for Chapter 7 Bankruptcy Liquidation," *Columbus Business First*, January 14, 2016, http://www.bizjournals.com/columbus/news/2016/01/14/healthspot-files-for-chapter-7-bankruptcy.html

lxvi Rishi Madhok, "Postmortem: Healthspot," *Telemed Magazine*, March 23, 2016, http://www.telemedmag.com/startups/2016/3/23/postmortem-healthspot

Chapter 6: Growth via Culture

i Peter Cohan, "Silicon Valley's Culture Doctor," *Forbes*, November 4 2011, http://www.forbes.com/sites/petercohan/2011/11/04/silicon-valleys-culture-doctor/#70285cf15461

ii Daniel Kahneman, *Thinking, Fast and Slow*. (New York, Farrar, Straus and Giroux, 2013).

iii "Possible Review of Chapter on Growth through Culture," October 28, 2016 E-mail from Wendy Murphy, Babson College Associate Professor of Management.

iv I introduced this concept in Peter Cohan, *The Technology Leaders* (San Franciso, CA: Jossey-Bass, 1997).

v "Intuit Stock Price," *Google Finance*, accessed October 9, 2016, https://www.google.com/search?sourceid=navclient&ie=UTF-8&rlz=1T4GUEA_enUS605US606&q=intuit+stock+price

vi Peter Cohan, "Intuit Stock Soars as It Disrupts Clayton Christensen," *Forbes*, March 11, 2016, http://www.forbes.com/sites/petercohan/2016/04/11/intuit-stock-soars-as-it-disrupts-clayton-christensen/

vii Peter Cohan, "Can Scott Cook Revive Corporate America?" *Forbes*, February 20, 2012, http://www.forbes.com/sites/petercohan/2012/02/29/can-scott-cook-revive-corporate-america

viii Peter Cohan, "Can Scott Cook Revive Corporate America?," Ibid.

ix Peter Cohan, "Can Scott Cook Revive Corporate America?," Ibid.

x Peter Cohan, "Can Scott Cook Revive Corporate America?" Ibid.

[xi] Peter Cohan, "Can Scott Cook Revive Corporate America?," Ibid.

[xii] Peter Cohan, "Can Scott Cook Revive Corporate America?," Ibid.

[xiii] Vindu Goel, "Intuit Sheds Its PC Roots and Rises as a Cloud Software Company," *New York Times,* April 10, 2016, http://www.nytimes.com/2016/04/11/technology/intuit-sheds-its-pc-roots-and-rises-as-a-cloud-software-company.html

[xiv] Peter Cohan, "Intuit Stock Soars as It Disrupts Clayton Christensen," Ibid.

[xv] Peter Cohan, "Intuit Stock Soars ss It Disrupts Clayton Christensen," Ibid.

[xvi] Peter Cohan, "5 Reasons IBM Is Buffett's Biggest Blunder," *Forbes*, February 29, 2016, http://www.forbes.com/sites/petercohan/2016/02/29/5-reasons-ibm-is-buffetts-biggest-blunder/

[xvii] "International Business Machines," *Morningstar*, accessed October 10, 2016, http://www.morningstar.com/stocks/XNYS/IBM/quote.html

[xviii] Peter Cohan, "5 Reasons IBM Is Buffett's Biggest Blunder," Ibid.

[xix] Peter Cohan, "5 Reasons IBM Is Buffett's Biggest Blunder," Ibid.

[xx] "A Culture of Think," *IBM.com*, accessed October 9, 2016, http://www-03.ibm.com/ibm/history/ibm100/us/en/icons/think_culture/

[xxi] Dan Bobkoff, "IBM: When Corporations Took Care of Their Employees," *Marketplace.org*, June 13, 2016, https://www.marketplace.org/2016/06/08/world/profit-ibm

[xxii] Robert X. Cringely, "What's Happening at IBM (It's Dying)," *Cringely.com*, March 8, 2016, http://www.cringely.com/2016/03/08/whats-happening-at-ibm/

[xxiii] Dan Bobkoff, Ibid.

[xxiv] Peter Cohan, "VMTurbo's Tripling Revenues Are IBM's Loss," *Forbes*, July 23, 2013, http://www.forbes.com/sites/petercohan/2013/07/23/vmturbos-tripling-revenues-are-ibms-loss/

[xxv] Peter Cohan, "VMTurbo's Tripling Revenues Are IBM's Loss," Ibid.

[xxvi] Peter Cohan, "VMTurbo's Tripling Revenues Are IBM's Loss," Ibid.

[xxvii] "Benchmarks by Company—IBM," American Customer Satisfaction Index, accessed October 10, 2016, http://www.theacsi.org/index.php?option=com_content&view=article&id=149&catid=&Itemid=214&c=IBM

[xxviii] Author interview with 10-year IBM veteran, October 9, 2016.

[xxix] Author interview with 10-year IBM veteran, October 9, 2016.

[xxx] Peter Cohan, "$100 Million Startup Reveals Innovation Weaknesses at IBM and Oracle," *Forbes*, February 22, 2016, http://www.forbes.com/sites/petercohan/2016/02/22/100-million-startup-reveals-innovation-weaknesses-at-ibm-and-oracle/

[xxxi] Peter Cohan, "With SimpliVity Surging, Can Nutanix Hold Its IPO Gains?' *Forbes*, October 10, 2016, http://www.forbes.com/sites/petercohan/2016/10/10/with-simplivity-surging-can-nutanix-hold-its-ipo-gains/

xxxii Peter Cohan, "Execution Machine: Doron Kempel's Six Keys to Getting Stuff Done," *Forbes*, October 20, 2012, http://www.forbes.com/sites/petercohan/2012/10/29/execution-machine-doron-kempels-six-keys-to-getting-stuff-done/

xxxiii Peter Cohan, "With SimpliVity Surging, Can Nutanix Hold Its IPO Gains?," Ibid.

xxxiv Peter Cohan, "With SimpliVity Surging, Can Nutanix Hold Its IPO Gains?," Ibid.

xxxv Peter Cohan, "With SimpliVity Surging, Can Nutanix Hold Its IPO Gains?," Ibid.

xxxvi Farhad Manjoo, "Zenefits' Leader Is Rattling an Industry, So Why Is He Stressed Out?," *New York Times*, September 20, 2014, http://www.nytimes.com/2014/09/21/business/zenefits-leader-is-rattling-an-industry-so-why-is-he-stressed-out.html

xxxvii Farhad Manjoo, "Zenefits Scandal Highlights Perils of Hypergrowth at Start-Ups," *New York Times*, February 17, 2016, http://www.nytimes.com/2016/02/18/technology/zenefits-scandal-highlights-perils-of-hypergrowth-at-start-ups.html

xxxviii Farhad Manjoo, "Zenefits Scandal Highlights Perils of Hypergrowth at Start-Ups," Ibid.

xxxix Farhad Manjoo, "Zenefits, a Rocket That Fell to Earth, Tries to Launch Again," *New York Times*, October 12, 2016, http://www.nytimes.com/2016/10/13/technology/zenefits-a-rocket-that-fell-to-earth-tries-to-launch-again.html

Chapter 7: Growth Trajectories

i These case studies are based on my analysis of 1,348 publicly traded global companies in the *Forbes 2000* database both in 2009 and in 2014 ranked by their five-year average annual revenue growth rate.

ii "PNH—Paroxysmal Nocturnal Hemoglobinuria," *Marrowforums*, accessed October 30, 2016, http://www.marrowforums.org/pnh.html

iii Matthew Herper, "How A $440,000 Drug Is Turning Alexion Into Biotech's New Innovation Powerhouse," *Forbes*, September 5, 2012, http://www.forbes.com/sites/matthewherper/2012/09/05/how-a-440000-drug-is-turning-alexion-into-biotechs-new-innovation-powerhouse/

iv Jonathan D. Rockoff, "Alexion Pharmaceuticals Promotes COO to CEO Post," *Wall Street Journal*, January 29, 2015, http://www.wsj.com/articles/alexion-pharmaceuticals-promotes-coo-to-ceo-post-1422569733

v Alexion Pharmaceuticals, S-1/A, sec.gov, April 4, 1997, https://www.sec.gov/Archives/edgar/data/899866/0000950110-97-000600.txt

vi Matthew Herper, "How A $440,000 Drug Is Turning Alexion Into Biotech's New Innovation Powerhouse," *Forbes*, September 5, 2012, http://www.forbes.com/sites/matthewherper/2012/09/05/how-a-440000-drug-is-turning-alexion-into-biotechs-new-innovation-powerhouse/

vii Herper, Ibid.

viii Herper, Ibid.

ix Alexion Pharmaceuticals, 10K, *SEC.gov*, February 29, 2008, https://www.sec.gov/Archives/edgar/data/899866/000119312508043592/d10k.htm

[x] Alexion Pharmaceuticals, 10K, *sec.gov*, February 23, 2010, https://www.sec.gov/Archives/edgar/data/899866/000119312510037748/d10k.htm

[xi] Alexion Pharmaceuticals, 10K, *SEC.gov*, February 11, 2013, https://www.sec.gov/Archives/edgar/data/899866/000089986613000060/alxn10k12312012.htm

[xii] Herper, Ibid.

[xiii] Alexion Pharmaceuticals, 10K, *SEC.gov*, February 11, 2013, Ibid.

[xiv] Lysosomal Acid Lipase Deficiency (LALD), *liver.ca*, accessed November 5, 2016, http://www.liver.ca/liver-disease/types/Lysosomal_Acid_Lipase_Deficiency_(LALD).aspx

[xv] Alexion Pharmaceuticals, 10K, *sec.gov*, February 8, 2016, https://www.sec.gov/Archives/edgar/data/899866/000089986616000226/alxn10k12312015.htm

[xvi] David Hallal, *Alexion.com*, accessed November 5, 2016, http://www.alexion.com/about-alexion-pharmaceuticals/alexion-leadership

[xvii] "Alexion Reports Third Quarter 2016 Results," sec.gov, October 27, 2016, https://www.sec.gov/Archives/edgar/data/899866/000089986616000369/ex991_102716.htm

[xviii] Brett Molina, "The Long, Troubled History of Yahoo's Top Execs," *USA Today*, July 25, 2016, https://www.usatoday.com/story/tech/news/2016/02/03/yahoo-ceo-history/79753262/

[xix] Brian Womack, "Yahoo to Sell Web Business to Verizon for $4.8 Billion," *Bloomberg*, July 25, 2016, https://www.bloomberg.com/news/articles/2016-07-25/yahoo-agrees-to-sell-web-assets-to-verizon-for-4-8-billion

[xx] Yahoo 10k, *sec.gov*, March 30, 2000, https://www.sec.gov/Archives/edgar/data/1011006/000091205700014598/0000912057-00-014598-d1.html

[xxi] Brad Stone, "What Sank Yahoo? Blame Its Nice Guy Founders," *Bloomberg*, July 25, 2016, https://www.bloomberg.com/news/articles/2016-07-25/what-sank-yahoo-blame-its-nice-guy-founders

[xxii] Stone, Ibid.

[xxiii] Stone, Ibid.

[xxiv] Todd Spangler, "Yahoo's False Prophet: How Marissa Mayer Failed to Turn the Company Around," *Variety*, May 24, 2016, http://variety.com/2016/digital/features/marissa-mayer-yahoo-ceo-1201781310/

[xxv] Alexei Oreskovic, "Yahoo is stuck in a never ending drama vortex," *Business Insider*, December 5, 2015, http://www.businessinsider.com/history-of-yahoo-troubles-2015-12

[xxvi] Spangler, Ibid.

[xxvii] Womack, Ibid.

[xxviii] Brad Garlinghouse, "Yahoo Memo: The 'Peanut Butter Manifesto'," *Wall Street Journal*, November 18, 2006, http://www.wsj.com/articles/SB116379821933826657

[xxix] Peter Cohan, "Hungry Start-Up Strategy," Berrett-Kohler, 2012

xxx   Nutanix SI/A, September 28, 2016, https://www.sec.gov/Archives/edgar/data/1618732/000119312516722284/d937439ds1a.htm

xxxi Peter Cohan, "Nutanix Beating EMC, Says It's Cutting Customer IT Costs 62%," *Forbes*, November 21, 2014, http://www.forbes.com/sites/petercohan/2014/11/21/nutanix-beating-emc-by-cutting-customer-it-costs-62/

xxxii Cohan, Ibid.

xxxiii Peter Cohan, "Nutanix Founder Bullish on IPO Prospects," *Forbes*, September 14, 2016, http://www.forbes.com/sites/petercohan/2016/09/14/nutanix-founder-bullish-on-ipo-prospects/

xxxiv Peter Cohan, "Nutanix Founder Bullish on IPO Prospects," Ibid.

xxxv Peter Cohan, "Nutanix Founder Bullish on IPO Prospects," Ibid.

xxxvi Peter Cohan, "One Word Propels This Startup's 200% Growth, $2 Billion Valuation," *Inc.*, December 18, 2014, http://www.inc.com/peter-cohan/one-word-propels-this-startup-s-200-growth-2-billion-valuation.html

xxxvii Peter Cohan, "One Word Propels This Startup's 200% Growth, $2 Billion Valuation," Ibid.

xxxviii Peter Cohan, "One Word Propels This Startup's 200% Growth, $2 Billion Valuation," Ibid.

xxxix Peter Cohan, "One Word Propels This Startup's 200% Growth, $2 Billion Valuation," Ibid.

xl Peter Cohan, "Mobile App Marketer Fiksu Boosts Groupon," *Forbes*, August 12, 2013, http://www.forbes.com/sites/petercohan/2013/08/12/mobile-app-marketer-fiksu-boosts-facebook-groupon/

xli Jim Schakenbach," Tech Luminary: Micah Adler," *Boston Business Journal*, November 16, 2012, http://www.bizjournals.com/boston/blog/mass-high-tech/2012/11/tech-luminary-micah-adler.html

xlii Kim-Mai Cutler, "Q&A: Fiksu CEO Micah Adler on How Acquiring iOS Users Has Changed After Offer Walls," *SocialTimes*, July 28, 2011, http://www.adweek.com/socialtimes/fiksu-adler-user-acquisition-mobile-developers/511929

xliii Peter Cohan, "Mobile App Marketer Fiksu Boosts Groupon," Ibid.

xliv Peter Cohan, "Mobile App Marketer Fiksu Boosts Groupon," Ibid.

xlv Peter Cohan, "3 Secrets for Growing From $1 Million to $100 Million in 3.5 Years," *Inc.*, August 11, 2014, http://www.inc.com/peter-cohan/3-secrets-to-grow-from-1-million-to-100-million-in-3-5-years.html

xlvi Paul Sawers, "Mobile Marketing Tech Company Fiksu Acquired by Asset Management Firm Noosphere," *Venture Beat*, June 2, 2016, http://venturebeat.com/2016/06/02/mobile-marketing-tech-company-fiksu-acquired-by-asset-management-firm-noosphere/

[xlvii] David Harris, "Qualcomm-Backed Boston Tech Firm Sold to California Marketing Agency," *Boston Business Journal*, June 3, 2016, http://www.bizjournals.com/boston/blog/techflash/2016/06/qualcomm-backed-bostontech-firm-sold-to-california.html

[xlviii] Allison Schiff, "The Fiksu Acquisition In Four Words: 'It's Tough Out There'," *AdExchanger*, June 6, 2016, https://adexchanger.com/mobile/fiksu-acquisition-four-words-tough/

[xlix] Schiff, Ibid.

I

Index

A

Actifio CDS, 48

Activist investors, 2

Adjunct Lecturer of Innovation & Entrepreneurship at Northwestern University's Kellogg School, 29

Advanced Technology Ventures, 48

Alexion Pharmaceuticals, 190–191, 193

Alignment By Objective (ABO), 180

Amazon, 4, 92–95, 168

Andreessen Horowitz, 48

Android Market, 52

Apple, 4, 15

Apple App Store, 52

Atypical hemolytic uremic syndrome (aHUS), 193

Avon Products, 64–68

B

Bank of America, 40

C

Capabilities, 14–16
  Apple, 127–132
  application, 162
  Commonwealth Dairy's founders, 155–159
  companies, 124
  DVD-by-Mail to online streaming, 138–142

GM files, bankruptcy, 132–134, 136–138
GoCrossCampus (GXC) fails, 152–155
growth, 125–127, 163
HealthSpot, 159, 161–162
industry, 124
News Corp. acquires Myspace, 142–147
product, 124
SailPoint's exceptional product, 148–151

Cisco Systems, 3

Color Labs, 52–55

Criteo, 33–34

Critical Software (CS), 82–84

Cultural, Administrative, Geographic, and Economic (CAGE) framework, 58–61, 67–68, 71–72, 74, 81, 83–84, 86–87

Culture, 16–19
  growth
    CEO's values, 166
    customer benefits, 166
    employee innovation and growth (intuit's culture), 169–173
    employee magnets, 166
    growth-at-any-cost culture, 183–185
    IBM bureaucratic culture, 173–176
    principles, 166–168, 186
    SimpliVity execution culture, 179–181, 183

Customers
  age range, 25
  appetite for risk, 24–25
  growth principles, 26

© Peter S. Cohan 2017

P. S. Cohan, *Disciplined Growth Strategies*, DOI 10.1007/978-1-4842-2448-9

Customers (*cont.*)
  income, 25
  industry, 24
  large and powerful distribution channel, 27
  large companies seeking growth, 27
  price sensitivity, 24
  product, 23–25
  purchase process, 25
  size, 24
  small companies seeking growth, 27
  well-run company, 27
Cut-rate film from Japan, 36

D

Department of Industrial Policy & Promotion (DIPP), 73
Digital photography, 36
DuPont, 2
DVD-by-Mail market, 139

E

Earnings before Interest Taxes Depreciation and Amortization (EBITDA), 104
Eastman Kodak files bankruptcy, 34–37, 39
Enobia, 196
Enterprise Resource Planning (ERP), 6
ESPN, 95–98

F

Facebook, 98–100
Fast Company, 52–53
Fiksu, 4
Foreign Corrupt Practices Act (FCPA), 74
Foxconn, 15

G

Geography, 12–13
  application, 86–87
  Avon Products, 64–68
  CAGE distance, 87
  case studies, 59, 61
  Critical Software, 82–84
  framework, 58
  growth, 58–59
  India Thwarts Apple's, 72–75
  MiniLuxe's geographic expansion, 76–78
  Netflix stock, 68–71
  Pacific Sunwear's slow motion wipeout, 78–81
  Sweden's Rdio, 84–86
  T-Mobile, 61–64
GoCrossCampus (GXC), 152–154
Go-to-market model, 49
Greylock Partners, 48
Growing faster matters, 2
Growth
  challenges, 3
  opportunity, 4–5
  via culture, 165–186
Growth road maps
  capabilities, 229–233
  customers
    CEO characteristics, 211–212
  diagnose culture, 234–235
  envision growth culture, 235–237
  execute growth culture, 238
  geography, 217–222
  growth strategy
    diagnose, 213–214, 217, 222–223, 229
    envision, 214–215, 218–222, 224–227, 230–232
    execute, 216, 222, 228–229, 233
  growth trajectory, 238–239
  independent consultant, 234
  products, 222–229
Growth trajectories
  Alexion Pharmaceuticals, 193–197
  application, 208
  case studies, 191, 193
  company, 209
  customer segment, 189
  effective growth, 190–191
  Fiksu Revenues, 205–208
  new capabilities, 189
  new culture, 190
  new geography, 189
  new products, 189
  Nutanix, 202–205
  Yahoo, 198–202

H

HBO, 50

Hewlett Packard Enterprise, 3

Homejoy
cleaners, 45
Facebook and Google, 44
financial statements, 44
growth strategy, 46
last-minute cancellations, 45
social network, 43
supply chain and operations, 45

Hyperconverged infrastructure (HCI), 179, 202, 204

Hypophosphatasia (HPP), 196

I, J, K

IBM, 50, 177–179
bureaucratic culture, 173–176

Imercive, 111–115

India Thwarts Apple's, 72–75

The Innovator's Dilemma, 7

Instagram, 99–100

Instant photography, 35

iPhone, 15

L

LinkedIn, 1

Localytics, 117–119

Lysosomal acid lipase deficiency (LALD), 196

M

Massachusetts-based Genzyme, 195

McDonald, 26, 28–29

Microsoft, 17, 115–117

Middle market, 33–34

MiniLuxe's geographic expansion, 76–78

Mobile and Communications Council (MCC), 72

Myths
acquisition, 9
big companies, 7–8
capabilities, 14–16

culture, 16–19
customers, 10–12
geography, 12–13
industry, 8–9
products, 13–14

N

Netflix, 15–16, 50, 68–71

Net promoter score, 77

New products
AOL/Time Warner, 100–107
application, 120
AWS's sheer scale, 92–95
capabilities, 121
case studies, 91
CEOs, 89–91
ESPN's new programming, 95–98
Facebook, 98–100
Imercive, 111–115
Localytics acquires Splitforce, 117–119
Microsoft, 115–117
New Relic's Six-Year Journey, 107–111

New Relic, 108–111

North Bridge Venture Partners, 48

NPV, 105

O

Online streaming, 138–142

Oracle, 17

Orphatec, 196

Over the top (OTT), 96

P

Pacific Sunwear's slow motion wipeout, 78–81

Paroxysmal nocturnal hemoglobinuria (PNH), 193

Products, 13–14

Q

Quantum Value Leap (QVL), 5, 201–202, 205

Quebec-based pharmaceutical manufacturer Valeant Pharmaceuticals, 2

QuickBooks Online, 169, 172

Quicken, 17

R

Railroad cars, 5
Research and development (R&D), 2
Rhapsody streaming service, 62

S

SAP, 7, 17
Saturn, 134
S-Curve, 6–7, 15
Securities and Exchange
        Commission (SEC), 74
Seibel's product, 6
S/4 HANA, 7
SimpliVity, 3
Small and Medium-Sized Business (SMB)
    Actifio's products, 48
    Actifio's strategy, 50–51
    CRN UK, 50
    EMC, 49
    first-time supplier, 49
    Massachusetts-based data
        management, 47
Small-and Medium-Sized
        Enterprise (SME), 48
SMARTS, 175
Social Finance (SoFi)
    adapt to rapid change, 43
    Bank of America, 40
    business, 41
    community support, 39
    customer experience, 40
    higher deposit rates, 40
    JP Morgan, 42
    lower loan rates, 40
    market segmentation, 40
    offer career counseling, 41
    participate, huge market, 42
    rapid response, 41
    segment, customers, 43
    sponsor social events, 41
    spouse finding, 41
    turn customers, 43
    Utah Bank, 42

Social network, 39
Specialty products, 2
Splitforce's development, 118
Subway, 26, 30–31
SunGard, 50
Systrom, 99

T

Taligen, 196
Technology Crossover Ventures, 48
Tiger Global Management, 48
Time Warner Cable's NaviSite, 50
T-Mobile, 61–64
Toyota Motor, 17
Traffic acquisition costs (TAC), 33
TurboTax, 17

U

Unattractive industries, 105
Unilever, 50
United Auto Workers (UAW), 133

V

Value-added resellers (VARs), 182
Venture capital magnet, 51
VMTurbo, 176

W

Washington Post, 30
Worse off, 105

X

Xero, 171–172

Y

Yahoo, 190–191, 198–200

Z

Zenefits, 183–184

Get the eBook for only $4.99!

Why limit yourself?

Now you can take the weightless companion with you wherever you go and access your content on your PC, phone, tablet, or reader.

Since you've purchased this print book, we are happy to offer you the eBook for just $4.99.

Convenient and fully searchable, the PDF version enables you to easily find and copy code—or perform examples by quickly toggling between instructions and applications.

To learn more, go to http://www.apress.com/us/shop/companion or contact support@apress.com.